CITY OF IMMORTAL SHADOWS

T.J. SWACKHAMMER

CITY OF IMMORTAL SHADOWS

ISBN – 9781777334000

First edition printed in Canada by BookPrint

For myself, for fighting tooth and nail to feel this dream in my hand.

<u>Part One</u>

death,
with his skin so cold and
hands so crooked
was the first, and only,
to show me the sweet poison of mercy

he said, 'sleep now, child,
for I will swallow your sins
and pick your soul from my teeth

and when the dawn of new life rises,
you will bring me new souls to eat

might I have
lost this meal
but I have earned a feast'

1

Moribund

I was always told that when you die, your spirit and your body become two distinctly separate forms: a ghost and a corpse.

This turned out to be entirely inaccurate.

There are three things I paid vivid attention to the day that I died. One, it was hot. Hotter than it should have been allowed to be when housing human beings- so hot that I felt every uncomfortable shift in my sheets and every cling of fabric to my skin. Second, the air felt brittle when pulling it into my lungs. Before the Institute, I'd never known air to feel so sharp against your throat. It was like inhaling glass. Caressing splinters with your tongue. It was, quite simply, torture.

Three, I felt awake when I woke up.

If I had been anywhere else- at any point in history- I wouldn't have questioned that. But it had been four years, seventy-odd days, and two hours since the last time I'd felt as though I could see clearly.

And I didn't like what I saw.

The first thing I saw was the sun. This in itself was not a surprise. The windows above my bed did absolutely nothing to stop it from blazing through. It was an almost angry thing, wringing the saliva from my mouth until I could almost convince myself there were balls of medical-grade cotton stuffed in my cheeks. I groaned, groaned, groaned, and rolled over, trying to pull the sheet over my head to filter some of the worst of it away, but it was hopeless. This fucking place was committed to giving the worst residential experience possible, and boy, did they deliver. The first night I was here, I'd tried to peel the glue off the edges of the window and just open one, for the love of all things holy, but with all my hoping that I could somehow fling it open with sheer will alone, it stayed put. I soon figured out that the only thing that ever made it through an independent window was the same sunlight that blasted through every single morning at the crack of dawn. If it had been a tangible thing in the room with me, I would've tried to fight it. Weak body and all. I rolled my body to the edge of my bed, dangling my fingertips towards the floor to escape it. It was the sight of my hanging fingers that invited a memory to smudge what might've been a perfectly ordinary morning where I was in the midst of being lightly tortured in a cramped bed and a private room.

Today was two weeks since the death of Richie Parker.

I squeezed my eyes closed and flopped back onto the bed right side up, this time ignoring the sun while rubbing at the short fuzz of hair sprouting anew from my scalp. How could I have a right to complain, when Richie would never see the sunlight again? Was that not the act of an inherently selfish person?

He was a smart boy- he knew the same as everyone else: the windows didn't open, or move and never tilted, bent, or swung. No matter how hot you got, or how unbearably heavy and sharp the air felt as you sucked it into your pathetic lungs, they didn't open. It was a brand of slow torture that began the first night they locked you up, and you didn't even realize how bad it could be until you clued in a year later that it was killing you worse than anything at all. I could hardly blame Richie for trying, but that wasn't my apprehension. I smacked my lips together, and the dryness of my tongue made the sound almost inhuman.

Richie. God, his name hurt. I closed my eyes against the throb of pain. Richie had probably been the last good thing here. He'd managed these small smiles to me while we waited in line in the cafeteria and would always move to let me go before him. It was more kindness and humanity than I'd seen from anyone else in this place. He was so small, almost half the size of me, and he'd still let me at the food first. I chuckled slightly, even though the sound felt raw and ragged as it tore from my throat. It would have been funny to see the two of us together if something like hanging out had been allowed. The top of his head barely reached my chin- we'd have looked like two separate species. They'd call us Big and the Tiny Head, or something. The chuckle quickly subsided into a frown because I couldn't think of good things about him without his corpse showing up in the most remote parts of my psyche.

He was so goddamn *small*. He'd never have been able to wrench the metal chair from where it was welded to the floor, let alone swing it with enough force to shatter both the wall and his spine. I couldn't even do that.

But that's what they said, and that's what we were supposed to believe.

Supposed to.

It took less than two hours for all of those chairs to be removed and replaced with plastic models. Frantic workers we'd never seen before busting in, wearing bizarre white jumpsuits that covered their faces like being half a foot closer to us would be the final thing to sign their death certificate. It was the first time any one of us had seen the Council under any duress. Even our power-tripped floor Senator had looked disturbed, perspiring heavily beneath the lights as they carted away Richie's frail, bloody body in a clear plastic bag, hand dangling to the ground, fingertips dragging against the tile.

I knew with a certainty I usually reserved for things with undeniable fact behind it that there would never be any relief from the memory of his eyes staring opaquely towards the ceiling as they wheeled him past. This would always haunt me-Richie, sweet and tender as he was in life, would never exist again. There was nothing left of him but a fleshy husk with dark, hollow eyes.

A corpse without a spirit.

Just the way nature demanded.

I forced myself to swallow and raised my arms to the ceiling, rotating my wrists. They clicked like the throaty ticking of the clock that hung on the wall and tirelessly consumed the time I had left before assembly.

It was all the same except... not. Everything was different now as if the entire world had shifted slightly off its axis and moved two inches to the left. It shouldn't have done what it did to me. I knew death. If you lived down there, on the plate, you knew death with a sense of intimacy most wouldn't unless they were in battle. Enough of us had grown up watching our families and friends die around us.

But that was out there.

People weren't *supposed* to die on the inside.

That was why we wanted to come here at all, wasn't it? That's why we put ourselves through this shit. Safety. Quality of life. We brushed elbows with the elite and competed against each other for a permanent spot as a Patron. It was the opportunity of a lifetime for all of us.

All of us, except a boy from the South with kind eyes and soft hands. A boy so desperate to leave, he'd be willing to break his neck in the process.

Were 'opportunities' supposed to end with a body bag in an empty hallway?

And that little thought had niggled its way into my brain and was laying eggs faster than whatever they were pumping into me could stop it. It was spreading, infiltrating, like a disease. I found myself unable to stop it and, even more so, unable to want to. This new knowledge was a drug, one that I actually decided I wanted, one that I had signed at the door for, and when I began to see some holes in their system, I began to see them all.

There were too many things we weren't supposed to do, especially in the wake of a crisis. The spreadsheet for protocol ran a half-mile long, fine print. There were too many rules to follow, and too many of us to watch to make sure we followed them. So, things slipped through the cracks. Me with my doubt, and the other kids with their taste for drama, to name a few. Though the Institute wielded a profound discouragement of gossip and fraternization of any kind, it didn't seem to matter. It was forbidden, sure, but some of them loved to talk. Kids will do that.

I'd like to say we all grieved. I'd like to believe that, too. It would be easier to see my peers as good people if they had. The truth was, most were more baffled than anything else, looking down on Richie for an act of perceived cowardice.

"Much better here than dying on the streets. We are fed, clothed, sheltered here, don't know what his problem was," were statements I heard more than once. They were careful to keep their voices low, but they still carried through the hall. I heard it, no matter where I sat.

The thing was, Richie hadn't thought so. Something had pushed him to try to throw himself through that window. Maybe he knew something we didn't. I wanted to say it, but I hadn't. You weren't permitted to show disloyalty to the Council like that. So, I buried my nose further in my copy of *The New Emaldin- A Society, Rebuilt*, and tried to stop thinking about it. I couldn't, though- I thought about it long and hard. I thought about everything we weren't allowed to know while we chased after a dream force-fed to us. And I got angrier and angrier until fury rose like bile in my throat.

The loud blare of the horn crashed through my thoughts with a cataclysm of vibration and sound. Suddenly jerky, I swung my legs over the side and misgauged, bashing my bare feet on the cold panel floor. When I stood, my knees trembled, and a wave of dizziness, accompanied by the unfortunately familiar blow of nausea, nearly caused me to double over. I sucked in a sharp breath and tried to shake it off. There was never any time to bitch and moan about my illnesses that somehow never got cured, despite all the fucking medicine. Breakfast would be served in twenty minutes in the hall, whether I was there or not. And Lord, help me if I wasn't. With movements slow and sluggish, I grabbed the small ivory brush off the vanity and rubbed it over my fuzzy hair. The soft brown curls sprung up like hopeful seedlings and brought my heart into my throat because, for a second, it was like existing in a timeframe that I wasn't here. It was like being *free*.

"No," I tried to say it firmly, though my voice was weak and tinny. It wouldn't be long now before it was shaved again. In a movement that was felt with the most rebellion I could muster, I threw the brush back onto the flimsy table, feeling some primal satisfaction from the clatter. It was so damn quiet here. I hated it. *Hate, hate, hate.* I shivered.

There was something in me that was hungry. Pacing. I scrubbed my hands over my face. *Come on,* I thought as my feeble arms shook from the effort. When had I gotten so weak?

I was wasting precious time. I should have been using the extra minutes to ensure that I was presenting in an appropriate manner that was conducive to the Institute. It was what they wanted. I didn't know why, because I figured it didn't matter all that much when no one ever really looked at any one of us. Then I thought maybe that was the point- if none of us really looked or sounded like anything in particular, then it was easier to erase us. Of course, if I said anything like that, out loud, to anyone, they'd sell me out faster than a red-handed thief. There was a time where I could've said those things to Caleb, but not anymore. Somewhere in the last four years, he decided he loved it here.

Gritting my teeth, I undid the clips from the back of my nightshirt- one at the neck, second at the shoulders, third at my spine. They released with 'clicks' like seatbelt locks, sending the boxy dressing to a heap around my feet. Fine that he did. All the better for it. I wouldn't want Caleb to hate his life, would I?

I made the mistake of glancing down and winced at the sight. *Fuck.* My already willowy body had become gaunt, the skin stretched so tightly over crooks of bones that the spiderwebs of my veins had swollen into fat purple rivers.

I turned to the side and adjusted my posture, pulling my shoulders back and aligning my chin with my toes. Ribs jutted from my stomach like they were stretching for air, fighting to be free from the thin membrane.

If I was outside, if I was free, my skin was a dusky olive that could hint on warm honey, but since I'd been here, it had turned a watered-down shade of grey that teetered precariously on translucent. I looked... sick. Like bad sick- the kind of sick that made your neighbour lock the doors of their home and refuse visitors until eventually, you'd catch a smell in the air and think, *'Well, there he went.'*

The specks and dots of dark colour across my nose and cheeks had almost faded into oblivion. With an obscene sense of sympathy for the small freckles, I brushed a thumb across them. I know how you feel, I thought, staring just a moment too long in the mirror. *Fading away.*

The sun shining through the tinted windows wouldn't be enough for long. I grunted, pressing the heels of my hands against my eye sockets. I was cool, calm. Collected. There was nothing I couldn't do. It was right to be here. It was right to be here. I repeated it to myself until it was all that was in my brain, drowning the feeling of restless fear with its pointy edges. I was fine. I'd be fine. Caleb and I would graduate, and we would be fine again. It was just a problem to be fixed. I would see about getting an Outdoors pass, and I would suddenly feel alive again, and the world would make sense.

It was going to be fine, I thought again, but I couldn't rid the feeling that somehow I was at the end of the line. Something awful was going to happen today.

I just knew it.

I tried to focus on going outside, on seeing Caleb, and it did just enough to lighten my mood that I felt capable of crossing to the narrow shelving unit and fumbling through the act of retrieving my daytime wear.

As I removed them from the wardrobe, I was careful not to grip them too tight. Wrinkles? Demerit. Creases? Demerit. I was shaking my head at it even as I carefully undid the buttons of the high-necked blouse and shrugged into it gently. The material was horrific- crunchy, inflexible, and more than a little stiff- it was able to render me nearly entirely shapeless. The pants did a similar thing, leaving me with long, straight lines instead of the human body's natural curves and slopes. It was a carefully cultivated image, created in the same way our hair was shaved to the skin or our fingernails clipped close. We were not supposed to have any markers of who we once were, clothing or otherwise. Somewhere after being clubbed over the head and before being thrown in the back of a collection van, we'd made that deal with them. Hell if I could remember agreeing, but that was life, I guess.

Everything I'd had on me had promptly been disposed of upon arrival. All I got back was two sets of outfits: two daytime, two nighttime. Every Thursday during our bath, these new clothes were taken to launder. And, like clockwork, a precise forty-one minutes later, they were hanging in our wardrobes as if they had never left.

I fastened the final button on my blouse, tucking it so snug against my chin that the coarse material chafed against the tender skin behind my earlobe. I could do this. I was fine. A small curl popped up from its place of rest, springing up above the flatter, tamer strands and called attention to itself. Frustrated, I aggressively massaged it with a finger until it, too, lay flat against my scalp. There were times I looked in the mirror now and didn't recognize myself, the close crop bringing such harshness to what were soft, childish features- it left the high crest of my cheekbones an exaggeration and made the goggle of my eyes all the more predominant. It left me, I thought briefly as I made my way to my door, looking a bit like someone drawing a person from a child's memory. All shapes and angles that don't seem quite to fit.

I punched in my code beside the door, setting off the predictable series of small beeps in response. Since I was early, I peered out the small rectangular slot at the top of the door. The lights hadn't yet flickered on, so it was a darkness that taunted that nothing existed beyond this room. In all truthfulness, it might as well not. Alone in here was the only time I felt like I even had bits of myself left, even if it was hidden behind my molars like a meal from two days ago. I let a growl rumble in my throat as I rechecked the clock. It had barely moved.

My punctuality had become a borderline obsession in the last couple of months, and I was really hoping it would be something useful in my official request for getting a deck pass. If I could convince Caleb to use his merits too, we could both go out to the Outdoor Area. My lips creased in a small, broken smile as I hugged my arms against my chest. He'd grumble, inevitably, but he loved to stand above the rushing water just as much as I did, even if it was just to try to catch the sounds of life through one of the Pod's vents.

"One day, that'll be us, 'Cia." He used to say wistfully, leaning against the thin wire fence, back when we still did things together. We could barely see anything from where we were, but it didn't matter. The Outdoor Area was little more than a small spot above the draining route for the Pod's pipes- but we'd occasionally hear the rumble of the elevator cars or the cadence of Patrons' voices, and it was a glorious relief that there might actually be an end to this. I never wanted to get ahead of myself in those moments, but it had been hard. Caleb was so much closer to being done than I was. He was set to graduate in a matter of weeks, but I hated thinking about how much time would be between our ceremonies.

We weren't supposed to speculate on life inside before we got our permits, but the more you learned of it, it was hard not to. It was the endgame. If you paid your dues, followed the rules, and took every bit of medication pushed and pushed on you, then you graduated to join the Patrons. I'd leave this circle of unblessed hell and finally exist again.

There were people, people in charge, that didn't want us speaking of it because there were kids who wouldn't make it, and the competition could cause conflict inside our quadrant. But I didn't buy it. It was ugly, but we all knew what it was going into it.

The unmistakable sound of the swelling alarm began to pour down the hallway like liquid tension, informing all of the Hub's occupants of retrieval time. I could hear my room neighbour through the thin walls, scrambling in her room to type in her code before the alarm signal could reach our far end.

She was one of the street people that just couldn't seem to get their mind off of it. It had been almost two weeks, but her struggle functioning within the Institute's strict structure became increasingly apparent as time went on. There was a part of me that hoped she could, but equally, any attention she was getting, I wasn't. I turned and faced the door with a carefully neutral expression on my face. I couldn't risk the attention, not right now, not with the rate of kids that were being moved in and out. It used to be a new batch every quarter, and we'd lose maybe three before the next group came, but these days it seemed people were dropping like flies. It made you wonder a little bit if they'd gone the way Richie had, just that there hadn't been anyone around to see it. I hated that thought but when they all but disappeared in the middle of the night and got replaced almost instantly, how could I *not* find that suspicious? How could anyone not? Was it as simple as ignorance, or perhaps, something worse, like they just didn't care about why the Council would be so desperate?

I heard a clatter from the neighbour's side again and almost wanted to slap the wall to remind her to shut up, but I set my jaw. Damn it, I wasn't going to let the last four years be for nothing.

"People bred by the values and beliefs of the Outer City don't make for a happy city," Justice Crawley had said on the first day, "Either you change, or you don't make it. It's a simple thing."

A simple thing. The bile of sickness stung the back of my throat as the alarm thrummed through the hallway. It was too loud, almost deafening, due to the proximity. The vibrations sent the signal to the lock system and began to release each bar off the door at a painstakingly slow pace. It took sixteen long seconds for every bar to open, so in the interim, I smoothed the front of my shirt and made sure the buttons were lined directly down the center of my body. The door hissed open. I'd done this a thousand times, and it never got any easier. I felt like I was playing a damn role with no direction except 'shut up' and 'obey me.' It was too bad I'd always been awful at doing both of those things.

The door snapped open. Compared to the blindingly bright rooms, the hallway was dim and dingy as if being transient between rooms came as an afterthought to the rest of the Hub. The plastic ceiling sagged with a swollen belly in the middle where rectangle bar lights had been weakly stapled to the malleable material.

The Retriever was a tall, slender man with a white mask tied over his face's lower half. His walk was robotic as he traveled down the hallway with a rod straight back and a blank stare. A group of residents, traipsing behind him in sync with the Retriever's pace, halted as he stopped in front of my doorway. My eye twitched. Had it always been this fucking creepy?

Puffing out my pathetically scrawny chest, I raised my arm with my tag closer to his awaiting scanner. It would be green. It was always green.

I was always green.

He waved the white cylindrical wand in front of my chest, and once the green light winked, he sent me to the back of the long line. A boy in the middle met my eyes for an instant, but quickly averted his gaze, the only greeting I had from any of them. It wasn't unusual, but today the blank stares called to mind Richie's empty eyes, and it left a pit inside my stomach. How far were we, really, from the dead?

My neighbour was late to leave her room. I wondered if she knew about Richie, and how close she was to his death site. I wondered if she would've cared.

The light on the cylinder was yellow when they scanned her chip. I almost forgot to speculate on what it meant.

The last room on the left was Richie's. Two doors down from mine. As we neared it, it felt as if the mutual exchanging of oxygen in our lungs halted with one intake of breath. The air was tense and heavy as the Retriever banged out his final signal. I'd like to imagine that it was all of us half-expecting Richie to walk out of his room as he had for the last four years, a whisper of a grin still glimmering on a cherubic face.

But he didn't.

Because he was dead.

We remained as silent and stiff as corpses well into the dining hall, long after we fell into line, and our plates were served.

I picked idly at the white lump on my plate, spreading it into an inedible mush across the ceramic. It made a soft, wet squelch as I sunk my fork into it. Caught in my thoughts about Richie, the Spillout, and the yellow light, I spun it around, creating tiny crop circles in the chop. A hand landed on my shoulder with a heavy thump. It shook my whole body.

"You wouldn't be playing with your food now, would you?"

I jerked to attention, dropping my fork onto the table with a resounding clatter. Heads raised to look at me. Hundreds of vacant gazes turned my way. My heart knocked erratically in my throat. "No, sir." My voice was as pathetic as I was. *Rage.* Senator Griggs loomed behind me, his broad forehead shadowing the slope of his eyes, making him look like a thing of nightmares. Fuck, who was I kidding? He was a nightmare, all on his own.

"Is there something wrong with the food?" A tight-lipped smile oozed across his face. He wrapped his thick hand around the back of my neck, digging his blunt fingernails into my skin through a barrier of the Senator's uniform gloves. I sometimes thought they only wore them so no one would know who they'd been touching.

How they'd been touching.

"You know, some people don't have anything to eat at all. You want to be back there, with one of them?" His fingers pressed harder, the seams of his thin gloves eating at my flesh. I wanted to gag.

If this had been a different place, I would have told him that I was sick of eating mashed up gunk every morning. I would have told him I was sick of taking medication that didn't help me feel better and sick of pretending I didn't feel like a compressor was crushing my chest. I was just sick, period.

My jaw tightened. My teeth ground together. And then, slowly, I lifted my fork mechanically to my mouth, shoveling the flavorless grub into the back of my throat. I would've preferred ramming the utensil into the good Senator's eye socket. *Rage.*

Unaware, Griggs offered me a curt nod and moved to continue his rounds.

As he turned to leave, I noticed the boy trailing behind him- Eli. None of us had seen much of him since Richie's rendezvous with the window in the room they had occasionally shared. They had been one of the first to be paired up, though it hadn't seemed to quite stick. Eli was with Richie for less than a month, and even then, he'd been escorted in and out like he was subject to whatever whim the Council had.

Even disregarding the anti-fraternization policy, I never interacted much with him. A sulky, scrawny beanpole of a boy, he kept to himself even more than I did. He had a mop of loose, dark, glossy curls that managed to completely cover his one eye-which was a blessing because two of those yellow-amber eyes would probably have enough impact to make people dry heave-and spiraled around a face just lighter than his hair. I wondered, and not for the first time, why he hadn't gotten his head shaved. I watched him pad softly in the Senator's footsteps. And what made him the Senator's lapdog? *Bootlicker*, I thought, unpleasantly.

The painful twinge in my stomach was unexpected, but I was leery of another interaction with any Senator (but especially Griggs). I directed my focus back towards the plate and attempted to push the strange, sullen boy with the hauntingly beautiful eyes from my mind.

After breakfast, we headed to the infirmary with our tags tied soundly around our wrists. Tired nurses administered medication with quick slaps to the inside of our elbows and three-inch needles. If we weren't vaccinated, there would never be a chance of us entering the city. Nobody had ever been sick there. Any one of us could bring an undiscovered illness into the Pod. If we didn't get better, or our bodies didn't accept the transition, we would be rejected, and our applications disposed of.

We all knew it, but we wished we didn't, so we pretended. We took every shot with a grain of salt, and when we awoke again, we headed to our respective study hall. On the third day of every week, we were relieved from lectures and allotted a small amount of freedom to roam the library. It was my favourite day if you could have a favourite day in here.

My heart swelled as we approached the main doors- a double set, as tall as they were full, with a simple handprint scanner aside the hinge. Plenty of what they built here appeared to be at random, with no apparent rhyme or reason.

As with the individual rooms and hallways, the library was kept in a polished and neat fashion, in stark contrast to the dimly lit hole in the wall we knew as the feeding hall. I was reasonably sure they'd constructed the building as cheaply and quickly as possible, just to get the program up and running.

Every year I thought they'd get sick of traipsing around in a mismatched shithole and do repairs.

Every year they didn't.

The Retriever laid his palm against the panel. His knuckles retracted in a bizarrely slow roll, executing a movement reminiscent of an old, rickety wheel. His pinky was the first to hit the glass with a small thud, then the others followed suit with a distinctly unsettling beat. The pad of his thumb hovered it over the last fingertip sensor.

A bead of sweat slithered along the nape of my neck. I only barely resisted tugging at the collar of my shirt, suffering as the dampness spread.

Damn, it was *hot.* I looked around at the others, searching for at least one distinctly human reaction in the crowd. I swear, sometimes, it was like nobody actually felt anything here. They stood still as statues, frozen like prey at the feet of their predators. Stuck in time as if any movement could cause them to be struck down and wheeled from the hall with unseeing eyes. It was like everything that made them human was just wiped out, as if we were all stripped bare. At this moment, I forgot that we were supposed to be on the same side. I hated them.

They remained as still as they did at this moment, unblinking and unwavering until the doors slid open, and everyone started to move again. Grateful, I quietly began to fall into place in line when I noticed my neighbour for the first time since her late exit this morning. She was a few inches closer to the wall than the rest of us, leaning her hand against it to support her weight. Fuck. I glanced at the Retriever, but luckily for her, his attention was trained on the scanner's blinking lights. Ready to be rid of us, undoubtedly.

I dropped my pace slightly and let the boy behind me pass. His eyes flickered in my direction as he furrowed his brow. Though nothing was said, I could feel the message loud and clear.

Don't.

I let a few more people pass until I was closer to her. Her chest was heaving.

"Hey," I hissed at her. She glanced up, bleary, and disoriented. She looked up at me with the same look I'd once seen on the face of an infected street cat. "You have to get back in line."

My voice was barely a whisper, but it still seemed too loud for the hall. She looked up and opened her mouth as if to speak, but her jaw merely hung open like a man gasping for his last breath. "Come on," I muttered again. The panic was rising in my throat as the others in the line began to take notice of us. Every murmur and stolen glance brought it closer and closer to the doorway. I wanted to strangle every single one of them. Didn't they know to keep their mouths shut? Didn't they care? "You need to move now."

Staring at me with bulging eyes the colour of deep earth, she started forward, dropping her hand from the wall and stumbling into me. Her fingers sank into my flesh as she bore her weight onto my forearms. My body shook with the effort it took to keep us both upright. I wasn't strong enough. The thought made me choke back an unwilling sob because I knew, I knew I couldn't save her. But I didn't let go.

"Please," she said, the tenor of her voice resonating through the hall. "Please, no. I'm so scared. I just want..."

I went to shush her, but I knew it was already too late. The Retriever turned his head away from where he had finally laid down his hand on the scanner, his cold gaze resting on the disruption.

"Please... I want to go home," she wailed. "I didn't want to be here. I don't feel..." She collapsed to her knees, still gripping me, fat, ugly tears sliding down her face. "I can't..." Black, slimy mucus began to dribble from her mouth, dripping down her chin and tarnishing the white blouse. "Please," she moaned again. Her hands slid from mine and fell limp at her sides. It was the only warning I had before her body twisted backward and began to convulse. The Retriever appeared beside her like a ghost. I hadn't even heard him move.

He whispered something, I thought at first to himself, but soon after, a Senator came through the doors of the study hall.

"All of you move- now!" The Senator bellowed with his broad chest puffed out.

The remaining residents flooded forwards. Someone hit me from behind, but I couldn't stop staring at the girl on the floor. Her body was still jerking sporadically, though her eyes were closed and her face even. I hardly registered the Senator reaching us and muttering to the Retriever, who floated away like smoke after the exchange.

The hallway was now void of everyone but me, her, and the Senator. My feet stayed cemented to the ground.

"What is your registration number?" He said to me. His voice was a low rumble. I finally tore my eyes from the stiffening body.

"What?" My voice sounded so very far away. *Where's your head?*

The muscle in his jaw jumped. "Your registration number, resident," he said, but he made it sound like a slur.

"Two..." I started, my brain still moving slowly. "Two... seven... nine... three."

He clicked his tongue against his teeth and stepped over her body like it was a pile of discard, close enough now for me to feel his breath against my cheek. "Two seven nine three?"

I nodded mutely. Why the fuck had I not followed the crowd back? What had I done?

He repeated the number into the egg-shaped walkie-talkie clipped to the front of his shirt. The response sounded like unintelligible static. He was still mumbling into it when he pulled a scanner from his back pocket and gave no courtesy as he yanked my arm towards him.

When he scanned it, it was yellow; I was yellow, she was yellow, and now she was dead. I blinked rapidly as the lights swam and bobbled in my vision. What would that make me?

"Did she touch you?"

I thought of her desperate grip and the bruises from her fingers blooming on my arms. "No, sir," I replied, but my voice trembled. *Yellow*. How was that possible? My heart constricted. I was never yellow.

He grabbed my chin and turned my head towards the ceiling. I stared at the grooves in the tile. "You're certain?"

"Yes, sir."

He left his hand around my throat for a few moments longer, his steely gaze bearing into me. “Fine.” He dropped his hand to gesture towards the entrance. “Go.”

It felt impossible, but I found it in myself to drag my feet the fifteen meters to the door. Still, I couldn’t resist looking back to see the Senator was crouched beside her body, prying her eyes open. A hand grabbed me from behind the door and pulled me away, though not before I saw that the white of her eyes had blackened to the colour of soot.

“Jeez, Valencia, what the fuck are you doing? Are you trying to get yourself thrown out?”

Numbly, I turned my head to see Caleb’s face, full of concern.

“No, I just...” I shook my head to clear it. “She just... collapsed...”

“Okay, just relax.” He pulled me into a narrow aisle to hide from surveillance and cupped my face in one of his hands, the gentle mirror image of the way the Senator had grabbed me in the hallway, even the scratch of his athletic gloves a parallel I didn’t want to draw. *Don’t touch me*, my mind screamed. *Don’t fucking touch me.* I blinked it away.

“Are you okay?”

“What’s going to happen to her?”

He grimaced at the question and dropped both hands to his sides. I stared at the one that had been touching my chin just seconds ago. Thought about ripping off that glove, finding that scar on his palm that I'd etched there almost a decade ago. Prove that we were more than this.

More than stupid yellow lights and dead girls in hallways and everything wrong and twisted about this place.

"You've got to leave it alone." I flinched at his voice. "What's done is done."

"You don't care." I meant to ask, but it came out more like a statement. Caleb sighed and rubbed tersely at the bridge of his nose.

"She's sick, Cia. There's nothing you or any of us can do about it. The Council will deal with it appropriately."

That brought my mind to Richie on the wheeling table again. Was that dealing with it appropriately? Where was the boy who demanded answers, who questioned everything? Who was braver than I could ever be?

A small boy entered the aisle and began rifling through the tabs. Chagrined, I exhaled slowly. For now, Caleb could be right. I could give this to him.

I looked at him, really looked at him for the first time since the conversation began. The last of the adolescence had left his face, which, when nearing your second decade, was to be expected, but it still gave my heart a small twinge to see sculpted cheeks carved into his dark skin. He was not a boy anymore. Not *my boy* anymore.

"You're right, I'm sorry. I'm okay."

There was no conviction in my tone, but he let it go, offering me a toothy grin.

"That's it. Just be careful. Things are getting serious. We're so, so close." His dark eyes skipped across my face, dancing in that way that always convinced me to take his side. I didn't feel so compelled this time. "I wouldn't want you to get caught up in anything you shouldn't and sabotage yourself the way you used to."

I wrinkled my nose, but I didn't reply. Between the two of us, Caleb had always been the smart one. Now it was beginning to feel as if there were things he didn't see.

Or rather, was refusing to.

The tag on his wrist beeped, and it reminded me of the little yellow light that had come from mine. "Oh, shoot, okay. We're being collected now." He smiled again, a dazzling array of pearly white teeth. "I'll catch you later," was tossed out as he began to stride out of the aisle.

My heart sunk.

"Good luck," I called out.

"Don't need it." He said, glancing back at me with a twinkle in his eye. "Remember what I said. Be good."

And then he was gone, and I was alone, left with nothing more than clammy skin and a pounding headache.

Attempting to leave all parts of the interaction behind me, I headed to my favourite section of the library- the history section. It was the only part of the institution that had books, real books, bound and written on pages, and was the only place that alluded to life before the Reckoning.

I trailed my fingers along the spines of the old, faded dust covers and felt the grooves and indents of each letter as if they too, reached for me. I had read every book in this section at least a hundred times, which only left me greedy for more. Sighing, I settled on one and crossed to an empty table in the centre of the hall. When the chair scraped against the ground as I pulled it out, I cringed. The last thing I needed was a disruption citation over my head too. I observed the other residents carefully as I took my seat. Most had their eyes closed and their tablets linked, so they paid no notice to me. I had never gotten used to the idea of plugging your brain into a sheet of plastic and wires to hear a story. I did it when I had to, but not during free study.

I opened my book to a page at random, then flicked to the beginning of that chapter. *Jebediah Hartnell; The Man, The Legend, The New God.* I blanched at the title, as I always did at these. A man calling himself a god didn't make him one, even if he had copious amounts of money. Something people often seemed to forget.

I skimmed the introduction.

Hartnell Industries began as a plastic manufacturer in the early 2030's and took the industry by storm, offering a cheaper, more accessible synthetic blend. By 2055, approximately ninety-five percent of North America had pure Hartnell Plastic replacing all appliances in their home.

Boring. I dragged my gaze to the next paragraph.

Company founders Olivia and Christian Hartnell were found dead in their Los Angeles estate on October 17th, 2056.

There were no signs of a break-in and no evidence of foul play, though the cause of death was never determined.

Immediately following their death, their son, Jebediah, became the company's sole proprietor and was forced to end his study in the North early. Hartnell never spoke of what he was studying, but inside sources suggested he was following a new organic material lead. This mystery material is rumored to have contributed to the bonded plastic known as Synthopolymoxin.

I paused, hearing the strains of a conversation in the aisle beside me. I craned my neck to see past the shelves but could only make out the back of one of their heads. At least there were some people here who still had something to say, though they'd best be quieting soon. It was only a matter of time before the Senator returned from the disturbance in the hall.

My brain was throbbing dully against the hollows of my eye sockets, so I let my eyes drift shut. Every day, I became a little more accustomed to physical ailments. I hoped that one day I would not flinch when harm came to me. I hoped that one day, pain itself would no longer feel like pain. Wouldn't that be a dream?

I set my teeth to their familiar grind and opened my eyes. Though my vision shook, I dragged my eyes back to the book in front of me, where the words swam like tadpoles in a sea of yellowed paper.

Synthopolymoxin hit the market in early 2060 with an affordable cost and impeccable quality, leading many business and production facilities to abandon previous plastic suppliers and open contracts with Hartnell Industries.

From his eagle-eyed perch in his penthouse, Jebediah Hartnell was making billions. This revolutionary product was estimated to break records for any supplier's highest-grossing profit margins in all known history. Synthopolymoxin was the future. Its skyrocketing success was second to none, with nothing getting in its way.

Until the Reckoning.

The Reckoning was a 40-day phenomenon that displaced over eight billion people and ravaged all 195 countries, beginning in the North. The North Pole saw the loss of icebergs and the rise of freshwater that swallowed species of plants and animals alike. This formidable tide continued to climb, rapidly approaching the Arctic, where many people had made their homes. It wasn't until the loss of human lives that people began to take notice.

The news of the flooding caught the attention of several high society members, including presidents, dictators, scholars, and the wealthy. Concerned for their well-being, fortunes, and place in society, the US embassy hosted an emergency conglomerate of foreign powers.

Jebediah Hartnell was one of many to attend. In transcripts and recordings of the event, he was acknowledged to have spoken few words and kept to himself even as tension rose between other occupants. While other leaders of the free world became impassioned and panicked, Jebediah maintained his impenetrable cool despite the knowledge of the things that loomed just outside the door.

Unaware of, or perhaps, unaffected by, the scrutiny, Hartnell left the building with not just a sense of purpose, but an idea. With only thirty-four days left before the forecasted end of the world, Hartnell Industries halted all production and sales of all Synthopolymoxin. They withdrew all products derived from it off the shelves.

Many of the populace were affected as they sought supplies that were quickly selling out, and without Hartnell Industries creating more, there was a vast shortage of survival essentials. What had been such a riveting success was now a hindrance.

At first, it was met with baffled irritation, but as more distributors' supply ran dry and more people were left empty-handed, the anger grew into a type of mania. Hordes of people surrounded the company building's outer security fences, and soon, the noise became deafening. Unbeknownst to them, Jebediah had predicted this movement, long before it had budded in their brains.

I sat up straighter and rolled my shoulders back. A horrible habit, curling forward like I did, making my best impression of a page of a book, touched by too many hands and unable to keep its form. Mid-roll, it occurred to me that the hall had lapsed into thick silence. The pair in the aisle must have dissipated or moved on to another section—all the better. I'd been involved in more than enough drama for the day. If they were to get in trouble, I'd prefer they did it far away from me.

I rubbed the page of the book between my thumb and my forefinger. The smooth plastic lining slid away with ease; the slipperiness was enhanced by the oils of my fingers. I reached into my memory, trying to imagine what paper felt like- real paper- before shaking my head to clear the thought. This, right now, was a form of innovation. That didn't matter anymore. As the Council always said, if things were not changing, we were not moving forward.

I glanced at the band on my wrist. The second bar had yet to move from the green. Since everyone else was still reading, I, too, dragged my gaze back to the page.

... Hartnell quietly gathered his top scientists and developers and moved to a remote location, unbeknownst to anyone outside the tightly knit group. He began construction of the project: a massive, protective Pod that could withstand any natural phenomenon. It was a waterproof, lightweight, near-invincible oval perched upon a flat metal base drilled deep into the earth's crust and protected by a wall higher than its tip.

A mere fifteen days before the projected end, Jebediah and his team opened the Pod for boarding to the summit attendees with a simple alert that bypassed their messaging filters. The rules were simple- if you were a member of high society, you received an invitation. You and your immediate family (spouse included) could gather four personal artifacts and join the crew just North of Sead for processing. The first oversight, one of which Jebediah could have forecasted had he had any need for them himself, was the accounting of a thing just beyond family- friends. The second was-

My wrist vibrated unexpectedly, the red light pulsing against my skin. My head shot up, and I scrambled to shut the book in front of me. How did I miss the call? How could I...

I stood up, clutching the book beneath my arm and nearly toppling as I rounded the corner to the Historical Section. My shoes scuffed at the floor with a quiet squeak. I cursed quietly, resenting that I was never able to execute the grace and diplomacy expected of scholarship kids.

"Come on, come on," I impatiently muttered as I scanned the shelves for the gap where my hardcover belonged. My heart thumped in tandem with the squeeze of my band as the alert became more and more insistent. There! I stretched up onto my toes and slide the book into its slot with a thud. In a flurry of white, I whirled away from section and towards the front door, where Gideon, the Department Head, gathered the rest of the quadrant.

My fellow residents swarmed around him, their small heads bobbing and swimming at the height of his chest. It was a reminder that though we all might've felt as if we had reached adulthood, we were hardly more than children. Gideon raised a single hand flat against the air, and everyone halted movement. He rolled his neck to the side and closed his eyes as his head swayed on its mount. It let out a stomach-churning *'crik.'*

Many things about Gideon were stomach-churning, though I couldn't quite place a finger on what it was exactly. He followed the same physical blueprint everyone in the Council shared. Still, somehow on him, the strong brow and gradually sloping forehead seemed aggressive and confrontational instead of romantic and classic.

He flitted his eyes across the sea of people in front of him with mild disinterest. A shudder raced down my spine when his gaze settled on mine. There was no small world to describe how I felt when I saw him. The closest? *Terror.*

His eyes were a cold, metallic blue-grey that reflected the harsh overhead lights with impossible sharpness and lacked all depth and response.

"As you all know," he began to speak in a commanding tone that stomped heavily upon each syllable. "There was an incident involving a resident from your quadrant this morning. They have been moved to Solitary and will not be returning."

My hand curled into a fist at my side, my weak grip only pressing the tips of my fingers lightly into my palm. *Dead, dead, dead girls. Everywhere.*

"I implore all of you to move on from this with a renewed, sharpened sense of focus and complete your studies accordingly." Gideon glanced at his watch. "Assemble into proper formation. You are due."

I had been number thirteen in the straight line for three months now, behind a fair-skinned girl with wide-set eyes and a bowed mouth. Spotting her, I slipped in behind, my nose almost brushing the back of her head as someone nudged me from behind. Afraid to take a step back and cause a ruckus, I stayed there, breathing against the nape of her neck where her peach fuzz had begun to curl. She shifted her head and shuddered, perhaps in response to the unwanted close contact, and the fine hairs rustled in a way that bordered on hypnotizing.

Up ahead, Gideon was punching in the code for the door with his broad shoulders successfully shielding the panel from view. I resisted the urge to roll my eyes at the scene I saw every day. Nothing ever changed. The doors slid open as if it had been accessible all along. On the other side, our Retriever was waiting, rubbing his spindly hands together. It made me sick watching them glide over each other, bony fingers trailing behind, so I turned back to Peach Fuzz and followed along mechanically when we began to walk.

Peach Fuzz was probably going to be the first from our group to graduate. She was the closest to a Patron. They wouldn't like her curly hair, but she had the skin for it. They always picked the pale ones first.

Not that I was necessarily dark either, especially since being institutionalized. Not that it mattered- my skin would never be that creamy ivory that all of the Senators boasted.

The group took a sharp turn into West Hall, our slippers making barely audible scuffs on the stone floor. The Retriever's footsteps made no sound. Their feet must touch the ground, I knew that, but the way their hooded figures glided made it seem as if they didn't. I caught a glimpse of the side of The Retriever's face when he halted at the Lecture Hall and shuddered. His cheekbones sliced through the air, leaving two hollow caves where the skin had stretched itself so thin across that the light silhouetted the outlines of his rotted teeth from the other side. I almost thanked the Gods when he turned away. Seeing his face was different than knowing in concept what lay beneath the hood.

What was that phrase that used to be so popular? 'Ignorance is bliss'? That one. I closed my eyes for a moment while we waited for the Senator to unlock the door. I could hear the soft whoosh of Peach Fuzz's breath and the nervous clicking of The Retriever's long fingernails against one another. Beyond that, there was nothing. Big, fat, fucking god-awful ugly nothingness.

I wanted to live in the moments where there was something again. I wanted to hear voices, laughter, conversation. I wanted to listen to clashes and bangs and the scraping of rusty wheelbarrows and the whirr of rickety wheels as they raced down bumpy roads. I wanted to hear life again. Not this poor replication. I wanted it so badly I thought I might fall apart, right here.

Someone nudged me from behind with a solid thud, and I pried my eyes open to see the doors sliding open and Senator Gideon taking the stage. The Retriever bowed slightly, his spine curving into the shape of a question mark as he held out his hand for the release scan. Gideon waved his panel atop the Retrievers, and it beeped in response, blinking green. In a barely intelligible hiss, the Retriever thanked the guard and backed away in their quiet, eerie manner.

Gideon waved us in, scanning each of our panels as we passed into the room. I avoided eye contact when he did mine, and instead, stared ahead of me into the room that unfolded like a toppling tower of cards.

The seats climbed the slanted walkway with the spaces in between each skinny and near nonexistent. Personal space wasn't a concept here. We weren't worthy of it.

We took our seats in the order we entered, so the twelve others and I scaled the ramp to the line of seats along the back wall. I spared a quick glance behind us. I'd rather be up here than up close and personal with the Professor. When I was still #27, my row was second from the front, and I made eye contact too often to blend in. All I ever wanted to do was blend in. On that thought, I slid into my seat and rubbed a hand over the fluff on my head.

I caught myself and smiled thinly, remembering how Auntie used to get so angry with me for always playing with my hair. She said a restless person was a person with no resolve- a person who was weak-minded needed distractions. A formidable person did not. I dropped my hand, but I didn't feel formidable.

The wave of pain in my temples was sudden but not unexpected. My headache was back. It was relentless today. I pressed my tongue against the roof of my mouth and tried to channel my pain through the pressure.

"Welcome back."

My neck rolled my weighted head to face the front, where the Professor had taken residence. He was a small man- much more modest in appearance than Gideon- with wire-rimmed glasses that frequently slid down his narrow nose despite his jerky efforts to shove them further back against his eye sockets. I doubted his incessant nervous perspiration helped his cause much. Out of everyone the Council employed, I probably liked the Professors the best. As an enemy, they were a meek one.

"As most of you know, I am the Professor." He wrung his hands together like a damp rag. Twist, twist. Release. "For those of you who don't, my role here is to educate you on what it means to be a Citizen."

Those of us who didn't... curiously, I peered down at the front seats, looking for new faces. To my surprise, there were three. That on its own was not incredibly strange- new kids came in rotations of three to five, on referral by Scouts' from their expeditions into the outer circle- but it was a Thursday, and drop-off was always Tuesday. We'd already gotten our new set this week. I scanned the crowd for the four kids I saw yesterday. Only spotting two of them, I rubbed a hand over my brow. Had I counted wrong?

No. I distinctly remembered four. Three of the kids had obviously been from the South. They had all looked so similar, which was odd because there was a significant rarity of outside people having familiars. We were all mixed with everything, so nothing ever came out looking the same. But I remembered them because they did.

I looked back at the one, the boy, who had come in yesterday, perched in seat twenty-four. His pallor was a mere shade or two darker than mine, and the fuzz on his head was coiled tighter. I imagine when he arrived, he would've had a mane of wild, unruly curls that bounced off each other in the holiest of matrimonies. Self-consciously, I touched my own once more. I had always wanted my hair to have more life.

Valencia, I cut the thought off with a silent scold to myself. *What the fuck are you going on about?*

It felt like my mind was on a wheel today. Scrambling, scrambling, scrambling, and never ending up anywhere in specific. Just running.

"Today, we will be watching an instructive film that will delve into life in Emaldin and the requirements of each citizen. Immediately following the film, I will be passing around an information sheet on each of the newer vaccinations mentioned, to which you will sign your understanding." He blinked rapidly. "So, without further ado," he turned from us and dimmed the lights, flicking the switch on the projector.

The title scene marched high across the wall in a minimalist block font, 'QZX-22'. I shuddered involuntarily. The QZX bracket was a bracket full of fast switching images, strangely even tones, and overlapping chatter. It barely came as a surprise when a kid last month had a seizure during 17. They pulled him out on a stretcher, and we never saw him again.

I squirmed anxiously in my seat and stole looks at my peers. They all sat impossibly still with their wide, unblinking eyes trained on the screen. The movie hadn't even started yet, not that it would be interesting once it did. I know it wasn't supposed to be and that we were to learn something from it, but I could've easily summarized it after the first two times, let alone the seventh.

The Pod is good.

Citizens of the outer city are bad.

Bad is not allowed in the Pod. I tapped my finger anxiously on my knee. Nothing was allowed in the Pod except perfection.

We knew. We'd heard it a hundred times before.

Here, in Emaldin, we strive to create the best possible life for our citizens.

A woman with a sleek cap of platinum blonde hair lifted a child up from a highchair, effortlessly balancing them on her hip in her slate grey suit. The child gurgled happily and clapped its chubby hands.

Our goal began the same as any- to keep the ones we love safe, warm, and healthy.

The camera dropped the woman's image and pulled up footage of a narrow white building with a simple red cross above the door.

Illness, even that of a simple cold, has a vaccine that ends it on its track. We guarantee that you and your loved ones will never be ailed again.

So let me ask the question before you do- what do doctors do when there's a cure for everything?

The screen changes again, abruptly switching to a dimly lit scene with humans' silhouettes around a table.

Now, we push the boundaries of what it truly means to be alive. We help you become your best self. Faster. Smarter. Stronger.

The screen flickered through images of equations being scrawled on chalkboards, to a man swollen with muscles and broad shoulders pulling a stack of bricks behind him.

I turned my head to my seatmate, ready to send a look that encompassed my, 'get a load of this,' attitude, but her eyes were glassy as the screen reflected in the circle of her pupil. Her soft cherry lips mouthed the words soundlessly.

There are no limits to what we can do.

I gritted my teeth together and tried desperately to bring the world into focus. But the discomfort did not subside. My breath was coming out in deeper puffs as I tried to pull the oxygen into my lungs.

Come with us on this journey.

The collar of my shirt rubbed coarsely again on the skin of my neck, and I slipped a finger beneath it to yank at it impatiently. Sweat was beading on my forehead in thick, massive drops that slithered down my face and left slimy trails of excretion in their wake. Above me, the narrow-bladed metal fans worked weakly against the suffocating heat, rattling where they hung from the ceiling. Their metal chains swung laboriously from the head, sending the ends clacking against each other in obnoxious melody.

Ask yourself when you have the chance...

The frog in my throat grew ever larger, tickling my uvula with its ribbed back. A cough brewed deep in my tonsils and pushed against the walls of my chest. I cracked my neck. Tensed my fingers. Shifted again.

Wouldn't you want to be on the

right side

of evolution?

The presenter had yet to see me, his attention remaining drawn to the screen, like a moth to a flame. The pad of his thumb rubbed the textured scroller as the speaker vocalized from the small cube.

I would ask myself a hundred times why I suddenly found the room insufferable and the poor excuse of education impossible. I would ask myself a hundred times why that day I couldn't sit still for another moment and just get through it.

The sweat-soaked through the underside of my blouse and left damp grey blemishes on the crisp shirt. My heart rate had skyrocketed and had begun the fight to free itself from the prison of my ribs. I rolled my shoulders backward and brought my head to the curve of my left collarbone to dissipate some of the restlessness, but to no avail.

And then I did the worst thing I had done up to this point. Worse than any of the stolen goods, the pillaging, or the looting.

I stood.

For a brief moment, no one seemed to notice, and I wondered if I would be able to slip out of the lecture hall and make it to my room unprovoked. This was a foolish thought.

My seatmate with the glassy eyes made a noise in her throat, prompting the row to look for the origin of the disruption.

Disruption. A Class-3 punishable offense.

My feet cemented to the floor.

It took all of three minutes for the presenter to gather that the focus had shifted, perhaps picking up on the unmistakable buzz in the air. His beady eyes sought out the disturbance and quickly zeroed in on me.

I knew I was going to die at this moment.

I had never broken any rules before. I had never rebelled. I was always green. I was always green, I thought with a touch of mania. I was grateful to be here. Wasn't I grateful to be here? My palms began to tingle, and I wiped them urgently on the sides of my thighs. It did little to rid me of the squirming feeling. I couldn't stop thinking about the boy who had the seizure, and how after he disrupted the class, it was like he never existed in the first place.

My knees remained locked together as I stood ramrod straight in my aisle, the flat of my seat pressing gently against the back of my legs. I wanted to exist.

A painstakingly slow minute crawled by with the cantor of a snail on heavy gravel. I was holding eye contact with The Professor when he first made the call. His hands trembled with uncertainty as he pressed on his pager and contacted a Senator over the small device. I wondered if it would be Gideon. My brain buzzed quietly, a steady, monotone sound that shook the walls of my skull in a gentle tremble. I hoped it wouldn't be Gideon.

My joints finally loosened, and I took my first, shaky step down the stairs. It felt like the first time I had ever walked. I couldn't remember how to bend my knee. Did I do it while it was in the air? I stumbled drunkenly on the third step.

Every eye in the auditorium zeroed in on me. I could never get used to attention, even when I was still in the Outer City. Caleb would always demand I come out of my shell. I pressed the palm of my hand against the slope of my temple. I never wanted people to see me. Would he be mad if he could see me?

I took another step, then another. I barely remembered that person now. Everything felt far away. Had I anything left? The only thing I felt anymore was this sickness, weaving its way through spider web veins and embedding itself into my bones. I dropped down the final step.

The Professor's face warped into an expression of horror and puzzlement. His upper lip curled backward to show a set of impossibly small, pointed teeth. His tongue darted out wildly to moisten his scaly lips as he nervously clicked the button on his pager three more times.

One.

Two.

Three.

I cocked my head. He didn't know what to do, I thought to myself.

I turned on my heel and gazed upon the wide eyes of my comrades and their wells of deep, empty sadness. No one did.

I had, but minutes before the response team made their grand entrance. If I begged for my forgiveness and pleaded a sad case, it was plausible to get off with isolation and a hearty slap on the wrist. All I had to do was go back to my seat and plead insanity.

But I didn't. I could've. But didn't. I took loping strides to the door and stared blankly at the panel and all its flashing gimmicks.

"Res-." I turned my head and slated a sharp glance at the Professor. He recoiled from my direct gaze. "Ah. Resident," his voice shook, "Return to your seat immediately."

Somebody laughed, and the light, breathless sound danced its way to the ceiling. It took me another moment to realize it was me.

I ignored his request and reached out to the glass panel. My fingers had barely grazed it when the backlight changed from the crisp blue to a blaring red. I was too far gone to be nervous about it. Either I made it out, or I didn't. Either way, I was as good as dead. I leaned my weight into my fist and set it in the centre of the panel. The screen rippled around my fist in rainbow-colored stripes. I pressed harder, and the colours dimmed. I just wanted out. I needed out. I couldn't be here anymore. I couldn't. I blindly swung my fist, landing it smartly where I had leaned it. Then again. And again. All that existed was this anger. Pure and unadulterated, the rage coursed through my entire body. I swung once more. The glass splintered beneath my hand, sending slivers in between the slopes and dips of my knuckles. Blood trickled from my skin and onto the floor, leaving bright red splatters on the white like roses in milk.

Out.

Out.

The panel meekly beeped as I swung for a final hit, bashing the flat of my fist into the mechanism. *Out.* My head swam as the blood poured from the pale, thin skin that lazily held my flesh together. I was in the middle of deciding if collapsing on the floor was the only viable option when the doors hissed and slid open, the gears groaning in a vast array of confused noises.

"No way," I laughed breathlessly. "No way."

It was impossible. It was... I took two shaky steps towards the main hallway, entranced by the yawning mouth of architectural creation and the ghosts it held. I had never been in it alone.

We were forbidden to go anywhere alone.

But here I was- alone.

A faint scuff of shoes on the floor came from around the bend, presumably a group of enforcing guards, judging by the pace and heaviness of their step. I broke into a clumsy jog deeper down the length of the hallway. Idiots, I seethed, baring my teeth.

I took the way back towards the banquet hall because it was a route I knew by heart, so when it appeared, I plowed into the silver-plated door without hesitation and let the vibrations wreak havoc on my weak frame.

“There she is!” Someone yelled from behind me, but the whole world was a blur, and I couldn’t determine the origin. I kept running, past the feeding tables that stretched with endless abandon and scrambled over the cracked linoleum.

My lungs ached for air - real air, the kind we got a taste of once a month when we opened the windows. Not the air they blasted through the vents that didn’t even taste like air. I used my shoulder to launch myself through a set of doors on the opposite end and tumbled into a room adorned with slim ladles that swung from the ceiling like pendulums—the kitchen. My breathing was ragged as I registered the swinging doors and the grand oven.

“Shit,” I muttered. It wasn’t a way out. Of course, it wouldn’t be so easy. So foolish. Always foolish. I was always fucking foolish. I curled my bloodied hand back into a fist, thought about plowing it into the wall.

A sharp clatter from the other side of the kitchen sent my heart further into my throat until I could taste blood on the back of my tongue. Ice swam through my veins with the potency of a hearty man’s bourbon.

Someone was in here.

Fighting against panic, I twisted, desperately looking for a place to hide. For a kitchen, the room was decidedly sparse. The shelving units along the wall stood a mere two feet high, packed with nondescript boxes and unmarked, grey packages. My taste buds remembered the heavy sludge from this morning and led a revolt in my mouth.

Trembling, I reached for a mallet that was atop the counter and clutched it in a weak fist. I had never been a fighter. I wasn't a fighter. *"It's a good thing you have me," Cal said, his eyes glimmering from above the smudges on the peaks of his cheekbone. "Otherwise you'd just run away from everything."* I sucked in a sharp breath, blinked into reality.

Footsteps tapped along the tile.

I backed up until I was flat against the wall, the mallet braced in front of me. Of course, in the Outer City, we all had to be fighters in a way. My chest heaved with wheezing breaths that rattled my lungs. But Cal was right. I was a forager. I was the sly one. I was the runner.

The handle of the mallet slips slightly in my sweaty palms. I readjusted and shifted, swallowing thickly, heart running wild.

The figure appeared in front of me, shifting back and forth in a way that inspired deep feelings of unease. They weren't quite a Retriever- not quite as thin and the skin not nearly as faded- but something else entirely. Their bulging, owlish eyes scanned over me, drinking in the uniform and my panel before the sparse brows lowered into a glower.

"You."

It surprised me with a human voice, though it shouldn't have. A slight whistle sounded as they settled their mouth at the end of the single word. Their jaw cracked as they cranked it open again. "You shouldn't be back here."

My tongue darted out to wet my lips, catching a salty droplet of sweat that had sunk its way into my cupid's bow. The mallet weighed heavily on my weak arms. "D-don't come any closer," I said shakily. The handle slipped into my palm.

They stared at me from their spot a few feet away, still swaying, unable to keep still. Their bulbous head, made more apparent by the lack of hair, teetered on a thin neck in an almost comical way. They reached for their belt, and I lifted the mallet in a warning. I wasn't about to get taken down by a mutant kitchen-maid. Not now. I was so close. I just needed out. They needed to understand that. I set my teeth. "I don't want to hurt you," I said, this time without the stutter. And it was true. I just wanted *out.*

The creature dropped its head to its shoulder and left it there, pulling at the thin elastic at their belt loop. It grunted softly. Intrigued, I found myself taking a small step forward.

For the first time since I had entered the Institute, the fear was ebbing, leaking through the soles of my feet into the Institute's foundation. I imagined it like a toxic spill, spreading along the internal structure, eating at the beams.

"What is it?" I asked, my voice sounding suddenly childish in my ears.

They pulled at the item on their belt again impatiently. Uncertain, I glanced around the room. It remained to be the two of us and no way out. Keeping my eye on their rolling head, I took another step forward until I was close enough for their impossibly hot breath to feather against my skin.

"Take it," it said.

I looked down at what they were holding in the bruised and mangled hand. A slim, white card dangled from a silver clip. "I take this," Shakily, they raised their other hand to wrap around the forgotten mallet and gently tugged until I released, "And you take this." They pressed the card into my palm.

"What do I..."

The creature held a finger to its lips, then turned from me, using the same finger to point at a wall section in between shelving. It took me a few moments to clue into the small silver box that I had previously mistaken for an item on the shelf in my state of confusion.

"You're letting me go? Why?"

They tilted their head again, a human movement not dissimilar to the one I had used earlier to dissipate my initial restlessness. When they didn't reply, I took the extra steps to the side wall and began to scope out the mechanism.

Like the lecture hall, the door was held in place by a gear system, triggered with only the valid security passes. I cast another glance at the near whimsical wisp of a thing. On the card, they were labeled as a kitchen staff member, but it was difficult to imagine it being able to perform such duties. They must be so terribly ill.

I lifted the card below the scanner. It blipped quietly, and I stepped back, but nothing happened. Had I done something wrong? No. I had seen this done hundreds of times. The only ones requiring supporting entry were our rooms and primary exits.

"Hey," I asked into the dark room, "Is this a trick?"

But they were gone, disappearing as soundlessly as they had appeared. I approached the panel for the second time, inexplicably irritated, similarly waving the card as I had before. Blip, it said.

"Come on," I moaned breathlessly. "Why would it-."

The door groaned in a sound reminiscent of a wounded prisoner and rumbled from its place in the wall. Dust fell slowly from the ceiling in a thick film as it worked itself open. How long had it been shut? Surely the staff would use this corridor to go in and out.

I stared into the yawning cavern, unable to breach the threshold. It was dark- darker than anything I'd ever seen before. My heart started beating heavier in my chest like a steel drum in a broken cage, shaking my body like a bag in the wind. I was trying to remember the feeling of anything else- the ground beneath my feet, the tickle of dust on my nose, the key pass in my hand- but I could not reach it.

Valencia. A whisper from somewhere above me. Below me. Around me. *Valencia. They are coming. Hurry.*

"Hurry," I said dully. Why was I hurrying? Where was I going?

I pressed a hand to my forehead, wobbling precariously.

I had been running. Running. I looked down at my legs and imagined them in the form I had seen in the mirror this morning. Blotchy, discoloured, and skinnier than broom handles- it was hard to believe they still could carry my body anywhere with any impressive cantor. It was even harder to believe that they could bring me any farther.

And so, I stared into the darkness. I stared until my vision creased with spots and an ever-growing vignette.

Then, I stepped forward.

The dim light from the kitchen reached its weak arms as far into the darkness as the shadows would allow, allowing me to watch the shape of my feet disassemble and slip out of focus the deeper I went.

The open hallway echoed my breathing back at me as I scrambled forward. I was losing the light in front of me now, so I kept my left hand against the wall's cool plastic. It was such a contrast to the ever-swelling heat. A part of me wanted to stop running and press my face against it, hopeful to chill the burning flame that crackled beneath my skin.

But there was no time to stop. The alarm had spread into the food hall, and the sound of the chairs being knocked aside was unmistakable.

I could picture it in my head. Griggs, with his silvery black baton, and Richard by his side, pulling out chairs, one by one by one; tossing them into the aisle before peering beneath the tables. Looking for me. Hunting me

"Bastards," I muttered through gritted teeth, stopping as my fingers bumped into a raised panel. I wasn't hiding.

Using both hands, I felt my way to the slender bar that stretched across the door.

I wasn't hiding. Not anymore. I exhaled slowly.

I wasn't a coward.

I raised my head forward and braced both hands against the mechanism.

I was a runner.

~~~~~~~~~~

My heart was no longer an enemy, but a friend, the flurried knocking against my ribs, urging me forward. *Go, go, go, go*, it said with each thump.

I ignored the mash of voices as they grew behind me and launched myself out of the darkness into the sticky air and blazing light.

It hit me like a ton of bricks. The sun was vicious against my suddenly vulnerable eyes. I shaded them using the flat of my hand and squinted off into the horizon. The door had let out on the opposite side of the tarmac. Across the yard on the left, I had
~~~~~~~~~~

a clear view of the electric fence behind me that signified the edge of our 'Outdoors Area.'

It had been years since I had been beyond it. I moved away from the exit, still unclear in my plan, jogging lightly across the pad. There were access bridges that stretched around the Pod, connected the Institute to the other work centre across the way. They reached and stretched around the Pod's outside like rings around a planet, blocked off by secure gates and electronic blinking. The other building was always silent, stoic.

No one ever saw any movement from that side.

Two emergency ladders rolled up in tight cylinders and bundled with safety cords were kept on the other side of the Outdoors' Area. It was almost like bait, keeping it within view of the residents but far enough to be untouchable- unreachable.

Caleb and I had studied them from inside the barriers, and released, it would let out by the dam. I would have to drag it to the edge of the bridge without being caught, and God knows how heavy one of those cast-iron things would weigh. The fear had seeped into my skin now, sending my thoughts spinning into an abysmal whirlwind.

What had I done?

Four guards came sprinting from the doors near the fence. Their sturdy legs ate up the ground meter by meter with the grace and ease of dancers. So ugly, so wretched, so wrong, and yet.

And yet.

My eyelids felt heavy, so unbearably heavy. They drooped and cut off the upper quarter of my vision.

The men descended towards me in a sloppy crescent. From the distance they were at, gaps were still between each man, but they were moving, and moving quickly. Could I find a way through? Slither my way through the loopholes, they left as if they were asking for me to try?

Runner. I closed my eyes. I was so, so tired, but I needed to run.

"Valencia!"

I jerked at the sound of Caleb's voice as if a bullet had struck my spine. I caught his eye from his place inside the Resident Perimeters. His expression was one of terror, warping his beautiful face into something I almost couldn't bear to see. His fingers dug into the links of the fence.

My shirt clung to my back. Why was it so damn hot?

"Drop to your knees and put your hands on your head," an officer shouted. He was approaching me, almost on top of me, reaching for his gun from the holster on his hip. I wanted to say there was no point. That he would shoot me anyway. That no matter what position I angled my cruelly decrepit body in, I was nothing but waste. But I was tired. I was tired, and it was hot, unbearably so, and there was nowhere for me to go.

Caleb frantically pulled at the links of the Parameter, his screams shoving their way past the breath that was tearing raggedly from his lungs. "No! Valencia, no! Please, oh God, no. Don't do this!"

I had never heard him scream like that. I had known him for years, more years than I could count on my hands, but I had never heard him scream the way he screamed for me. He was a man, but right now, he was just a boy. A boy pleading with a God he didn't believe in.

A boy begging the world for a bargain it would never give.

Where are you, Valencia? I curled my toes in my shoes. *Are you in the clouds?*

I shook the voices of the dead out of my brain and stared at the man barreling towards me, his face twisted in an expression of pure and foul rage. The flesh of his face wobbled like jelly thinly tethered to the bone of his skull.

After what felt like an eternity, I called my cement feet into action and began to clamber in the opposite direction. It didn't take long for me to pick up speed. With my blood pumping hot in my ears, I ripped the collar of my shirt to free my neck as it sucked the boiled air into my lungs. The first shot they fired tore into the flesh of my arm, beading small orbs of blood until they leaked together into a crimson river.

Tears welled in my eyes when I saw the edge of the bridge ahead of me. My feet slapped in a sludgy puddle, spraying muddy residue up the back of my legs and dirtying the last clean part of my suit. I scrambled to the edge and gazed at the flush river below me.

The place it all began.

Pushed it too far. Went too far. They all said the Spillout was too far.

I twisted back, seeking Caleb's eyes, but he was gone now. They took him. Tears stung my eyes. They *took* him.

"I'm sorry," I whispered as the guards swarmed me. Griggs was there, cool and maniacal, not a drop of sweat in his collar. It was a hundred fucking degrees, and he didn't even have the nerve to sweat. My head swooned. "I'm sorry, Caleb," I whispered, my throat raw with grief. I'd failed him. Isn't that what I always did? Always disappointing him. I should've done more. I should've been...

The second shot rang out like the crack of a whip and split the air directly down the middle. I forget to breathe here, at this moment.

The last thing I saw was Griggs' cursed face creasing into a wicked grin from behind the bold silver weapon with an emotion I couldn't quite place.

The bullet tore into my chest. I took a step backward, teetering on the edge of the roof. Griggs raised his weapon again.

No, you know what, I knew that face. I had seen it before, on the cruel boys Downtown, who would swarm and taunt you like birds over a carcass.

Glee.

It was glee.

The last shot plunged into my gut. Instinctively, I brought both hands to my stomach, my mouth drooping into a slack O. I waited for the pain, but it never came. The blood spilled between my fingers, running rampantly down my front. I swooned and lost my footing, desperately trying to get the useless feet flat beneath me, but I couldn't find the earth.

Stumble,

Stumble,

Fall.

The air enveloped my body in a windy embrace. I could see nothing in front of me and nothing behind me. The world was cloaked in black velvet, and the sweetest humming sound kissed my ears as I fell. Was it out there? Or was it inside of me? My eyes drifted shut. It was so impossible to tell.

I wasn't hiding anymore.

2

Resurrection

My first impression was one of weightlessness.

There was a dull rocking around my limbs, the only assurance that they were, in fact, still there. I couldn't feel the throb of my head or the ache in my bones. There was nothing, except this gentle rocking.

This peace.

Then, belatedly- oh, shit, I was fucking *drowning*.

It had taken a bit for my lungs to kick in with the panicked message, but once they had, it was all I could feel. It felt like I was swelling, water crowding my organs, climbing up my spine like a ladder to my brain.

The entire time I was thrashing, I was thinking over and over again how stupid I was for never learning to swim. For not following Cal into the water when he told me that the water could get me worse than anything.

My face broke the surface entirely by accident of momentum when I'd managed to flap my arms in the right angle that had me surfacing above the churning waves.

"Fuck," I garbled out, blinking the grime out of my eyes.

I'd finally clued into the way kicking my legs worked to keep me afloat, and the waves seemed smaller as a result, but by no means less violent.

It appeared the only reason my body had been stopped was due to the grate behind me. I hadn't noticed it touching me before- again, I only had the dullest awareness of even being A Body- but when I turned to hook my fingers into the slots of the rusted, slimy grate, I realized how far I'd been carried downstream. Even though it was grimy, I laid my forehead on the slimy metal and tried to slow a suddenly frantic heart.

It was still hot- so, so warm, the sun reverent and blazing, but I had the oddest sense of it not being the same day I'd fallen out of. Maybe it was the pliancy of my skin, the deep pruning of my fingers, the way I felt like I might start shaking and never stop, but whatever the reason, I felt like I'd been pulled in circles for hours and hours.

I sucked in a deep breath, flexing my fingers in the grate's knotholes. I needed out of here, out of the water. The next gulp of air burned like hell like my lungs had been well and truly fine in death, and now here I was, dragging them back to work.

I swore again because that was kind of the way it felt to pull my frame out of the hungry water with nothing but my knuckles. I was so close to the top, if I was just a little longer, if I could just dislocate my shoulder and send my arm up an extra inch, I'd be out.

My ribs, my shoulders, everything was screaming as I scrambled to get hold of the edge. When I finally made contact, the praise of God slipped through numb lips as I managed to hook both hands on the side of the Spillout.

I grabbed hold of the ledge with numb hands and began to sink into the thick, slimy grout that shoved itself beneath my fingernails and into my wounds. Crying out in exhaustion, I dug my knuckles further into the soft waste until I had enough power to hoist my body to the height of the cord.

The weight of my sopping uniform was nearly unbearable. It felt like the wet clothes were made of old stone, the material determined to drag me back down into the water that would sooner see me drown than be freed. It wouldn't have surprised me if the Council intended it that way.

Groaning, I locked my arms straight and pulled my body onto land.

For a blessed moment, I laid entirely still on my back, staring blindly up at the silver-lined sky.

A cluster of surveillance birds flocked together and soared across the sky in a V formation, their wings beating mechanically in a synchronized program every few moments. I remained motionless- incredibly so- unable to cultivate enough energy to scramble undercover.

A modest breeze broke through the oppressive heat and stroked a gentle hand over my wet hair.

Was I dead? Is this what comes after? Heaven?

I held out a hand above me, blocking the sun. After a beat, I spread the webs of my fingers open and let the blaze shine through. It all felt so real, but I felt so different. So... *wrong*. Soiled.

The dry turf rubbed coarsely against my exposed skin, and the wind whispered back quiet relief. Perhaps I was meant to stay here, this clearing amongst the garbage. There must be some kind of metaphor in that.

Irrevocably fatigued, I closed my eyes against the sunlight and attempted to slow my breathing. Couldn't start running if you were exhausted, Caleb had always told me. That was the first rule.

I inhaled slowly, then released before opening my eyes again. The water beside me was still turning viciously, splattering water off the mud wall and misting my legs. From here, I could even see the faint horizon of the roof and the mangled link fence that surrounded the Resident's Area.

It was but a speck in the distance.

Shuddering, I dragged myself upright. No, certainly not heaven. Feeling no pain, I looped a few fingers into the tear on my pant leg and peeled the clothing back. The seams split easily and unraveled into loose strings against the skin of my thigh. Confused, I looked back at where I'd fallen. The edges of my memories were jagged and torn, like puzzle pieces that wouldn't quite snap together, but I remembered running, and Caleb's devastation, and... shots? Shots fired. I jerked my hands to my chest and felt for the holes I knew were there. I didn't want to look, but I needed to know.

The wounds were there, as undoubtedly as they had been when I fell, but they had long stopped their leaking, the edges soft and grey like rot.

"What the fuck?" I exclaimed as if expecting something to come out of the silence with answers. What the fuck?

Was I dead? I waited to feel the thud of my heart again. After a few moments, I stopped holding my breath. Did it matter? To everyone I'd known during my stay, I was. I'd be just another room they felt uncomfortable passing during attendance.

Just like Richie.

People would believe that I jumped just like they did with him. Strange how easy it was to gain perspective when you found yourself living out the last few minutes of someone else's story.

Had it been Griggs, I wondered, who'd cracked Richie's neck the same way he fired those shots?

I lifted myself shakily to my feet and made a few swipes at the grunge from the front of the jumpsuit. It stuck stubbornly to the wet cotton, and I laughed breathlessly at the sheer futility of it. There was no salvaging any of it. Not a goddamn piece.

Sighing in frustration, I tugged free the remaining shreddings of a sleeve and tossed it aside. I was going to need a change of clothes, or lord knows, I wasn't going to get far. There were few things more suspicious than a bald-headed girl with a damaged uniform and open sores. God, I was like a wandering leper. A damn leper who didn't know left from right.

I rotated in a slow circle to get a better view of my surroundings- tall beams. I squinted as the sun reflected into my eyes: tall beams, a low and crookedly built overhang. And, because I had yet to see another person- sparse population. Out of habit, I reached to rub at my temples, as I often did to soothe my chronic, pounding headaches. It occurred to me mid-rub that there wasn't any pain to rub away.

God, this was all fucked.

I glanced back up towards the Pod. Even though I'd traveled towards one of the canals- the water traveled freely in a circle around the Pod's base but split off into four separate channels that divided our city into quadrants. Since I had my head craned back and could just make out the very last of the Outdoors Area in the far left of my peripherals, I'd somehow ended entirely South of where I'd once made my residence in the Institute.

"Could this get any worse?" I said aloud, to no one in particular. My words came out like bubbles were still in my throat. "Okay," I tried to speak calmly, to centre myself.

It wasn't the end of the world. It was a pisser to be all the way over here, but really, the whole city was the same if you had no one waiting for you. Everything was dirty, grimy, and miserable- and I was counting what I remembered about the people in that. Same. Shit.

If I was, say, looking for a real change- the kind of change that would make everything feel new again- I'd have to play around with the distance I was to and from the Pod- never moving in a circle. There might as well only be two directions- closer and further. It was a shame that the best advice I ever got was to not go looking for things in the far other direction. Things got a lot screwier the further away you got.

I rolled my shoulders beneath the uncomfortable bridging of my blouse's seams. And how much more of that could we really afford?

The only people who would willingly leave a life for one further away were people that knew they had no chance. People who were forced out.

Was I to belong there now too, with the rejects- the people that couldn't- and wouldn't- ever be successfully scouted or contracted out? Now that I was without a scholarship, registration, or a license to save my life, what was there for me to return to downtown?

If I had been my choice, my real choice, as in: if I had been allowed to merely... exist with my autonomy and make decisions for my own livelihood, I liked to imagine that I would've chosen something noble. Honourable, maybe. Good, hard, honest work.

Distracted, I thrust my fingernail into my mouth, and I was mid-gnaw when I realized it was still full of grime from the slime alone the side of the Spillout, and that was what I was tasting.

“Fuck,” I said, spitting into the dirt next to the path. “Nasty.”

I was hunched over, back curved like a scythe and cragged hands resting on my knees, and I just couldn’t stop thinking at that moment that I was such a liar. I wouldn’t have done the ‘right’ thing and zipped my mouth up and worked in a factory or slaved in production, and I would never have upheld a law I didn’t agree in- there weren’t any honourable jobs for dishonourable people, whether it was here or not.

The majority of people leaned towards working the plugs when they couldn’t make it through the Institute’s filtration process- they had to be young enough to be scouted, and skilled enough to be noticed. I was pretty sure it was probably damn near everybody’s failure because I’d never once heard of someone celebrating some great success.

We were just there. I was just there. I was there, for no good reason, selling out a quarter of the length I’d been alive to come out the other side weakened and with less applicable skills.

I made a noise somewhere between a scoff and a snort and wiped my mouth with the back of my hand. Better, my ass. There wasn’t a good option. The Council just gave us a bunch of shitty ones and let us all get too distracted arguing with each other about which path was the ‘right’ one to take. And now I’d been booted off the only thing I'd been fast-tracked one since adolescence, albeit unwillingly.

"Perfect," I muttered, wincing as I crossed through a gash in the Overhang, and the overwhelming sun glared through.

I'd never been much of a planner. Not much of a dreamer, either. Maybe that was why I never got caught in the idea of this mysterious Better Life that everyone swore was *Only A Few Steps Away!* I could never draw the lines to connect the dots between our situation and their privilege and make it anything but crooked.

Maybe it was the fact I had someone, my person, to stay up late with and talk these things through. The real kind of pull it apart talks that could only happen when the rest of the world was slipping into sleep, and you could feel their energy leaving the air to make room for your own.

My mind flashed the image of Cal's face. The grief almost choked me, so I deliberately began building bricks between me and the image of his face.

We used to call the Institute a reset. Never wanted it. Swore to each other we'd die before they took us. We'd said it right up until we were locked inside, then something happened. *Something.* I glanced at the Institute behind me. The cool glass exterior betrayed nothing, but I knew- I knew I hadn't fought a single day I'd been in there. And I should have.

I should have wanted to.

I should have wanted to with the clarity that I earned from shattering bones in my body and being shot in the stomach, but I...

Hadn't.

Chest aching with an intangible and indescribable pain, I wrestled the memory back down and faltered while stepping deliberately into the Overhang. With all the crap around me, the stumble nearly sent me flat on the ground.

Goddamn feet. Didn't know how to work. I wiped the sweat from my brow with my damp sleeve. It was still fucking hot, but it was a little more survivable, with some of the sun covered. 'Course I couldn't have picked a more agreeable earlier quarter of the year to take a nosedive.

That would've been too convenient for me.

I peered at the outstretched pathway ahead of me. There was no way of knowing if I was moving in the right direction or if there even was a right direction anymore, but I figured if I just kept walking, I'd either end up in the City Centre or I'd loop back around to the other side. And then... I scratched my head. It too hard to think, to plan, to be practical when my brain was one part,

"Holy shit! I'm outside! I'm out fucking side! I'm walking! I can see the sky! My feet are on the ground! Holy shit!"

And another part,

"I'm a corpse, but I'm walking. I'm a corpse, but I'm alive and well. I'm dead? I'm dead, and this is my final hallucination before I disappear from this mortal form forever and-."

I should have known better than thinking that I would get lucky two times in a row, so when I did trip this second time, I couldn't even be mad when I landed on my one knee.

There was shit everywhere down here. People from both sides- civilians and representatives for the Pod- dragged down whatever they couldn't sell or use and just left it here, along the Spillout, waiting for a day of heavy rain to kick it in there and send it through the floodgates into the Outside.

Someone had been here recently to dump, that much was obvious. The boots I'd tripped on were damn near new. I rose to my haunches and leaned to dust them off. They appeared to be a wider, flatter style shoe typically found on the men's garment shelves, but I wasn't about to bitch about a free and convenient pair of shoes. It had been a long ass time since I'd been out, but the Plate was the Plate no matter what year you were facing, and you never looked a free gift in the face and said no.

I tied the two sets of laces in a loose bow and slung them around my neck like the world's worst piece of jewelry. If I wanted to, I could've put them on right there and then, but I wasn't feeling confident in leaving any evidence on my path, which primarily included garments that were exceedingly specific to little dead resident girls.

A breeze slithered beneath the shingles of the Overhang again, dropping a chill into the air in the wake. I shuddered and cupped both my elbows, pulling them closer into a hug across my chest. It was a welcome, if not unfamiliar comfort, my hands emanating a soft warmth that soothed. How long since I had felt something as simple as human contact? As warmth? As embracement?

It'd been too long, for any of it, for both the chill and the relief from it. I was woefully underprepared. If this heatwave was the start of one of our weather peaks, the temperatures would be in the low digits by nightfall.

And I'd be fucked.

Royally.

I quickened my pace. I was still a long way out. As far as I could see in front of me, there was only debris and nothing as new or usable as the boots. Everything looked old, rotten. Decaying. I had no idea where I was headed now, but I was reassured by the fact I was moving away from what was intended to be my grave.

And that was a mighty fine marker if there ever was one.

~~~~~~~~~~

The Beamline was roughly two miles of path, running parallel with the Spillout for approximately one and a bit, then doing a quick curve towards what would eventually be the primarily residential area, then the downtown.

As more distance passed between I and the Spillout, there were lengthier breaks in the mounds, yet the dumps were more valuable - these were things people needed rid of but weren't
~~~~~~~~~~

destroyed. A perfectly lovely brown jacket that someone probably wore to a robbery, a discarded briefcase that once housed documents not to be seen by light. Someone would probably eventually come back for things like that, I imagined. But not until the memory of the object was blitzed from the memory of state.

The Overhang was always an excellent place to stash things unless you were worried about Scavengers. They weren't patrolled by any form of guard, and no one would be shaking you up for a license when you were knee-deep in trash unless they really, really wanted to fuck with you.

Scavengers were the only deficit of dumping grounds like this. They always liked to push things as far as possible and take whatever they could get their hands on. Nothing was ever enough.

I knew that, I thought as I walked, because that had been me.

And it had been what had got us caught.

I traveled further. When the Overhang ended, so did the stashing. I made a conscious choice here, a separation of being a dead thing and an alive thing because I kept going, out into the sun that felt too bright for my eyes that were used to the dark.

I tossed it a glance.

Constructed out of broad, flat shingle-like materials, it dipped low in the middle and was tethered to the mass of signal beams with a braided rope. It blocked out BirdsEye for the two miles but evidently must not have caused too much of a hindrance since no one from the Council had ever tried to take it down, in all these years. If there were more beams, we could've made a lot of more secure paths like that one. It was too bad every shaft that was inserted had been done before the Reckoning ever came.

There wouldn't be anymore. Ever.

I was rubbing sweat from my stinging eyes when I entered the residential area. Everything had changed so abruptly, I actually spun around to take a second look to make sure I hadn't somehow walked through a portal of mystical origin.

The yawning mouth of the Overhang stared back at me like the throat of a python, less than twenty feet behind me. Twenty feet and I was already at the first set of South residences. There was something seriously wrong with this picture.

I shook my head and kept moving. The laws had always been to give a thorough girth between the Spillout and our homes, to provide leeway to higher water levels and maintain neutral levels of toxicity. I'd read that law a hundred times.

Why would the South have different safety measures than we did?

It didn't follow.

Everything else appeared to be the same. The houses were the same low, grey buildings with sagging front porches, boarded-up windows, and lawns of the same patched dirty turf I had woken on. When made, the artificial grass was a brilliant green, born out of vanity and a selling point when advertising the low-profile, high-rent area. Long forgotten, like everything else, the turf was dusty and browned and worn thin where workers' shoes had tracked over them, day in and day out.

I toed at the corner of a lifted square and shook my head when it crumbled. It was just another gimmick.

If Hartnell had had his true way of things, there wouldn't even be a place for us to live at all. I remembered that much- the Plate's only purpose had always been to stabilize the Pod, a balancing system beneath the ghost town to alleviate some of the ever-shifting tectonic plates' pressure.

At some level, he must've known people would flock to the abandoned city once the rest of the world began to crumble. He was the smartest man alive. I stopped walking, resting my hand against my head. Or was he?

Could I ever truly be sure of which thoughts were my own now, after everything? Everything I learned up there, all the information crammed into the orifices of my brain, soaked up by the porousness of the human psyche. Soft, waiting, willing to be molded, and changed.

After everything I learned, from every book and article I read, they never once claimed that Jebediah had been planning a rescue for us. And they'd been so far up his ass they were coming out his mouth, so if they weren't even trying to speak complimentary about something, it had to be so far from the truth.

In my head, the scenario went like this: the Plate wasn't meant for any great thing, for anyone other than the people in the Pod. Auntie and most of the elders had believed that he'd planned to leave the empty, walled-in city and the metal disc to their own devices. The change came from the people from Outside, who found a way in and shook down the Pod and demanded protection, demanded assistance.

Demanded salvation.

And, facing a mutiny, Jebediah did what every wealthy, important man had done in the face of adversity: feigned cluelessness, and made a half-hearted attempt to alter reality (but only enough for it to still benefit him).

And this is where our debt lay, I thought as I scanned the houses for movement. Our debt was in these ramshackle homes, this dirty turf, and the sky-net above us, filtering the worst of our storms.

We all knew this City, Jebediah's Outer City, was the only reason we were still alive.

He owned it.

And so- he owned us.

~~~~~~~~~~

The path leading out of the Overhang had been nothing more than a long strip of tracked bare turf, made from the pounding of citizen's feet as they rushed to the water edge. Now, as I neared the residences, it was laid with slabs of stone that fell sturdy and flat beneath my feet. It was a welcomed relief after the harsh grittiness of the dirt had started to scrape through the
~~~~~~~~~~

soft bottoms of my slippers. I could feel every grain of sand and stone chafing into the pads of my feet.

The houses, like the path, had gone through a similar transformation. In contrast to the dingy grey siding to the few I had seen on the buildings nearest to the Beamline, some of these new ones were adorned with splashes of colour- a blue shutter here, a red chair there. A handful of clotheslines winked at me from behind a few, faded material flapping in the wind. It looked cozy. Well-worn. I whistled lightly through my teeth. I wondered if their soul covered the deposit or if they'd had to take out a loan.

I would be running into one of them soon, I was sure. Should I ask for help? No. I shook my head at the thought. It was ludicrous. They'd recognize the uniform, at the very least, and no one was going to aid and assist someone on the run. Going against the Council was like signing your own death warrant. Of course, I should have thought of that before I'd gone and leaped.

Huffing in frustration, I zeroed in on the visible clothing lines. If I could manage to snag a few things off a line without bringing attention to myself, I might be able to get closer to the Centre without arising suspicion or notification to the court. My biggest problem was going be getting through the backyard fences. The netted walls were erected to a height that varied between roughly six and seven feet tall and surrounded the entire properties. The boundary nets were not an unfamiliar practice for people of the Circle, as the Council had long forbidden a perimeter that would close off your quarters. They required a full view of the front and back of your home at all times, and the linked tarp was a convenient loophole.

Right now, it was anything but.

Making a sound in the back of my throat, I moved to walk along the property lines and access the backyards, hoping in vain that someone might've left their gate slightly undone.

The first four I tried were tightly sealed, the closures all obsessively wound shut as if someone had gone over the magnetic seal with the fastener several times. These people were damn careful. Either they were important, or this neighbourhood had one hell of a problem with looters. I snorted out a laugh. Who was I kidding? The whole circle had a crime rate that left you vulnerable at every turn. You didn't take care of what was yours, and you'd wake up one day, and it wouldn't be anymore. That was true when I'd been roaming the streets, and I was sure it was even more so now.

My luck changed at the fifth house I approached. A worn yellow string had been tied and looped over the top of the wire post, embellished with a few matte beads that dangled directly in my face. I tapped at it, watching it swing like a pendulum. Someone had lost their fastener. They'd lost it, and God knows, it wasn't worth the arm and the leg the Council would charge for a replacement.

I grinned and blessed them quietly in my head for being so absentminded. Another moment spent in these sopping wet clothes would be a cursed one, as far as I was concerned. I gave the string a quick tug, but the only response from the seal was a quiet squeal of fabric against like.

"Dick," I muttered under my breath and peered past the wires and into the backyard. An eclectic mix of objects tumbled over one another for a coveted spot on the barren ground. Judging by the smaller tools, clothing, and general disarray, it was safe to assume the building housed at least a few children. Probably already working. No one would keep kids that didn't pull their own weight. At least- I hoped so because I really didn't want a kid counting witness. Kids had big mouths. They were the worst keepers of secrets.

I wiggled the string a bit side to side, waiting to hear the uncomfortable squeal I had heard moments before. When it shrieked, I froze. Waited for someone to come flying from their neighbouring homes, weapon in hand. Then, of course. I laughed. Nobody who made this much money would be in their homes midday.

The Council put up the factory postings daily at dawn, and whoever got there first was lucky enough to snag the lucrative ones. Time alone stood to be the difference between processing mechanical parts and shoveling human waste, which was an obvious choice for most people. Boring meant safe. Boring meant you got paid, and you got to come home to a house, and a yard, and a locked door.

Disreputable jobs wouldn't get you that. You'd get paid- but everything would be under the table. Apply for a contract for one of these houses, and they'd claim you'd done nothing to participate in the economy, even if you'd been maintaining properties for twenty years. And if- a strong if, all in capital letters with a broad, thick stroke- you were so lucky to get passed licensing, scanning, credit checks, you still wouldn't be home during the day because you'd need to be working fifteen-hour days to handle the extra taxes you'd have to pay. You'd never get to enjoy the goddamn thing.

I twisted my hand until I thought my hand might give way before the seal did, but thankfully, the snaps clicked open. Giddy with the first inkling of glee I had felt in ages, I allowed myself a small squeak of victory before pulling the flaps open.

The guilt was sudden and unexpected. Chills raced along my body. Stepping into this yard was stepping into someone else's life and dragging my dirty feet across it. Such a beautiful and poignant rarity it was to have a place to feel safe in.

It was, in a strange way, humbling and shameful to be the one to ruin that.

Haunted by the unfamiliar feeling, I crossed to the clothing line and reached out to gently drift my hand along the clothes. Soft to the touch, they swayed gently in the breeze. So many shapes, I thought to myself. So many colours. It had been so long since I had experienced clothing that wasn't the horrible stiffness of the Institute's uniform.

I passed by the sweaters and denim without so much as a pause. The sun didn't need any help keeping me heated. I shaded my eyes. It was doing such a good job already.

A large, faded red t-shirt caught my eye. It was perfect- the dusty colour would blend in, and it looked old enough that no one would think I had fat pockets. I yanked it free from the clothespins and carelessly let them fall to the ground. I continued along the line, scanning for bottoms. It didn't take me long to locate a simple pair of brown woven shorts with a braided string tie.

Now holding both the shirt and shorts limply in my left hand, I squinted into the house through the dingy patio doors. When the shadows remained still, I shimmied what was left of the damp uniform down the length of my body. It left a fresh track of moisture in its wake, somehow turning the humid wind crisp. Shivering, I dropped it in a pool at my feet and pulled the shirt over my head, reveling briefly in the feeling of fabric warmed by the sun.

After years of wearing the starchy jumpsuit, the short, loose sleeves of the t-shirt felt as if I was still unclothed. I both hated and loved it all at once.

I gathered the lump of shed clothing and pushed it into a dripping, musty ball. I'd have to discard it somewhere before Downtown, but it couldn't be left it in the backyard of someone's residence.

No one wanted to come home to Council branding. You just don't mess with stuff like that. I rubbed the scruff of my head. Not even clothing. You see something, you phone it in, get your token, and a slight approving nod. Then you forget about it.

You forget about it, or they make you forget about it.

I paused at the seam. The feeling of intrusiveness was still pricking at my spine. It was a few moments before I relented, heaving a sigh, and returning to the yard. It wouldn't hurt to, at the very least, keep the lawn kept and their remaining items in place. Those small differences could make the slight sting of a minor robbery significantly less irritating (God knows how long it'd taken them to procure a wardrobe for four people).

The clothing pins were blown downwind from their spot on the clothing line and rested their tips in submission near what might've once been a fire pit. It had a crisscrossing of durable tape across the top of the only standing stones: REMOVED BY ORDER OF LAW 17B.

I made a tutting sound. How long, I wonder, did the Council let these people have their fire before they figured out how to restrict access to that too? Use the stove, use the energy, fall behind on bills, lose the house.

It was at-the-top-of-my-lungs-stupid. And that was a rating I didn't use lightly.

In an action I might've deemed weak and inane had I been watching someone else do, I clipped the gathered clothespins back onto the empty stretch of wire, leaving one hanging loose in an attempt to create a scene of which the items were merely whisked by the rambunctious wind.

"That was silly. I know it was," I muttered, as I moved confidently back through the yard. I'd never cared about things like that before. Probably a little late to start now. I skirted out through the seam, slithering comfortably in silence. I was rusty, admittedly, but I could still slink with some of the best.

Not that it mattered. Despite all of the residences, I had yet to see a single person emerge. What was a skulker if they had no reason to skulk? I curved my lips into a whisper of a smile, refastening their net seam to the best of my ability. *They'd just be odd, Val*, I mused to myself as I balled the uniform into a wad and pressed it tightly against the slope of my waist. *Just odd.*

I raised a foot in a step that never fell- hovering above the pathway on one leg in a disciplined display of balance and self-control. The silence that had brought me comfort and assured me of my secrecy now buzzed around my head like a swarm of angry insects. Fuck, it was quiet. Another drop of sweat slid down the small of my back.

I turned my head to the skyline, seeking out the distinctive black shadows of BirdsEye that would be silhouetted against the dull blue, marring the colour with their tarnish. They'd be out today, surely. It would not only be vacuous, but careless, to pretend otherwise. I stared at the sky, and, as vast and unblinking as it was, reflected nothing but the thin lines of the net.

"Come on," I muttered, flexing my fist, "Show yourself."

When the view remained blank and unoffending, I lowered my foot. Those damn birds were programmed to be covert. They knew every limit of the human eye and how to contort and twist themselves around the edges. There was no way to avoid being seen. Cautiously, I started forward. All I had to do was to be an image that was inoffensive and unthreatening.

It might've not been too difficult, had I not been the only person meandering across in a barren wasteland. It was dangerously like having a bold red target on my back.

I inhaled deeply.

What was I before all this?

Who was I before?

I glowered from beneath a lowered brow.

What was normal? What did it look like?

A gust of wind snaked beneath the billows of my shirt. The creamy silence allowed the ripple of fabric to sing back to me in a whispering serenade.

What had I been?

The answer was a resounding chorus from the swaying world around me.

Afraid.

I was immediately aware of my stiff shoulders and rigid, unyielding spine. It would never pass as the gait of someone who was still full of cowardice. I forced the conditioned muscles to relax and unravel, slouching my shoulders into a gesture that reflected the submission and general weak disposition expected of a Plate Resident.

Duck the head, tuck in the chin, avert direct gaze. A shell of a person, disappearing inside of themselves. I'd spent my entire life wishing that I could have the cowardice wrung out of me, leaving it to drip from the tipped basin of my childish compliancy. The Institute had done that for me, but it was backward and wrong.

I'd wanted to be not afraid so that I could be... more.

But I'd come out so much painfully less.

3

This Hand; A Dagger

For six or seven blocks, I walked in the same, nondescript shuffle in a near-catatonic state in the middle of the pathway. It took me nearly that long to relax and accept that I wasn't in immediate danger. Just when I was finally getting into a rhythm, my stomach rumbled angrily. The cramps started shortly after.

The first round was survivable. The second pinching was more like a churning, and I doubled over with my arm braced across my ribs.

"Okay," I said, choked. "Deep breaths, Val."

It was the first pain I'd felt since I'd woken at the water's edge, and it was a sonic boom of the pain I'd felt in the Institute. For the moments that I was curled over, staring into the dirt, I thought that perhaps it was a delayed sort of dying and that this time, my intestines would simply consume themselves until I was a vomiting heap on the ground.

Then it subsided as quickly as it came on. I was shaking, my hands unsteady as I reached for the uniform I'd dropped below me. The purple blemishes were angry and swollen on my hands, splotching in little bursts of colour on my wrists. I sent out a quick prayer that it wasn't an infection, then straightened with the sort of careful resistance that only the previously profoundly ill could understand.

I hadn't eaten enough this morning. Had I known it would be the last dish I'd be consuming, I might've put a little more effort into it. *Shit*, I thought and pressed under my ribs. Though I couldn't be sure that it had only been this morning. I kneaded at my neck, and a few droplets of perspiration dampened my palm. It was impossible to know how long I had been tossed around in the angry current.

It was impossible to know how long I'd even been gone.

The Institute had only one distinguishable sense of time passing; a brief view of the sun rising and setting through the window slits lining the seam between wall and ceiling. I tilted my head back and gazed at the thin silvery webs that bound the outer dome. Even that was a dishonest affair, with the staff controlling when we saw the sun. I had forgotten how to tell the length and duration of not only moments but days. I'd begun to measure time in the most simplistic way of all, gauging it by the way even my most precious memories would fade and disappear into the infinite depths of my psyche.

The train of thought brought dread to a boil in my chest. I had lost so much- and yet, remained unaware of half of what was gone. If there was a crueler fate, I couldn't have imagined it.

Now here, as I will admit, I was careless. I was being careless, and my defense will remain to be that I was as good as new to this world, and I'd merely forgotten the way things were. I should have rushed to put the boots on, but in my haste to leave the backyard, I'd opted to keep them around my neck in the world's most awful statement piece, so it was no wonder that the sole of my slipper had scraped open, and my bare foot had used the best of its luck and ended up with something jammed to its point in my heel. In the centre of the murky grey fabric was a shred of copper jammed on its side, the sharp point piercing the soft shoe. My blood, which was a darker shade of red than I thought entirely normal, leaked down the side of the copper point, and the facing peeled and foamed in reaction.

Too exhausted and hungry to be concerned with its science, I surveyed my newest surrounding area. It appeared as if I'd made it to a sort of in-between place, not quite residences and not quite the downtown, the empty field was little more than a few dried weeds, and broken scraps and pieces from the rundown remains of a small production facility just north of where I was standing. With narrowed eyes, and a heartened refusal to watch myself do it (that would be crossing the line, even for me), I pinched the tip of the copper piece and yanked as hard as I could until I felt my flesh release suction of the little chiv.

Funny, how they would build those homes so close to the Beamline and pretend this travesty wasn't just a few steps away. I pinged the piece away from the path as far as possible and made the switch from slippers to boots. My neck, without the weight of them, felt a thousand times lighter. I was looping the laces around when I saw a rusted iron barrel toppled on its side, just a few feet off the path. A slimy, charcoal sludge oozed from the mouth of the container, seemingly eating away at the outer layer. I darted my gaze between the crumpled pile of clothing tucked beneath my arm and the container and decided to dispose of it in the slimy matter. If that shit could eat a barrel, it could eat a set of clothes.

I rose quickly, tossing the uniform sideways into the mouth and winced at the squelching sound it made as the mixture inhaled its newest delicacy. The clothes sunk in a flurry of gurgling bubbles that popped and hissed steam above the now useless fabric. I watched it simmer for a few more seconds until the last of the white was submerged in the thick jelly, and the Council emblem was nothing more than a memory. There wouldn't be any chance of identification now, and anyone willing to dig in an acidic pile of leaking garbage for a shapeless, soggy blob deserved it.

I allowed myself another casual peek, careful to seem inconspicuous in case I appeared on the cameras. The gelatinous sludge was burning away at the fabric's seams, melting it down to match the consistency. There was no way anybody would be identifying that.

I straightened myself and brushed at the front of my shirt. Between the freedom of the boot-necklace and the lack of my soggy carry-on, I felt entirely off-balance. But what was fucking new? Been feeling off-balance for over half a decade, be a shame to ruin the streak now.

~~~~~~~~~~

It didn't take long for the energy in the air to change. I wet a pinky finger and held it to the wind. I waited for the breeze, but the breeze never came.

I was close.

I used the same hand to shade my eyes from the sun's simmering rays and scanned the horizon. Gone were the lonely, desolate acres of still, quiet houses and the broad, yawning pathway. The buildings near the Downtown were tall, thin, and pressed so tightly against each other there was less than a foot to spare. The details of the faces were the only remarkable thing about them, stunning only in their impoverished mediocrity. Bricks poked their grimy, grey edges out from beneath a flurry of peeling white paint flakes and sent the casualties to drift
~~~~~~~~~~

aimlessly like ashes, settling along the thick, black wires that snaked along the sills.

They were the most accurate visual representation of the feeling you got when you entered the City. Broken. Heavy.

I let out a shaky breath. I was really here. Doing this. Out here. Fuck.

"Aye, mama."

Suddenly tense, I spun to the sound of the voice and clenched my hands into tight fists. Two boys, too slight to be men, stood behind me, their arms crossed in a near-identical manner, though one was quite a bit smaller than the other.

Sweat dribbled down my neck as the muscular one sucked on the cigarette hanging from his mouth. "What you doing down here all by yourself?" He curled back his upper lip, revealing a line of yellowed teeth, each whittled to a point. "You know it ain't safe to go nowhere alone."

There was no apparent threat in his words, but I felt it slithering between the lines, its tail flicking with venom as it stroked along each consonant.

They may have just been boys, but it was apparent they had never seen childhood.

Could there ever truly be youth if there was no innocence?

My heart thudded like thunder in my chest.

Did I even have the strength to run? I'd been so sick, I didn't-

"Leave her alone, Dru," the smaller one spoke from beneath a mound of unkempt dark hair that covered nearly half his face. "You're scaring the thing."

His voice, more bored and dismissive than gentle or merciful, seemed to tame the other boy back in from where he stood, frothing around his chain.

I wasted no time in my departure, kicking up dust in sloppy tornados from boots three sizes too big and legs three sizes too weak. Unease was my only companion, and she was rearing her god-fearing head, clinging talon-like fingers deep into the grooves of my skull.

I could feel their eyes trained on my receding figure like hungry birds. They had pardoned me from a gleeful torment, but I knew how people changed their minds. I might've not known much anymore, but I knew that.

No one could be trusted, and no one would ever be spared.

Relax, Val. Calm.

The whisper in my brain was a welcome familiarity. And it was right. I did need to relax. If I let every rugged person I came across shake me to my core, I would never make it across town. I indulged myself with another shaky breath and slowly raised each finger out of the tight fists I had made. With the newly freed fingers, I nervously smoothed the rogue, downy hairs that had sprung up back down to my scalp.

I was nearly calm when I approached the Downtown, though my heart was still heavy and palms damp with sweat. It was a relief to be entirely surrounded by the dilapidated buildings of the City. Being closed in was a lot safer than the wide open.

I had always been more of a Downtown kid. The ventures we took down to the Spillout had been few and far between, and we should have never risked pillaging against that kind of high surveillance in the first place. *Stupid*, I thought of it. A fire escape rattled on the building next to me. I cringed at the sound but did not falter. *Foolish.*

The streets were still empty, but the distinctive sounds from inside the buildings let me know I was not alone.

Garbage poured from overflowing bins into the street, leading me on a path that was both obstructed and wobbly. I did my best to avoid it, yet something still crunched beneath my foot. Glass, presumably, I mused as I looked at the first story windows. It appeared as if every window down the front line had been smashed and replaced with sheets of soggy cardboard and sodden planks. I hadn't thought it was possible, but it seemed as if out here had only gotten worse as I was on the inside. I scraped for knowledge of the past but came up with only droplets on my tongue when I went seeking for a gulp.

Wait. Was that- could it be? I turned an ear towards the sky. It was.

Voices.

I scrambled to the end of the street, ignoring the scraps of paper sticking to my still damp boots, and followed the curve of the road. Beyond the turn, I stumbled upon something I had been long without - life.

People milled around the pavement edges where the sidewalk met the walls, skulking with bowed heads and fumbling hands. Most, if not all, avoided any form of eye contact in its entirety.

Even the children kept to themselves, giggling as they ran in circles around each other, unperturbed by the dirt smeared across their noses and the holes in their clothes. A little girl clambered by me in a whirl of pigtails and baggy clothes, forcing me to stop suddenly as to not trip over her.

"Sorry," she called out as she passed, and I caught just a glimpse of her bruised, cherubic face before she disappeared into a narrow door. Buried deep in thought of what might've happened to her, I nearly missed the frail old woman sitting in a heap in the middle of the sidewalk.

"Excuse me, sir," she interrupted, rattling a tin can at me. "Could you spare a token or two? I just want to get something to eat."

I recoiled from her outstretched hand and shook my head mutely. She must've assumed I was a boy, from my haircut and bony frame. All the better, to be remembered wrong.

I had nothing to my name, but the clothes on my back and even those were stolen. Judging by her empty cup, it would seem that most people here were in a similar financial state. It was doubtful there would be anyone in this part of the Circle that had extra tokens to spare. She'd be better off hitting up the

Beamline houses or going out further to the areas near the factory entrances and exits. No one in the heart of downtown was making any real good money.

My stomach cramped again, forcing me to lean against the wall of a building for support. Dizziness and nausea raced against each other in a competition for who could bury the lead, with dehydration and heatstroke making a formidable effort in the mid-line. Two women passed me without sparing a glance.

"Did you hear what Rory's going to be bringing down?" The one on the left spoke with a low, husky tone that sounded like clouds of smoke were hiding in her lungs.

"No. I thought the Council put him away," her friend retorted, gripping her dusty purple purse with claw-like fingers. I spied the golden logo on the front of her bag and immediately recognized it as a luxury item. Someone had made an immensely lucky find in the junk piles. I took account of her attempt at groomed hair and patched heels and made the assumption it hadn't been her.

"Just his partner. Tried to get Rory on it too, but the bastard's slippery," she let out a full-bodied cackle. "Good thing partners are replaceable. Word on the street is he's bringing a fresh body down with him to Market."

My ears perked at the mention of the Market. There'd be food there and, hopefully, a way to contact some of my old gang. I pushed off from the wall, gritting my teeth with intense focus as the shift in weight caused my ankles to wobble. The two women continued to titter in an inane conversation between one another, breaking it up with only the occasional bout of nasal laughter. I dragged my leaden feet after them and desperately tried to match the pace in which the women were moving.

The heat that I'd forgotten demanded attention as we pushed into the magnitude of sprawling cement. It was passionately cooking each square of concrete until they were all simmering miserably beneath the blaze. My tongue felt thick and awkward in my mouth, sitting uncomfortably amidst little saliva. I fought to keep my head up. I didn't want to lose sight of the guides I had designated.

The Downtown plaza was crackling with the sheer force of overwhelming human energy, a tangle of voices buzzing excitedly amongst the sickly hot weather. That'd be why I didn't see a soul on my way over. I shook my head at my ignorance.

A seemingly endless line of booths was set up in the middle of the street, some paired together to squeeze into the small space. I was caught by the canopies' distinctive and vibrant colours, dazzled by the brilliant blues and deep reds of the thick, tarp-like fabric. How were they getting colours like that out here? How much development had I missed? Confused, I tried to force myself to focus, but I was losing grip and losing it fast. I understood less and less with every passing moment.

The two women I followed from the block over were already submerged in the crowd, their bobbing heads disappearing amongst the others. Ah, fuck it. I was probably far enough Downtown now I didn't need them, anyway. There wasn't much more they could show me that I wouldn't eventually figure out on my own.

It took me a little less than a minute to work out what section of the market I had entered in. The booths on the left and right were filled to the brim with flurries of wires and beads.

Crafts.

I pulled the one corner of my mouth up into a sneer and turned away from the creative hubbub. What good would a trinket offer at a time like this? Art wasn't for the desperate, lost, or sick. My stomach pitched against me, sending another stabbing pain into my lower intestine. I pressed my hand against the offended and tried to force it to dissipate with sheer will. When it didn't, I scanned the street for somewhere to rest.

I needed a break. And that annoyed me.

A few meters down, a recently vacated wooden bench in the shade of one of the stout booths caught my eye. At first glance, it appeared to be in a better state than everything else; glossy, sturdy, and carved with a degree of artistry that was most unusual. It wasn't until I neared that I realized one set of legs was significantly shorter than its parallel pair, leaving the seat to slope precariously left. Might explain why no one was scrambling for a chance to sit on it. I lowered myself onto it, unconcerned by the diagonal nature. From where I was, I was delightfully hidden from the humid commotion.

It was a minor degree or two colder in the shade, but the momentary relief was a welcome one. I wouldn't make it if I kept pushing like this. Not now, anyway. Who was I kidding?

I observed a family carefully as they passed. Their garish limbs were linked and woven together like pretzels, and their heads tossed back in nearly identical cackles of joy. Such a gift it was to find that glow and vibrancy here of all places.

I stared at my sallow skin. I was further from it than I had ever been. Sometimes when you think you're getting closer to something you're really just getting further away. And I was as far away from everything as I could get. I'd been out of the circuit for way too long to have any hope of getting back in my old ring. You needed an in to get jobs around here. I swore again. I needed a reference. I needed a ticket.

If I could figure out a way to get a hold of Miss May- she had given Cal and I jobs when we were a lot worse off than I was now.

It wouldn't work. I sighed heavily.

I hadn't a clue what grid block I was in, nor how far I was from the Pod, and there was no guarantee I'd be able to remember where my ring base was anymore. Four years was a long time to be gone.

It was a long time to be out of the game.

The gnawing reality settled in as comfortably as I had lowered to the diagonal seat. There was no way around it. I was lost. I squeezed my eyes shut as if the pressure could make me disappear.

I was lost, and any more time spent in denial of that was merely delaying the inevitable. There wasn't a way for me to seamlessly return to the old quilt I was once knitted into. Old Val had a place here in this world.

But did I?

My eyes were still shut when the warble of the Council's siren began. I didn't process it immediately, as it had been years since I listened and waited with bated breath for them whirl down my street.

The gears in my memory clicked on the fifth wail, and my eyes flew open.

The Council knew. They knew, and they were here to take me back. I would be thrown into solitary. Panic was growing and swelling in the air, infecting the people in the booths with its sticky fear.

The siren cut out as the ostentatious silver van pulled into a parallel park at the intersection a few booths ahead. The vendors swarmed frantically, babbling loudly amongst themselves. A tanned woman with skin folded like a leather satchel across the way dragged her arm across her small glassware and pushed it into a duffel bag. Her hands trembled so fiercely on the zipper that she wasn't able to yank it over the teeth. She gave up, threw it over her shoulder, and pushed off from her table, launching herself into the crowd.

I wasn't hot anymore.

A gangly Officer (not quite as important as a Senator, but better than those meathead guards) with broad shoulders but nearly impossible skinny limbs unfolded from the car in broken, halting movements. It was mesmerizing in its warped and crooked nature, looking and moving like a nightmare.

His long legs, two of them though I was somehow expecting more, ate up the ground as he walked into the crowd. The sea of people parted around him like he was a god, though objectively, I knew he was only a man.

"Nobody moves from this area until you've been verified. If you run, you will be chased and apprehended." The simple statement cut everyone to the bone.

I had seen this scene before. I stared down at my hands until my palms spun into spirals.

The Officer approached a small, mousy looking man across the road.

"Licensing and ID, please," he drawled. In the air now void of murmurs, his voice was puzzlingly both unpleasant and melodic to my ears.

"Really, Officer? We gotta do this every time?"

"Licensing and identification," the Officer retorted calmly. "Now."

Though obviously perturbed, the vendor fished for the proper documents in his satchel. The Officer was still, bearing no flicker of humanity or expression on his sharp face, but I had a feeling beneath his rectangular sunglasses, he was aware of everything.

In a moment of great triumph, the vendor found the badge and flashed it open, leaving the thin leather casing to float loosely in the wind. The Officer seized it from his hand in a robotic motion and lifted his scanner to the plastic card. I felt the crowd draw in a collective breath in anticipation of the light.

Yellow.

Everyone exhaled. I glanced at the flat grey panel on my wrist, just below my skin. The light was off, as it had been since I had gone over the edge. I was dead in the Council's database. Status; deceased. If I were caught with a dud, I'd be tossed away or executed for fraud.

What the fuck was I still doing sitting here?

Heart in my throat, I uncurled from the bench and took off towards the dimly lit alley nestled behind me between two storefronts with illegible signs.

I picked up my pace, taking loping strides to finish crossing the concrete strip and ducked into the alleyway. A barrel, much like the one I had encountered earlier, had rolled into the middle of the path. I glanced around wildly, seeking any sign of an exit in the alley. A brick wall, solid and formidable, stood at the two buildings' crux and blocked off what should have been the next street over. Couldn't go back, couldn't go forward. I scanned the ground, and my eyes landed on a tunnel hole, half-submerged beneath a rusted dumpster. I'd have to go down. I gripped either side of the metal atrocity and began to shove at it.

"Licensing and identification."

The Officer's muffled voice was drawing near, giving me no choice but to continue the seemingly futile pushing at the putrid-smelling dumpster. The pad of my foot slipped in the leaking garbage as I used my body's momentum to get the old wheels to rotate. It finally released and slammed into a large, cracked mirror, sending it to the ground. With no time to be concerned, I busied myself in the challenge of lifting the iron disk that covered the tunnel hole. My fingers scraped raw as I tried to pry it from its bed.

"What are you doing?"

I swiveled my head halfway towards a rapidly approaching Guard. I hadn't even seen him, but then again, that was the point of it. He was to protect the Supervising Officer at all costs. I swallowed the dust that filled my mouth. The cost to kill me would be next to nothing.

The scanner laid heavy in his one palm as he jogged towards me, his face now squashed into what might've been a scowl. The disk covering the hole was about an inch raised on the left side, almost enough for me to prop it out, but I hadn't enough time. I couldn't get away. I would have to fight.

I was mad, utterly mad.

Well aware of the impending danger, I scrambled to my feet. I needed a weapon. I had nothing. I never had anything. A fucking runner. I swung my arm blindly on top of the dumpster in search of the crooked pipe I had seen just moments before. The rust flaked onto my skin and peppered it like freckles. I blew air out of my mouth impatiently and strained until I could feel it brushing against my fingers. I almost had it...

The guard wrapped a gloved hand around my wrist. The fabric was warm against my bare skin.

I tried desperately to kick him off, still stretching for the weapon with my other hand. He gave my arm a hard tug and yanked as if I weighed nothing. The force sent me shuttling towards the ground.

"Identify yourself! Stop resisting!"

I could not speak even if I had anything to say. I was pinned to the ground with gravel and trash remnants being pushed against my teeth. He dropped to his knees with me and wrapped an arm around my neck, squeezing.

"Stop resisting!"

I gasped wildly for air and started to claw at his forearm, putting tears in his uniform. He swore, venomously, and profusely, as one of my nails ripped through and grazed his skin. I felt his saliva spray the back of my neck. Dizziness shook my entire body and turned my vision to static. In a last-ditch attempt, I swung my elbow back into his gut. He let out a grunt and loosened his hold around my neck, only slightly, but enough for me to slip out from beneath him. I crawled on my stomach towards the sewer hole and weakly pulled myself into a squatting position. Before I could gather enough momentum to rise, his hand was back on my shoulder. All it took was one careful flick of his wrist to send me flipping back onto my tailbone. I closed my eyes against the vibrating pain, breathing heavily.

"Oh, I'm going to enjoy this." He spat out from his place above me.

He wrapped his hand around my neck, squeezing with his fingers of concrete bone. The pressure hit me first. It was as if my head was placed in a vice. It crossed my mind that no man should have so much strength.

No man should have that much power.

I was tired, lord, was I tired, and my head began to droop, but there was this energy, this electricity, running through my veins, through my head. It was too much- it was overwhelming- my eyes started to roll back into my head.

"No, you look at me. You watch me while you die."

Blearily, I raised my eyes to his. He had lost his helmet at some point, and he now stared at me with soft hazel eyes, lightly decorated with wispy eyelashes, the shade of burnt straw. He had two freckles, right along the tanned skin of his nose.

He seemed so... human.

Disoriented, I raised my hand to grip his exposed wrist. The single inch of sticky skin clung to my palm as I wrapped my fingers around the forearm. *Human.*

The colour in his face started dropping immediately. Horrified, I dropped my hand.

"What-," I whispered hoarsely but never finished. A man, so strong in life- power swimming in his bones as blatant as marrow- seized in front of me. His mouth flopped agape and left his thin lips slack over pearly white teeth. Already becoming weak on my neck, he released me and dropped to his knees, clutching white-knuckled hands against his chest.

A strange gurgling sound bellowed from his chest, hypnotizing me with the sickening noise until thick, slimy blood began to drip and ooze from his mouth. I scrambled back against the dumpster, using my arms to brace myself, and watched with wide eyes as he keeled over. Blood poured from his eye sockets, mixing with the secretion from his mouth before pooling on the ground in front of him. His body followed suit and landed with a loud thud.

Then it was me, and it was a dead man. It was me, and a dead man, in a shadowy alley with the hot, sickly air all around us.

Inhale.

Exhale.

I'm not sure how long I sat there, staring at him. I'd never seen someone die so close, not by my own hand.

Sometimes, the Council members would come down to slums with their fancy guns and take their pick late in the evening. We'd wake up in the morning with a neighbour swinging from a beam, a rope around their neck, or a boy with a shot in his temple, and there wasn't anything we could do about it.

But this was different. This was my fault. Indubitably so. My hands shook.

His eyes were now enveloped by a thick white fog, leaving only traces of the colour that used to live there. His mouth was still twisted open, but now it was stiff and unmoving.

Inhale.

Exhale.

Something wet slid down my face. Instinctively, I reached up to wipe it away. Deep red stained my fingers. Blood.

God. I shakily wiped my fingers on the side of the shirt. The feeling of drops remained. Another siren began wailing in the distance. His panel would've gone out. They knew.

Rising on quivering legs, I stepped around him and weakly retreated back to my post at the side of the dumpster. Glass crunched beneath my feet.

I recalled the shattering of a mirror, but my memories felt fragmented and strange as if pieces had broken off and were floating around in space. I found the rest of the frame off to the side, face down near the sewer hole. Breaking everything. Always breaking everything. *God, Val. Why are you always breaking everything? Ruin, ruin, ruin.*

I squatted down and curled my fingers underneath the ornate border to pull it upwards. My body screamed against the effort. I leaned it against the wall and sought out my familiar face among the grime. I needed to see something I recognized.

Using the bottom hem of my shirt, I wiped feverishly at the dirt until a small circle is cleared on the pane.

A dull ringing sounded in my ears.

My veins were skinny blue snakes that swam in tangled webs and pushed against the barrier of skin stretched over my bones like a smudged plastic sheet.

God, it looked bad. It was bad.

I leaned closer, tilting my head to the side. The skin around my eyes was a dark, washed-out purple that only highlighted the piercing red of burst blood vessels that surrounded my left iris.

Since it was making me sick to look, I shoved the mirror away. What the fuck was happening? What was happening to me? I made the mistake of glancing at my hands, which, beneath the mud and blood from my scuffle, were a bloody, pulsing shade of maroon. The deep splotches spread their wine stain up my forearm, breaking off only to stain another patch of skin higher, above my elbows. When I flipped them to the light, the panel in my wrist was pressed so firmly against my skin that the square's edges were ridges against the bone. Thick black currents snaked into the palm of my left hand. Nauseous, I grasped the offender into a tight fist and pressed it tightly against my gut.

"Hey!"

I snarled at the voice, swinging my head towards the child in the archway. His dirty little face was earnest and eager, but he quivered under my gaze.

"What are..." He trailed off as his mother rushed to his side, swooping him beneath a billowing sleeve and pulling him to her breast.

She muttered something to him and avoided eye contact with me, half dragging him with her as she loped away. Her running told me worse things were coming.

I hobbled to the sewer hole and wedged a pipe in the gap, cranking it like a jack to prop it open.

The smell hit me first. It was a smell, more profound and putrid than repugnant human waste, more than the garbage bins' leaking juice behind me. It was like the smell of burning sulfur and rotting skin.

There were few men brave enough to enter the tunnels, and even fewer men to emerge afterward. It was the only piece of the City I had never been without Caleb by my side, and the only boundary I'd never enjoyed pushing.

I had no choice. I knew that. I was out of options. Still, I hesitated at the mouth, caught in a staring contest with an unblinking hole of shadow and rot.

Mucus gathered around my tongue and coated my teeth with an oily film as nausea heaved again. I had done worse things. I could do this.

I dropped my legs into the hole, searching for the ledges that signified the rickety ladder and held onto the ground for one final moment.

"Aren't the tunnels where men go to die?" I'd asked Caleb, the first time we'd ever stared into the hole.

"The tunnels," he'd said, "Are a test."

"A test?" I'd asked, my heart battering in my frail chest. I'd angled myself behind him, grabbing the fleshy bit of his forearm, trying to pretend I wasn't what I was.

"Yeah." He'd pulled his arm away from me and circled the opening, crouching down to drop his legs in. "Only the bravest of the brave will try to outrun it."

"Outrun what?" My voice had shaken.

"Death," he replied and sent me a wicked grin before he disappeared into the darkness.

Back in the alley with the dead man, I closed my eyes and tried to cling onto all the times Caleb and I had done just that. I could do this. I could do this.

All I had to do was run.

Part Two

a lost soul,
a wanderer of windowpanes
and old creaky floorboards,

a hollow longing; a vacancy

oh, my lacuna,
what else have you
stolen from me?

4

Servitude of the Broken

(2.5 years later)

The sun woke me. It filtered through the newspaper plastered over the window and slanted across the small, unsentimental bedroom directly into my eyes. I squeezed them shut, hoping I could wring a few more hours of sleep out of the day. Instead, the red glow continued to pulse softly and persistently beneath the sheet of my eyelids. That was the problem with living in the central city. The light always found a fucking way in.

I twisted onto my back and stretched my legs to the end of the bed, rotating my ankles beneath the scratchy fake wool blanket. Resigned, I cracked one eye open and gazed at the bumpy ceiling.

Look- I wouldn't complain. I never would. Not out loud, anyway. Not to anyone else.

I didn't have a bad thing going here. I really didn't. But waking up like this felt an awful lot like the last morning I awoke in the Institute. And that wasn't a day I especially wanted to live through again.

"Or die through," I muttered to myself in dry amusement.

My voice hung in the air like the ghost of someone that had passed long before this time. I so rarely spoke these days, and when I did, it was mostly to myself. Perhaps that's why my words felt so heavy when they slipped from my mouth: because the house was so goddamn quiet in the first place.

I wasn't always bitter about it. It was often one of the things I liked and appreciated most about Harris. She never poked her nose in my business or asked a lot of questions. I'm not sure we would get along as well if she did. The professional relationship worked for both of us. She kept me in my little crate, fed me and sheltered me, and in turn, I took care of a few things for her.

It was only once in a while that I missed camaraderie. I missed conversations, experiences, laughter. It was too empty of a word to say that I was lonely. It was more apt to say I was a mourner to my own passing—a visitor to my own funeral that never seemed to end.

I flung the blanket off of me and hissed as the frigid air bit at my skin. The heat from the main room's fireplace rarely made it to the upstairs, but the extreme temperatures would still catch me by surprise if I was fuzzy enough. Harris had put in an appeal for an additional heat cycler to be put in for the second floor, but it had been rejected after long months of waiting. It already cost an arm and a leg for the bare minimum, and even then, it had a tendency to break down without a moment's notice. I pulled myself to the corner of the bed and yanked the pajama top back down, protecting the exposed strip of skin from the nippy air. Thick, curly dark hair tumbled over my shoulders in loose waves that cascaded over my shoulders in a warm blanket. A breeze whistled through space beneath the perpetually open window and ruffled the paper. Right here, I thought to myself, cracking my neck, this exact moment and this moment only, it actually felt almost peaceful.

Of course, that'd never last.

Sighing heavily, I rose and padded softly towards the bathroom, scrubbing my hands over my gritty face. There was sparse time to relax, especially in the middle of the week. I had to complete most of my jobs earlier since it was much too dangerous to travel down on the weekends. The Council nearly tripled patrol then, in a desperate attempt to reach their arrest quota before Mondays' hearings.

Self-fulfilling prophecy, I thought. The Council would claim they wanted us to live these honourable, noble lives- but would just as soon break our backs over an illegal road cross to fill a ridiculously high registry. Making living against the law so they could throw us in jail until we died. I snorted derisively, kicking a lump of clothing out of my path. What a joke. Couldn't blame the lot who became actual criminals with a system like that backing you.

So that's the way it was: days like today, with Harris waiting downstairs with a name ready and an expectation it would be done before the second shift rotation. And I couldn't really complain.

I flicked the light on in the bathroom, and my reflection popped up to greet the light with sunken eyes and a crooked scowl. This vanity was a thing I wished I was no longer forced to experience; the vulnerable and indubitably human affliction was an embarrassing blemish on what I considered a carefully cultivated 'blankness.'

It was a shame practicality would never allow me the luxury of saying 'fuck it' to all of it, no matter how bad I wanted to. Heading into the Downtown circuit was plunging into an area of high scrutiny, and every person or building you passed could just as well be cultivating footage of you to feed back into the Guard. If I was planning on getting far without flagging suspicion, I couldn't be looking like a criminal. Grungy people pinged on their system.

I really didn't want to ping.

I splashed cold water on my face and wiped the sleep from my eyes. In my line of work, it paid handsomely to be invisible. It was necessary to do everything I could to get there, and I did, of course, but there remained to be a need to cover my ass in the event my brand of invisibility left something to be desired.

I had bought fake licensing from a guy down on Fourth that ran a shady business out of the back of his shed, so for me, it was only a matter of matching the description on my ticket. I had yet to be carded in my career so far, but I still didn't want to take the risk. Just because I hadn't been stopped before doesn't mean I never would. Carding opened the door to questions, and ask too many of those, everyone involved would end up dead in a ditch.

I shed my clothing in the hamper and hopped into the shower, cranking the faucet in winding circles until finally, water. The showerhead sputtered out an ice-cold spray that was damn near frozen, pelleting my bare skin with tiny arrowheads, and I winced, the expression creasing a face still stiff from a late night.

The sputter eventually petered out into a bearable trickle of room temperature, but I wasted no time lathering up and rinsing in case the heater decided to fail once more. There was no trusting anything out here, that's for sure.

In a beautiful allegory to my life, I managed to snort a pile of suds, the cheap soap stinging my nostrils with an almost unbearable stink of chemicals. The feeling of peace and sanctity was now entirely depleted, replacing it with the one I knew all too well. Already exhausted with a day that had barely begun, I punched the knob in and turn off the pathetic trickle of water. The darkness I held scarcely at bay was busying itself, twisting around my vessels and embedding itself in my lungs. I stepped onto the bathmat and wrapped a small grey towel around my hair, leaving my body bare as I traipsed across the small bathroom, letting the water slip carelessly onto the tiled floor. By intention, I avoided my reflection this time.

I hated seeing it. I hated everything about it- especially bare.

I hated the purple-black stains on my arms that spread to my elbows and the patch that had shown up just under my left ear. I hated watching it squirm, twitch, and wriggle whenever anything touched it. It had been two years and fifty-five days since I'd crawled out of the Spillout, and it had been spreading every day since. Slowly.

So somehow, it was more manageable to focus on the knobs of my knuckles as they flexed and released beneath the purple skin because somehow, they still felt like human things when I looked at them like this. They still belonged to me, even as pointed and severe as they looked coming out of my hands. The mirror told a different story.

Told me the truth.

I shuddered, my body suddenly unbearably cold. That was another unfortunate thing I'd brought back from the grave- I was always fucking cold. Growling, I reached for the ratty robe I had hanging on the back of the door. I needed to eat more- I know I did. But I was never hungry- not for sustenance, at least. If I managed to be, I'd probably be able to swing more than a little pooch at the crux of my pelvis and the jiggle I held in my thighs (more by genetics than indulgence). And that'd be a damn useful thing, especially in the cold season when food and heat were in short supply.

I nudged the door open with my foot. Who was I kidding? It was nice to dream, but realistically, I was lucky to get two small meals a day, and that kind of diet just wouldn't cut it if you were looking to pack on the pounds.

Walking back towards my bed, I unrolled the towel from my head and shook my hair loose from the bundle, dragging my fingers through it. I was on the better end of malnourishment than most, with the exception of Harris, who never seemed to be affected and was always in a perpetual state of husk and bulk, even with food shortage. And, I noted ruefully as the clock on the wall broadcasted my late sleep-in, it was husk and bulk I didn't care to piss off.

The process of readying myself was a quick one, and I was hoping it'd be enough time to allow my hair to dry. Harris was strict about self-presentation, and she hated when I set out with a, what she called, 'wet head.' We'd had so many fights about what she believed I should look like, there were a few things I decided to compromise on. This would typically be one of them, but even after tidying and making the bed, it became apparent the thick locks were as stubborn as they were unruly. I'm sure I had some long line of ancestry to thank for that.

Letting it go as a lost cause, I twisted the mess around my hand and secured it with a bald rubber band at the nape of my neck. I was tired, still. I closed my eyes briefly and breathed slowly. Would there be some merit to the old practice of meditation? Did anyone even do that anymore? As soon as the thought came, I was chastising myself. It was stupid to think about it.

No one around these parts knew any peace. Inner or otherwise. All that was a dying business.

I spared another glance at the clock. But the one I ran was not.

I grabbed the cloak off the back of my door and slung it over my shoulders, feeling the rumble of appreciation in my heart at the welcomed weight. The piece was both the first and most expensive thing I owned, and it had a right to be. I wouldn't leave my house without it.

I had felt somewhat rash in the months leading up to the purchase, scavenging every token I got, hoarding it beneath my bed in a cigar box like a child, ignoring the holes in my clothes and the growling of my stomach. But that small feeling of personal embarrassment was nothing compared to the sense of pride and security when I made my first legitimate purchase.

I might've had nothing, but then I had a damn cloak.

I tucked a loose curl behind my ear and grabbed the key off the shelf next to the door.

It had taken me a while to get used to the practice of locking my home door, though it in itself wasn't unusual to have personal locks in Plate Residences. Many of the larger houses hosted multiple groups of people, and more often than not, they didn't get along. It was best to keep a close eye on your belongings and an even closer one on your space. Especially when you were breaking the law as bad as I was, I thought as I clicked the door shut—the fewer people poking around me, the better.

I glanced at the panel on my wrist for only a minute before sliding the gloves over my hands, up above the length of my forearms. Hiding it- hiding everything. No one was permitted to know Harris' dead girl.

I stepped carefully out into the hallway, minding my step around some of the creakier floorboards. It was an older house, thought to be one of the first built on the plate, and the age was apparent in the slow but steady disintegration of materials. Harris had done all she could to keep on top of it, but without proper training or access to tools, the place was showing its wrinkles and sagging skin.

Despite all of its faults, Harris cared for her home fiercely. It might've been a shared space, but no one could make any mistake- this was Harris' house, and Harris' house it would stay. Rumour has it, a group of wayward thugs once challenged her for it years ago, but I wasn't sure I believed it. People knew not to fuck with Harris or her home. She was terrifying in her own, six foot two three-hundred-pounds-of-muscle way.

I spared a glance at a blue vase and its cluster of plastic flowers as I meandered down the way. The same few quaint touches had been in their respective spots since long before I came along. I've always thought perhaps the decorating gave her a small moment of warmth in such a hard reality, but when you actually met her, it was hard to imagine her arranging the little pink tulips with her scarred hands.

The only other decorative piece on this level was a painting of a girl on a dock, her silhouette framed against the softness of the setting sun. It was faded to a dull echo of the vibrancy it once must've been, something painted long ago when there was still sunsets and whimsy. The canvas was lumpy beneath my fingertips as I gently traced the protruding lines around her wild, cascading hair. What a lovely thing it must've been, to be free.

The quiet ring of the bell above the door shook me from my fantasy, causing me to drop my hand guiltily like a child caught in a cookie jar. Sending one last musing glance at the picture, I began to move away. It was a beautiful piece, and rare, at that- but I was sure its value was next to nothing. No one had ever even been by to see it, and Harris rarely made the trip up here herself to look at it. Despite that, I knew I wasn't to touch it, but there was something about the depth of the light across the water pulled me in, slowly and soundlessly before I realized it had happened. I tucked my hands into the pockets underneath my cloak and started down the steep steps, my feet sinking into the old, squishy carpet. The bell sounded again, and I cocked my head to the side, pulling my body close to the wall. I wasn't permitted downstairs if we had visitors.

"Is it true? That she's here?" The man's voice was feverish and desperate, tinged with madness.

I heard the unmistakable sound of Harris' spoon clinking against her ceramic cup as she stirred sugar into her tea.

"What is it that you're hoping to gain from this, Peter?"

Peter. It must be one of the brothers from next door. I strained forward, trying to catch a glimpse around the winding angles of the staircase.

"I need to see her!"

Harris expelled a sigh from her weighty chest. "What is it you need from her?"

"I don't have to tell you this. Where is she?"

The chair scraped loudly against the tiled floor. I imagined Harris crossing the room deftly, her shawl trailing behind her.

"As long as she is in my home, under my roof- everything she does is run by me. She belongs to me." *Belong to me.* I blinked spots out of my vision. "I will ask you one more time. What is it you need?"

"There is a man- I need him to be... taken care of..." He faltered in his speech, beginning a slur of indistinguishable murmurs. I took the first tentative steps closer, but only in time to catch Harris' dismissal. She made a sound in her throat like she was about to spit at him, but thankfully, I never heard the splat of saliva.

"You will leave my home. All requests are to be discreetly dropped in the mail slot between the hours of midnight and four A.M."

I didn't have to be in the room to know the threat that followed. The elegant end of Harris' cane would flip up, revealing a sharpened point. She would press it into the hollow of their throat, just enough to draw blood, before sending them on their way.

There had been speculation on my existence for quite some time now. Most too afraid to lay eyes on me, I remained but a myth to everyone except the mad and desperate. I held my breath until the door slammed shut again. They knew of me as one knows of a legend. Something they couldn't quite touch, couldn't quite understand... a thing made of shadows.

Harris' monster.

I'd asked myself more than once why I bothered staying. Why I didn't go somewhere else. But two and a half years ago, I crawled my way into the tunnels after killing a man with nothing but a touch. I had died and reawakened with twisted, rippling skin that emitted something so awful people would die from the briefest contact. That was how Harris found me- bloodied in clothes that did not belong to me, my grey panel without lights, and tears streaking my dirty face.

She took me in, and there was a sense of loyalty in that. She risked a lot in doing what she did.

"You can come down now," she said mildly. The chair creaked as she settled back in. "He's gone."

"You sure?" I hadn't heard the door slam.

"Yes girl, come downstairs."

I tentatively rounded the corner into the kitchen.

"What did he want?"

She sighed and sipped from her cup, hissing as the boiling water scorches her tongue.

"What do any of them want?"

I narrowed my eyes. Harris didn't like it when I questioned her, but she'd answer all the same. She had a tough exterior, but, just like everyone else, she was afraid of death. And in turn, afraid of me. I felt the faint glow of ego and did my best to smother it. *It did power no benefits to become arrogant.* That was her first rule. I tried to relax my brow.

"Peter Elvidge lost one of his brothers a few weekends ago," she said finally, shaking her head sadly. "He just hasn't been right since."

"Was it Councilmen?"

She jerked a shoulder in a shrug. "Can't be sure."

I took a mug off the top shelf and lifted the teapot from its spot on the stove, pausing to watch her with each hand occupied.

"But he thinks it is."

The sigh rolled out again. "Yes, he thinks it is."

My free hand balled into a fist, and I pressed it against my thigh. It seemed the business of vengeance was a booming one.

I sipped some of the bitter tea and fought the urge to spit it out. I'd never liked tea, but rituals were necessary, no matter how small.

Rituals made you feel human, even if you weren't.

I watched as Harris shuffled her papers, flipping through a folder as she mulled over the stack of names. I stopped prodding about Peter, though I wasn't done thinking about it. It was no use trying to engage with her once she started her process- she fixated on her task, and that was that. I might as well have been alone. I took another sip of the burnt tea and cringed at the flavour.

I was sure Peter was right about his brother. Councilmen just hated, recklessly and unapologetically. They needed no justified reason to pick us off. They'd just as soon make up a list of phony charges as an excuse to put a bullet in some poor man's head.

We could board up our windows and deadbolt our doors all we wanted, but it would never be enough. There wasn't any power against the Council. I doubt there ever had been.

People would talk about a different time, where they used to be honest and noble, but we all knew what they were- power-hungry machines, hell-bent on grinding every last one of us into the dirt.

"It's been chosen."

I turned to look at the spread on the table. The sheer number of files made me nauseous. Could there really be that many? Could I really take so many away?

I reached forward, uncurling my fingers from my palm. She pressed the square paper in the middle of my palm, and I moved to take it with me, my fingers brushing the tips of hers on the retreat. Through the gloves, she was safe from my touch, but still, her hand faltered in the air and trembled vigorously, before she dropped it back in her lap. I wanted to apologize for causing her fear, but the words fell down my throat before they reach my tongue. Did a woman like that deserve it? An apology?

"I will see you tonight, Valencia."

"Tonight, Missus Harris."

With that, she hobbled out of the room, her cane tapping the hardwood floor as she went.

Valencia. I mouthed it silently to myself. Yes, that's right. That was my name. Harris so infrequently referred to me by name. I thought maybe it made her uneasy, seeing me as a person. I crumpled the paper, then smoothed it on my thigh in meditative practice. It was folded in one place, directly down the midpoint. With a deep breath, I spread it open. In thick, heavy-handed scrawl, a name graced the top of the page. *Christian Diern*. His address was listed below it in smaller, lighter print. I stared at the card until the edges blur. Christian Diern was going to die today. Two warring emotions raced alongside each other. Guilt was, of course, present, but it was mixed with something much more sinister.

I couldn't call it hunger, as I would not suffer without it. I did not need to kill to survive. Like the sun, I was infinite- above death, separate from life. I was an abomination of any god's creation that you could imagine. It wasn't hunger, nor greed or revenge- no, it was one treacherous, haunting thing- something I wished I did not feel when I received my cards. Something I wished wasn't so sticky with glee.

Purpose.

This was my *purpose*. My belonging. Shuddering at the dark feeling, I flipped the card around the webs of my fingers before tapping it rapidly on the table. I hadn't much time to waste. I glanced at the clock above the old gas stove.

9:56.

I did up the rest of my cloak's buttons and grabbed a faded cross-body bag from the hook next to the table. Slinging it over my shoulder, I rifled through for my licensing, ID'S, and proof of citizenship if I should be stopped. My lighter colouring usually gave me a pass by both BirdsEye and the 'stop-and-frisk's, so I wasn't too worried about my papers' authenticity. I glanced back at the clock again.

9:59 a.m.

As I left them, my boots were straight in a row against the far wall, just above the cellar door. I looped the laces around and around until they were snug against my feet.

10:00 a.m.

"Goodbye," I whispered to the house. It felt nice to have something to say goodbye to, even if it was just plaster and siding.

The doorknob was a smooth, bald jewel in my hand, and I pushed on the heavy door. It swung open with a guttural creak and revealed a room with a wide hole in the ground. The first few steps of a rickety set of stairs were all that was visible before it stretched into a mouth of darkness. There were no lights in the tunnels. There hadn't been since well before my time. Long since the settlers abandoned the passageway, the lanterns they'd once fitted had been shaken down and crumbled from the elements. It was almost a death trap in its own right, and it fit the image.

The tunnel system was the only way a citizen could access a system below the plate, and it was, in my opinion, the best way to travel. The danger was what made it exciting.

I scaled the stairs with my hand against the side, wary of the planks that were inclined to become wet and slippery. I might have been dead, but it didn't mean I had a yen to slide down three flights of stairs in pitch blackness. I had little, but I still had my preferences.

I reached the bottom without incident and stared north. For now, it was all black. But I knew the further I walked, the more I would see. The closer I would be to light.

Accepting the darkness, I started out. The soft thud of my steps echoed ahead, and the steady thump began to sound like a soothing drumming. Sometimes I liked to think of the other people that walked this path before I did- whose hands touched these walls before I was even a flicker in the universe.

Harris said her granddaddy had pioneered the tunnel system's use, back when outsiders were refused supplies and left for dead on the fringe. They'd smuggle food and goods from the outside world and stored it underground, hiding from the elements when they could and living like rodents. They would wheel things from the torn and ravaged city they once lived back down to the cellars in little metal trolleys, praying that the echo wouldn't call the Council down from their Pod or trigger the tunnels quaking.

They were left abandoned, rightfully so, after the Department of Integration finally relented to the protests and signed the contract abiding by a human and labor rights law. The law put in place by Jebediah himself, actively signing off a Plate resident's livelihood, blood, sweat, and tears in exchange for a life on the plate.

Residents were provided with the first Sustenance queue and a general amenities area closer to the North quadrant's middle in the City Centre. Then three more popped up along the way, nestled in the middle of downtown like they'd been lifted and copied down to the notches in the baseboards. The food was barely edible, chemically enhanced beige slop, and the pharmaceutical prices were at least twice a resident's monthly pay, but that was more than our ancestors ever got. It made you feel a little guilty about complaining. In fact, made me more than a little sick to imagine what they must've had to do when the tunnels got a mind of their own and started twisting and squeezing around whoever didn't get to a safe cellar. At least I could leave if I needed to.

I reached the fork about a mile in. You hung towards the left, you would be let out by the main suburban area, where I first crawled out after my untimely departure from the Institute.

It was still a decent place to live, quiet, isolated. People in that area kept to themselves and kept their heads down, only heading out to work a sixteen-hour day before locking the house down and heading to sleep. Like drones, they stared unblinking at the ground and shuffled forward, their hands stained with grease from the factory.

They weren't bad people. They'd just given up. Sometimes I thought perhaps some things were too complicated for them to comprehend. Then I thought, maybe they just didn't want to know. Didn't want to look at it.

Since I was depressing myself, I returned my attention to the steady thudding of my shoes and the trickle of excess water down the storm drains. I was getting close now. I could feel it. The energy of the people buzzed in the air, sour on my tongue. It tasted the way a smorgasbord of voices sounded if they had all been tuned to a higher volume and overlapped.

The tunnel let out in the City Centre's boiler room- one of the four that held just over eleven individual booths but had several roped offline sections that wound their way out the door. Each line had a capacity for a maximum of eighty people, and we usually needed every inch. The wait times for the three dispensary units were abysmal. It was one of the reasons I opted to swap for what I could at the market. Might've been illegal but at least I wasn't stuck smushed against a hundred other people waiting for one Councilman to get his finger out of his ass and process my request.

Our City Centres were made useful in many ways aside from the one it was famous for- the very purpose of accessing the west doors was enough to sell me on its value. The exit leads directly into our Verity courtyard and would connect to almost all city complexes and routes. After that, it was just a matter of finding which one belonged to Diern.

I reached the crawl space and shimmied my way in on all fours before flipping onto my back for the final stretch.

Above my head, a rusted iron wheel hung from the low ceiling. If you weren't careful, as I hadn't been many a time before, it was too easy to whack your head off it.

I shifted in my awkward stance to settle onto the small of my back, needing both arms to crank the wheel. It took three groaning turns and strenuous exertion for the heavy iron door to give way.

I waited a moment, listening carefully for any sound of movement that rumbled above. The room was often vacant, but you could never take anything for granted at the Centre. People were always up to all sorts of unsavoury things in every room of that corridor.

I tapped the ceiling lightly twice.

When there was no response, and I was convinced the room was empty, I flung my already oddly bent body from the floor into a flop that landed me inside.

The place was a small one and only seemed even tighter at the movement; its minimal square footage housed a giant machine that was awake as it ever had been, sputtered sparks like gunshots. In the beginning, it was a thing that inspired a sincere and genuine terror inside of me- something that caused me to scramble back at my wit's end in anticipation of another blast. Now, the incessant scrape of the cast iron bellow invoked not even a shudder.

Things changed.

Still wary, I kept an eye on the fire that blazed in the belly of the metal contraption while striding across the length of the room, robe flapping behind me. Christian Diern, I thought to myself, before shoving the door open into a narrow hall. You're running out of time.

With the haunting sound of a clock ticking in my brain, I stepped into the dimly lit hallway.

Tick.

Tock.

5

The Wronged

I hated the Centre. I'm pretty sure I would've hated it even if I was as painfully alive as everyone else here. A woman went running by me, her slouchy potato bag connecting with the side of my ribs. Too busy chattering wildly into a walkie-talkie with long, talon-like fingernails curled around it, she didn't bother to give me a glance as she scurried past. She was talking so fast that she hadn't taken a single breath to allow a reply from the device, but even so, I knew that the crackling static meant there was no one on the other end. I gulped down the fresh wave of anxiety, not meeting her eyes as she turned her head as if sensing my scrutiny. Was insanity not knowing you're insane? If so, half the people on the plate were probably nearly there. Something in the food, maybe. I remembered her claws again and shivered. They made me think of those winged lizards that Harris had books about in her reading room. She was a damn ringer for one I saw on page thirty.

Focus, Valencia. "Focus," I hissed to myself, skirting around an information kiosk amidst the sound of shrill, upset voices.

Why couldn't that damned route let out in a quiet field? Or an abandoned warehouse? Even someone else's cellar would've been better. Any place that wasn't populated by the very thing I couldn't help but destroy. I recoiled as someone brushed my arm. That'd cause a scene, wouldn't it? Bunch of people dropping fucking dead in the middle of the hall. Tersely, I yanked my shirt further over my waistband and clutched the bag at my side.

"Devon, come here!" An exasperated woman called out to her daughter from the middle of a winding line. The kid, oblivious to both the concept of time and accountability, barrelled away from her mother and slipped out from beneath her grasp. I glanced at the woman again, waiting for her reaction. She hesitated anxiously, caught between the unwillingness to lose her place in line and her child disappearing. Making the decision, she stepped forward, only to be grabbed by the man behind her.

"You leave this line, you ain't getting back in it. Don't expect us to hold this for you."

Blinking tears from her eyes, the woman tore her arm away and chased after her daughter.

The throbbing in my ears increased along with my pace, both rising steadily now that I was no longer caught up in the sight of commotion. They must've been waiting for hours already. Surely there must've been something she could trade at the market instead of waiting in this. Everyone had something they could sell. Hell, she had herself, didn't she? Despite not being the most appealing alternative, there was little worse than waiting in this stuffy, humid building for hour after hour just to be scalped of both your savings and dignity.

My stride was interrupted by one of my feet, losing traction and slipping forward. Bewildered, I squinted at the tile to see what had caused the interruption.

"Oh, for fuck's sakes."

A slimy, chunky puddle of what I could only imagine was the contents of some poor man's stomach had been smeared across the floor, from the looks of it, not just by me. Disgusted, I pressed both hands against the sides of my face. Why was I so damn distracted today? Why couldn't I manage this energy flux? I needed to compartmentalize. It was the exact thing that made me so good at my job, and I was fucking it up today.

Too focussed on weaving through the crowds without contact, I had failed to notice I'd crossed into the third sector of the Centre. The pharmaceutical district.

Or, more aptly, the bacteria hubbub.

It was a sight that shook and trembled its way past disheartening. People of all ages swayed, barely able to stand as they dripped, oozed, and spewed from various orifices. A man, a few years older than I, pulled someone behind him in a wagon, the frail figure wrapped in a blanket with a compress over their eyes. Judging by the curve of the young man's spine and his pallor, he wasn't doing well himself. I wondered if they'd even last the assessment.

A person was ushered behind a large, grey curtain with his head bowed in both sickness and shame. They'd be picked apart and spliced back together before they even got a whiff of the medication they needed. This whole thing was just a front, and everyone knew it. The Council would strip themselves of power before they offered us their vaccinations. Our survival was based on little more than the hope that we wouldn't fall too ill. I surveyed the length of the lines. A lot of good that way of life was doing us. It seemed the sick doubled every year, no matter how much people spent on medications and preventative measures.

"Hey, kid, join a line or sod off," a man yelled from behind me, stabbing a sausage finger into my back.

The rage boiled my blood, but I resisted the urge to snap the finger off his calloused hand and merely snarled at the demand.

Kid. What a joke. Fat, bumbling idiot. I swallowed my tongue and smothered the urge for violence, disappearing in a flurry of cloak towards the double doors before I did something that really broke the rules.

Just a few hundred meters more and I would be free of this place and its overwhelmingly oppressive air. I quickened, slithering by everyone and stirring up dust before they had time to shift their bodies. There was a kind of art to it, I thought, as I dashed around a small family clustered in a huddle—an art to avoiding contact.

I heard Harris' voice, clear as day in my ears. *The touch of death.*

Few things warranted the caution that I treated my condition with. In actuality, a modest wardrobe would effectively do most of the work- giving me as much coverage as I needed, eradicating the fear of accidental physical contact. I'd tried the route of keeping my distance without making alterations to my attire at the beginning, but, as it turned out, it wasn't a reliable one. The second my sweat landed on someone's skin, they were dead. It didn't matter how little or brief the contact was.

I flung the weight of my body against the double doors and hurled myself into the sunlight. Shit, that season went fast. It was already getting warmer again.

The air had just taken a turn towards spring and warm dew settled on the leaves of the Verity garden, rubbing the petals softly with their tender hands. Everything was so unbelievably green here- the grass, the trees, the shrubs. They weren't real, of course, but the greenery of Verity Courtyard was the closest thing we'd find to nature on the plate.

I stroked an index finger over the vein in a leaf and watched the way the yellow rippled through the artificial stem beneath it. The Council had to draw in the people in some way. You'd almost forget what awaited you inside when you were busy being dazzled by its face.

Realizing I, too, was falling for the trick, I ripped my hand from the dangling plant and headed further into the Courtyard. In the middle of the clearing stood a peeling sign, held up by pillars aged much older than I. The large, dingy board displayed four lines woven together classified by bold, distinct colouring; blue for individual houses, yellow for apartments, green for shared living, and red for high risk communal. Along each line were several dots, labeled carefully with the names of the roads. I took the folded note slip out of my pocket and spread it open.

8B Lavellfield. Knowing Lavellfield was on the yellow, I scanned the line, following it with my finger until I found it on the map, smack in between Prudent and Buir.

I didn't really need to look, though I always did. I had garnered a decent enough understanding of the city's intricate webbing and the layout of the streets all on my own. It all worked together. My first week at the Harris place had me confined in the reading room, studying the city's maps night after night after night. How to get in and out undetected, which sites were most surveilled. Which areas were safe, which weren't.

The Verity yard was one of the former. Ironically enough, its proximity to the Centre made it equally safe from not only the Council but the citizens as well, because there wasn't anyone moronic enough to cause trouble with so many guards a holler away. Anyone using the path would check an address or route and be on their way, simple as that. I was probably the scariest thing these stones had seen, and I hadn't even done anything yet.

Not that I had too many opportunities to, with the glaring lack of people around. Being mid-work week and still shy of noon, it left the streets sparse and desolate. Most Council mandated jobs began with the rise of the sun and stretched into the evening, and the others started, at most, a few hours later.

Because I happened to have fallen in that small but significant timeframe, I decided to break a rule. I had no particular reason, except that I wanted to, but today... that was reason enough. I dropped my hood.

The breeze plunged into my hair with its deft, lilting fingers and lifted it from my collar, sending it billowing it behind me. The sky above me shone a bold and vibrant blue with but a few gentle brush strokes of milky white clouds fading against the thin, silver lines of the netting. I missed so much of the sky, always looking down. It really was the most beautiful part of coming downtown.

The skies near Harris' place could get so dark you could barely tell when it was daytime. The few loud, angry factories we had in our district pumped out endless amounts of pollution in huge billowing clouds that could block the sun in its entirety if the downwind was right. We barely got to see the sun down there, let alone a clear outline of the seams in the sky. It was for that reason that I so thoroughly and genuinely enjoyed the blessing of such a bright day while I had it. It made the journey a lot less bleak.

It took a few blocks for my eyes to fall victim to the harsh glow of the sun, but once they did, my vision was lost to tears of sensitivity. I halted in my step and squeezed my eyes shut.

A thing made of darkness could never spend too much time in the light.

The ring of a bell caused me to lurch guiltily to the side of the path, reflexively parting way for an all too enthusiastic adolescent to cycle by on a rickety, bent bicycle.

"Watch out!" He called behind him shrewdly as he zipped along the path. A bag of bread was strapped to his back with two thick straps of twine. Beneath it was two boxes of sustenance. Thick purple indents blemished his smooth, dusky skin from the weight. I imagined the tokens he must've dropped at the Sustenance counter and stifled a shudder. It might've been safer than what you could get on the street. But at the same time... I wrinkled my nose in thoughtful distaste. That all depended on who you trusted, and I didn't trust the Council worth a damn. It was all made in a lab whichever way you split it. The boy, now several feet ahead of me, took a cut-off through a hole in the fence.

I'd be coming up on the apartment sector soon.

I returned the hood to its rightful place, shading my face and delving into anonymity with one cloaked swoop. I had to be careful now. Such frivolous indulgences were better kept to my dreams. That's what Harris would say if she were here.

To my left, a high building crested the sky and split it into two distinct halves. The sharp point of the building was as good as a beacon for trouble. An eerie smile crept across my face in anticipation. It was time to go cause some.

I quickly split diagonally off the path and made way towards the split in the fence. Since most of it had been sawed or cut through, it didn't do much good as a fence. The remains made only the weakest of efforts to protect the land. When I fumbled my way to the other side, the broken metal snagged on my clothes and picked at my skin.

I spilled out towards the sharp grass and kept low as I skirted along the edges of the relatively well-kept yard. Keeping my movements careful, I slunk to the front, rotating doors, and peeked inside. Like most apartments, it was guarded by a couple of enforcers. The two of them sat behind a rickety plastic desk and used it as a rest for their legs that were tossed up in casual disobedience. Their arms were crossed against their chests in mirror images of the other, the muscles of their forearms pulled so tautly, they seemed raised beneath the skin. One said something to the other, causing him to slip a small smile.

There was only one other person in the front lobby. A woman, tall and trim in a faded blue pantsuit, checked her watch impatiently at the bottom of the staircase. I made an idle mental note that the elevator must be out again.

She had one item in her possession: a slim, black leather-bound briefcase that she pressed tightly against her side. Two brass padlocks swing from either clasp. I wondered what she was protecting and if it was worth stealing. People only locked things they were afraid to lose. I gave the door a nudge. It swung open.

Sometimes people didn't know when to be afraid. This was one of those times. Both men look up at me at the same time, their dark heads rising in synchronicity. Their expressions were flat, unassuming. The woman immediately shifted the briefcase in front of her and slipped into the stairwell. The door dropped shut behind her with a soft click.

Good call, I mused. I wasn't feeling particularly nice today.

I started forward, my shoes clicking against the cracked tile as I made a beeline for the stairwell.

"Hey! We need to see your building pass-." Something clattered to the floor as they scrambled to their feet. I didn't bother to turn around. They were going to catch up with me either way.

I was a breath away from the stairwell when I felt the presence of a body behind me.

"Don't take another step."

Only one of them, though. I tilted my head to the side, stretching out the kink in my neck. Interesting. The other must be calling it in. Little weasels. Snitches for goddamn hire.

I made a tut-tut noise with my tongue and pressed down on the door handle, pushing forward and crossing the threshold into the dimly lit hall. He grabbed my arm through the shifting fabric of my cloak.

"I don't want to hurt you."

Sure you do, I thought. You're a small man who wants to feel like he's not. That's why you signed up to be an Enforcer, wasn't it? Wanted to pretend you have some semblance of control in this shitty place? I twisted my arm and ripped it from his grasp, slithering along the wall away from him. Electricity was quivering on my skin, this hot, rapid energy that felt like tiny explosions on my skin.

He did not chase me.

He must've thought he had me.

The thrill raced down my spine. He thought he'd gotten the cat in the corner.

"What the fuck is your problem?" His hand landed on his holster, his finger stroking the head of the gun. "Are you insane or just stupid?"

I dropped my gaze and cast my eyes at the winding staircase, excitement welling in my throat. God, this is what I was missing. The thrill. The energy in my hands- in my body. The sheer power. Who was weak now?

"Walk towards me slowly, with your arms above your head."

He sounded young up close. A lot younger than he looked. I detected a slight quiver in his voice as it warbled on the last word.

"Are you afraid?" I hissed from the shadows. "Maybe you should be."

As if on cue, the light above us, already dimmed, flickered into blackness. I silently thanked the unreliable electricity.

"Turn around and place your hands on your head. I'll shoot!"

He would, that much I knew. Despite the trembling fear and the youthful glow, he had been trained for this. As low as all Enforcement Officers were on the totem pole, they were prepared to maintain control by any means necessary. This fearful kid wouldn't hesitate to drop eight shots directly into my skull.

He stepped forward towards me, where he believed me to be, and swung the gun around in front of him.

The radio clipped to his belt crackled loudly. The dialogue was barely audible through the tinny, poorly made equipment, but I assumed it meant a call had been made, and official Guardsmen would be on the way. I kept my back against the smooth stone of the wall, cautiously observing him as he plodded deeper into the stairwell.

I could make out the edges of his awkward figure as he fumbled at the radio, attempting to silence the sound.

I breathed slowly, relaxing my body until the whole thing felt like it was held together by dreams, floating listlessly in the twilight.

Seamlessly, I slid along the wall until I was behind him, my feet barely touching the ground.

Almost a ghost.

I pressed a gloved hand at the nape of his neck and hissed in his ear. "Careful now." He bucked beneath my hand and tried to swivel. "Uh-uh. You're going to stay," I paused as I pressed my fingers into the swell of his throat. "Right here."

I could've killed him right now. I told myself I didn't want to because I didn't want to leave a trail of bodies behind me. That's what I told myself, even as he twisted and squirmed to shake me off his back. Gentle in an impossible manner, I lowered my head and brushed my lips against his neck—less than a kiss, with no more pressure or movement than speaking.

His body went rigid beneath my grip.

"I'm going to need you to drop your weapon."

"M-m-muh-."

I clicked my tongue and crept my fingers to the back of his head, grazing the fluff of his buzz cut. It wasn't quite enough to kill him. Could've been, if I shifted my weight only the slightest bit. But I'd learned along the way how to disperse it properly. The weapon dropped to the floor with a loud clatter. If he behaved.

"You're going to let me go about my business now."

He shook his head weakly and tried to step forward and free himself from my grasp. Furrowing my brow, I sunk my nails deeper into the tender skin below his ear and felt my fingers push at the cotton barrier of my gloves. I kept my index and middle fingernails sharpened for this reason and this reason alone.

He yelped in pain, stumbling forward and landing on his kneecaps.

"I said," I enunciated my words carefully, pushing a foot into the small of his back, "You're going to let me go."

He collapsed from the gentle but persuasive pressure and released a choked sound from the well of his chest; it was hollow and watery, almost a cough but with something inherently disturbed about it. I briefly worried I had pushed too hard and killed the poor bastard, but he curled away from me and sobbed into his hands.

He'd broke, so I left him where he was. Stepping over the still whimpering pile of flesh, I began my ascent up the dreary stairwell. He had curled into a fetal shape and pressed his hands tightly against his sides as if to keep his insides from falling out. They wouldn't, of course. It would only feel like they were. He would return to normal eventually. Or at least close to it.

The stairs whined loudly beneath my weight, squealing as I rapidly took the steps two by two. Between the second and the third floor, the lights came back on, sending sparks into the air as they crackled back to life.

Using the opportunity, I paused on the landing and removed the folded piece of paper out of my pocket, smoothing it on my thigh. It took my eyes a few moments to adjust in the lighting to decipher the faded scrawl, but once I did, I felt the hair on the back of my neck stand up—the third floor.

How wonderful. I tilted my head up. The large, emblazoned 3 sat above the platform above me, pulsing from a faded fluorescent light behind it.

It was time.

It felt like a dream, as it always did. I watched my hand push the door open with a strange sort of third-party observation and felt oddly disconnected from my body.

Like the front lobby, the hallway was well decorated with different degrees of motion and weight sensors, lining the edges of the hall with thin, translucent wires. This, in addition to the several tube-like lights, made slinking in the shadows an impossibility. I hated being in the open.

Relax, Valencia.

My foot hovered on the edge of the doorframe, my breath caught in between the inhale and exhale. Christian was one well-off resident. This place was high class. For us, at least. I knew most engineers and scientists lived in apartments and complexes, but I'd never been in one quite as polished as this one. Behind the peeling paint and the slightly swaying lights, the building's structural integrity was better than anything I'd ever seen. I guess it made sense. The smart ones were the only people worth anything. Had to lock them up in one building to keep an eye on them, I'd bet.

After another moment of contemplation, I dropped my shoulders in a shrug and stepped out onto the carpeting. It felt strange and unnecessary underneath my shoes as I plodded like the ground was squishy and malleable. I hated it.

By the time I reached room 313, I was stewing with frustration and bubbling with irritation. Antsy and restless, I scratched at the lengths of my forearms. It felt like tiny bugs were crawling beneath my skin and laying eggs. I rapped my knuckles on the door in two sharp knocks.

"Yeah, yeah, I'm comin'."

I raised an eyebrow. He must've thought I was a Councilman of some sort. I could hear tins clattering to the floor as footsteps padded heavily towards me. I kept to the side, carefully staying out of the view of the peephole so that when he peered through- which he would inevitably do- he would only see the edge of a dark shape.

The chain slid in the bolt audibly. The lock clicked.

The ever-present ticking of the clock vanished from my brain as the door crept open. A broad, ruddy-faced man glared down at me. I took in his narrow eyes, the sagging stomach, the purple around his eyes, and his sickly pallor. He might've once been tan. Looked like he had the aptitude for it. I kept my eyes on his mouth and watched the thin, chapped lips pull into a confused frown.

"Christian Diern?"

"Who's asking?"

The words had barely left his mouth when I shot my hand out from beneath my robe, landing it in the centre of his broad chest and pushing him into the apartment. Cleverly, I slipped a foot behind his heel and sent him toppling onto an ass that had grown too large on the diet of someone pandered to.

"What's happening?" His voice was whet with worry, and I watched him through slitted eyes as I tugged off my gloves.

"Someone sent for you," I replied softly. I owed no explanation, nor had I ever given one before, but it came on the back of doing something I hadn't done since my first six months of working for Harris.

I was hesitating.

"The Council." His voice cracked, but it was a tone of finality as he pushed a hand through his greasy hair.

I was squatting in front of him, hanging over his legs with both hands dangling between us. Why did he think I was from the Council?

"Just tell me," he begged as my hand absentmindedly traveled up his buttons. "Tell me how much they know about what I've done. Please. Let this be my final wish."

I cocked my head, my hand loosely cupping the air where his throat should have already been. I wasn't supposed to listen to them. "What have you done..." I dragged a finger lightly down his cheek, and his body tightened, then shuttered, eyes still wide on my face. "...Christian?"

"I just wanted to save them." His chest was heaving faster now, his airway closing as he struggled for breath. "I- you-them..." A sharp inhale that sounded like it hurt his lungs to even do. "It isn't right. It's not right. The Centre... giving out... making... lying... to us...the sickness..."

I pulled my hand back, suddenly rife with doubt and snared in his story, hoping for bought time, but his eyes were dark and bloodied, his nose swelling black. At the sound of the squeak in his throat, I kicked the door shut behind me. It was unlikely anyone would be roaming the halls at this time, but I didn't have any idea where the second guard was, and the status of the call he had made.

"Fuck," I said aloud.

I pushed his head back, watching the life run from his eyes in thick, red tears tinged with black the shade of oil. "What were you trying to say?" I asked his head, shaking it with his hair. "What did you find out?" His body fell limp, and I released with a sigh, letting the dead weight hit the floor.

Well, that's goodbye, I thought with a quiet frown, crouching above him. His face, greyer and more faded than ever, looked like putty morphed horrifically around the wide-mouthed expression. I dragged my fingers over his eyes, closing his eyelids. What was he saying about the Centre, damn it? *Fuck.* I fell back on my haunches, pressing my hands to the sides of my heads. I hated this. I hated that I hesitated. I hated that I didn't wait longer. I hated that I did this at all.

Most of all, I hated that I felt warm. Alive. Had I stolen that from him?

"Chris?"

My heart's beat dropped to a halt at the sound of the woman's shaking voice from just down the hall.

"Shit," I whispered to myself. The panic began a steep ride to my frontal lobe, rocketing past my temples.

No, I shook my head, rising to my feet. That was the old Valencia. I was calm. Level-headed. In one swift movement, I flicked the light switch off and submerged us into darkness.

"What's happening? I can't see! Chris? Is everything okay?"

I quickly adjusted to the darkness and weighed my options. I could try to make a dash into the hallway, but there were more variables in an uncontrolled space. I flicked through the pages of my memory and the countless hours and days spent reviewing with Harris. I needed a secondary escape route. What was I, fucking new at this? I shouldn't have even given him a second to talk. Fuck!

I slithered across the living room towards a tall, narrow window and hunched my shoulders to pull myself smaller. I was pressing my fingers against the glass to see if it would move when a girl, clad in a long dress, padded softly into the room.

I couldn't let her see him. It would ruin everything. I'd have no choice but to kill her.

I felt the humanity buck in my throat. And if I didn't... no, if she saw him it would change her. Warp her.

I thought of Richie's body for the first time in years, and the way it had been folded and mangled over the thin stretcher.

Ruin her.

"Chris..." The young woman's voice wobbled again, but she had stopped moving. She spied me in the shadows and curled away.

A swift pang in my heart was unexpected. Was that... shame I felt? Remorse? Couldn't be.

That was not who I was. Not who I was *supposed* to be.

"Did you hurt him?" She angled for a look at the crumpled body but couldn't quite see past the front wall. She wasn't far enough in the room. I sighed with quiet relief. "Are you going to hurt me?"

Uneasy, I pressed myself further against the wall until my spine snapped rigid and high.

She balled her hands against her breastbone, squeezing her eyes tightly shut. "Please don't hurt me. I won't say anything. I have no loyalty here. My brother-." She choked out a sob, "My brother was not a good man. He's been cut off by my family. I know he's broken the law. I only came to say goodbye. Please. I'm not from here. I live downtown. I'm not even supposed to be here. I have no part in what he's doing. What he's been testing."

The words were shrill in my head. If I drew them, they'd all have knives for points and swollen bellies of regret. What had he found? What knowledge had he had, that I'd now taken from the world? What might I never know?

We stood in a moment frozen in time, the quiet whirring of the fridge puttering on—a dainty wisp of a woman and a monster.

Whatever I might have said was caught in my throat, thick and thorny around my vocal cords. She waited across from me, shaking like a leaf with her arms clasped in front of her.

I wanted to tell her I did not want to hurt her.

That she need not be afraid.

I wanted to tell her these things, but I was sure she wouldn't believe me, with her brother dead less than six feet from where I stood.

She shifted on the balls of her feet. I knew she was considering a bold scramble to the door. I could've stopped her. All it would take was the few steps to leave the shadows and swipe of my hand.

Instead, I curled the flaps of the cloak around me, pulling at the frame of the blacked-out window. Thin beams of light poked through the smudges of paint that had been wiped off. Dust danced in the sun in miniscule floating orbs, unable to settle as I tore through it. I had the frame nearly out when a force of impact from the side sent me barreling into the wall. The table next to me was taken down in the crossfire, a vase shattering on impact and spewing glass in all directions. Momentarily winded, I laid helpless beneath the weight, sucking in shaky breaths.

No, God, don't do this, I thought as she wriggled off of me and gripped a shard of glass from the shattered vase. Above me, she rose, brilliantly beautiful, in the slanting light with her arm raised defiantly above her head. As I lifted my own arm to defend myself, she angrily used her other arm to push at mine. I had just enough time to utter a soft curse before my sleeve fell, and her palm came in direct contact with my skin. The shard of glass fell from her hand as she became stiff and unyielding. Seconds passed before she began to convulse, frothing a dark sludge from her mouth. Horrified, I pushed her off and scrambled away. She continued to jerk listlessly on the floor, her bulging eyes trained on me as the blood leaked and stained the carpet with an angry dark smudge.

It had been a long time since I had hurt someone not assigned to me—a very long time.

'You have to be more careful,' Harris had said sternly to me. *'You kill too many, and people will look too close. The wrong people.'*

We had been sitting on the rooftop of the old Mill's factory, watching the sunset. We saw so few there, so this one was particularly remarkable, even after that day.

In a state of rebellion, I had run from her home into the street. I ran into a man coming home from factory work. He reached out and steadied me, then promptly crumpled to the ground.

He had a home. A family. A life.

I had stolen that from him.

You walk the line between what is good and what is bad- if you do not control your power, it will control you.

We had stared out at the sun as it sunk below the horizon, dragging the beauty away with it.

If you're not careful, you will lose your humanity forever. Is that what you want, Valencia? To be a monster?

I stared at the bodies that lay in a permanent sleep in front of me, their void gazes boring into me.

If you do not control it, it will control you.

I stood amongst the shattered glass, crunching it beneath my feet.

Is that what you want, Valencia?

I finished prying off the window cover and busted it open, breathing in the fresh air.

...to be a monster?

6

The Fracturing of Things

The evening was approaching rapidly, the sun taking a swift turn back towards the edge of the earth. After leaving the apartment, I'd wandered through the weaving streets back towards the downtown. Ordinarily, I'd abide by the strict rule to return straight to Harris' house after completing an assignment, but something was different today. It was biting at me, and I needed the break. Every time I fucking blinked, I saw Christian's face: tired, resigned. But not surprised, never surprised. He knew someone would be coming for him. But why was it me?

Why did Harris send me? I had twirled my hand in the centre garden pond and wondered why she would take out an enemy of the state. I sat in someone's abandoned makeshift hammock and wondered what side I was working for, really. I returned a ball to a child and thought of how the woman had begged me to see she had no part in breaking the law and died anyway because I wasn't the law. I had a relatively interesting, albeit brief conversation with an old woman on her stoop about how a line had been pulled from the Centre and thought about Christian's remarks about the Centre lying to us. Giving us... something.

I had thought of the woman speaking to no one and the people in the sick line that'd never make it out. What did he find out? Could I go back? No, I'd dismissed that thought as soon as it was born. The guards would have already arrived, already pulled his body. Cataloged everything. If there was anything to find, it'd be long gone now.

I gnawed gently on a toothpick. I couldn't go back to the Harris house, not yet. Nothing was going the way it was supposed to today.

So, I was faking my freedom. Sue me. I wasn't ready to stop feeling like a contract yet. I didn't want to stop being human. Stop existing.

A group passed me, their voices mingling with each other's and rising above the buildings. They must've just been leaving work. I peered at the breast pocket of one of their uniforms. Section B. Assembly line. Not the worst place to be.

Shorter hours. I'd say better conditions, but it was relative. Judging by the soot around the smallest one's eyes and the burns on the middle's neck, it must've been passable, but barely—the mad scientist's minions. I idly considered the possibility that they had developed any of Christian Diern's ideas. I wondered if anyone had heard of his sudden passing yet, then almost immediately, if he'd transferred whatever he learned to anyone else.

The group took a sharp turn towards one of the storefronts, nearly toppling over the high front stoop as they wrenched the door open. The sign out front was massive- almost ten feet across and four feet tall and broadcasted the obnoxious namesake of 'Big Ed's.'

Through the window, I had a direct view of a group of men sitting at the bar, their feet resting on the narrow metal pipe that stretched from one end to the other. All four sets of eyes were trained on the small, crackling television fastened above a wall of nondescript spirits.

No wonder it was such a popular establishment. I could count all the businesses with working electronics on one of my hands. Programs weren't much, but there was usually some brightly coloured animated series running on a loop. Entertainment was entertainment, whichever way you got it.

I tossed the toothpick into the trash can across the sidewalk and followed the group's tracks, yanking on the door. It swung open with a high-pitched squeal that drew the nearest patrons' attention towards the doorway and away from the flickering screen. Unaccustomed to the attention, I ducked my head and moved into the room. All but one averted their gazes. The bartender, a tall man with a stern and unforgiving face continued to watch me warily, a damp rag fisted limply in a scarred hand. He wiped it in a deliberate arc, clockwise, then back again, leaving his eyes on me. The jukebox in the corner wheezed to life and spat out the chorus an old jaunty tune, and the bartender's attention was snapped back to the job at hand- wetting the whistle of one of many eager civilians.

Relieved, I chose a seat in a booth nearing the far back of the restaurant, beneath a burnt-out lightbulb. The other flickered weakly beside it as if the absence of its partner had sapped it of its energy.

The booth was even less impressive up close, the cracked vinyl seat splitting into spider web lines that climbed along the backing and hung off it scaly peels. The table attached wasn't in a much better state, tarnished by a skinny scratch that stretched from one end to the next. I gently reached out and laid my fingers on the mark. It had to have been a knife that did it. Pocket or otherwise. If there'd been bloodshed, it'd been long cleaned up.

"Oh, Miss, you don't have to sit at this ratty old table. I'm sure we have a couple of better ones open." The waitress beamed at me as I turn, her full cheeks a pale burgundy color that complimented her soft tan skin. "This guy's just about seen his last days, I'm thinking."

"No, it's okay." Realizing my voice was coming out as an eerie whisper, I cleared my throat and dropped my satchel down on the bench. "I like my privacy, anyway."

"Ah, an introvert." She winked in good cheer as I slipped into the seat. "We get a lot of those around here. Can I grab a drink order from you, or do you need some time to decide?"

Not used to such cheerful service, it took me a moment to realize that it wasn't personal- the Council emblem above the door said enough. How had I managed to stumble into one of the only court-owned bars on this strip?

In a manner that I hoped was casual, I surveyed the beverages at the bar. All the bottles were unmarked. Of course.

"Whatever you've got at the ready is fine."

"Sure thing, doll." She sashayed away, her full hips swinging with each drop of her feet. Endearing, I thought, tapping my fingers on the table and turning my attention toward the screen.

Burly, poorly drawn men with cropped haircuts propelled themselves toward each other, an acorn-shaped ball tucked beneath one of their arms. When they collide in a campy explosion of colour, cheers, and laughter erupt from the seats.

The left side of my lip curled up in what could've been a smile, but without any good-natured bemusement. It was like waving a rattle at a baby—a pathetic distraction, nothing more.

"There you are now," the waitress said with another wide-toothed smile, effortlessly sliding the drink onto the table and a coaster beneath it. "Just give me a holler if you need anything else, alright? My name's Linda, by the way. I always seem to be forgetting that part."

Her tinny laugh was still ringing in my ears long after she'd left my table. The first sip of alcohol made my tongue pucker and chilled my teeth, but it wasn't horrible. I'd had worse. I took a second swig and swished it around in my mouth before swallowing.

Disillusioned by the channel selection, I turned my speculated gaze to the people in the room. There were men everywhere. Other than the waitress, there were only a handful of women in the room. I fought the unease every time someone shifted in my direction.

The men at the bar all looked vaguely similar, as if all their features had been hand-picked to match. They all shared a full brow, deep-set eyes, and a broad, flat nose, offset by a thin-lipped grimace and aged yellow teeth. Their eyes' color was the only thing that differed from one another, but they shared the same glazed, detached look while staring at the screen. I was caught up in it, in the unsettling-ness of it all, when the bartender slid a bowl of powder towards them. I leaned forward, curious. He had on a pair of latex gloves, the kind you would use for surgery, and he dipped a wet finger into the powder, then carefully trailed his finger around the rim of the glasses in front of the men. Only one of the men had turned away from the television to watch him, and his glassy eyes followed the circles the fingers went like it was the only thing he was ever meant to do.

Something felt fundamentally wrong about it, so I looked away, but the horrible feeling stayed in my chest. If my instincts had a voice, they'd be screaming at me to leave, to run away. To never look back.

No one ever talked about what it felt like when you started seeing. It was a cleave down the middle of your soul- and I knew it was denial to want it to stop, but I couldn't bring myself to be brave enough to feel otherwise. I wanted to go back to a time before I saw the lingering poison that bled like ink through the fabric of our society. Before it stained our auras like black, bloody vignettes and left us more feral and broken than ever before.

But that was the problem with seeing. There wasn't any going back.

I squeezed my eyes closed, bristled like a dog in the rain, shaking away the feeling the best I could, even though it clung to me. Clung to my clothes, my skin. I opened my eyes only when I felt as close to blind as everyone else and shifted my gaze away from the things I couldn't bear.

The group from before at a table near the entrance. They chattered excitedly as the redhead began taking something out of their bag. I immediately tensed, expecting at best, a close-range weapon, and at worse, an explosive device that would blow us all to smithereens. When it was merely a folded piece of cardstock, I leaned back, curious about the way they hunched over the paper.

I took another sip and forced myself to relax, easing my back flat against my corner. I had almost achieved comfort when I saw the man sandwiched between a wall and another wasted patron.

Tall and rangy, he leaned on his elbows at the crest of the bar and nursed a pint of unfiltered amber beverage. Long, dark eyelashes framed his light eyes and worked to enhance one another, creating an impactful gaze I wouldn't want to be the receiver of. Glossy black hair fell in waves over his forehead, only a few shades darker than the creamy tan of his skin. He might've been beautiful, but more than that, his energy vibrated in the small space. Dark, dense, and dangerous, it fell off of him in languid waves.

There was something inherently captivating about the way he moved; his body made up of sharp angles and geometric shapes, and yet, you didn't see him shift until he was suddenly in a new position. I couldn't hear the words he spoke to the man next to him, but the nature of the conversation inspired a quick furrow of his straight brow before he smoothed it into a pleasing, albeit detached, smile.

As if suddenly made aware of the attention, he straightened his back and tilted his head up, dancing his eyes across the length of the bar and landing them smartly on my face. I flinched involuntarily, before remembering the hood covered most of my face in shadows.

His lips curved into the ghost of a smile, and he lifted his drink toward me, cocking his head to the side. A warmth snaked through my body, leaving tingling streaks of life where it lay. I was overcome with a desperate and feverish sense of familiarity. Like I knew him like I wanted to know him. Like I needed to.

Irritated and embarrassed by the frivolity, my cheeks flushed, and I reverted my attention to the drink going lukewarm in front of me.

It took me just over fifteen minutes to finish it, and the second nearly thrice that. I was never much of a drinker, but as the night crawled on and the light outside dimmed, I was inclined to sip at it to keep busy, if nothing else.

Later, a live band replaced the tinny music from the jukebox, consisting of a hodgepodge of young, adolescent dreamers and home-made instruments that looked less than functional.

Though not entirely melodic, the music had an irregular beat and heavy bass that inspired tapping feet and swaying hips. It was, after all, real, and there was an appeal to that. It was a good thing to remember; that we were still people.

Before long, people were in the centre of the floor, arms above their heads, voices raised in incoherent songs. What glorious freedom, I thought as I finished off the last of the glass, but it wasn't for me.

For tonight, my little field trip was over.

I craned my neck, attempting to spot Linda through the barrage of people. Growing increasingly frustrated, I rose to my feet, pulling my satchel onto my shoulder. All I wanted was to settle my bill and get out of here. Big Ed's, being court-owned, wasn't exactly a place to leave a debt, especially when you weren't supposed to exist in the first place. Someone bumped into me, sending my hip into the corner of my table. I cursed softly under my breath and pulled my sleeves further over my hands before beetling through the horde. There was no need to pass this on to these people. They didn't deserve it.

Not tonight, anyway. Another day, another place, there might be. If Harris told me to. I swallowed the nausea.

Getting to the front of the bar at night proved to be much more complicated than it had been earlier, and it took me another four minutes to squeeze my arm through before I finally made my way to the front.

I slid a couple of tokens across the bar, leaning forward to reach the bartender. He had immersed himself in a conversation on the other end, but I called out anyways. I needed to leave, or things were not going to end well.

"I'm just settling my bill," I spoke sharply, barely breaking through the wave of voices.

When he ignored me, I huffed out a breath.

"Hey!" When he failed to respond once more, I repeated myself louder still. No one paid me much mind in the mix, but his head finally snapped up, and he wandered over to me.

"What the hell do you want?"

Exasperated, I held the tokens out and lay them flat in my hand. "I'm trying to settle my bill. If I leave 'em here on the counter, someone will take 'em."

He twisted his mouth in a quick corkscrew before greedily snatching it from me like he was a starving man, and I'd just offered him food. "Okay. Thanks."

I was slinking away towards the door when someone grabbed hold of my arm. Thinking it was an accident, I tried to pull away but was quickly made aware of the purposeful grip.

"Hey," the man slurred. His voice was a resounding warbling echo in the caverns of my ears. Indignantly, I whirled, ready with a snarl.

Wait- that face. I knew that face. Feet propped up on a bent and faded desk, twinkling dark eyes. Even through the slick glaze of alcohol, I'd still be able to recognize them. I never forgot a curse.

The music continued to throb as bodies mashed around and jostled us. I yanked my arm again, this time with more enthusiasm.

"I know you."

"You're mistaken," I said coolly.

"You were there," his eyes were manic now, bloodshot with angry red veins that bulged around his iris. "You were there today. You did something to me."

The pressure from his fingers sunk deep into the flesh beneath my sleeve, bursting veins the harder he pressed.

"What did you do to me?" He asked, his voice the worst kind of cocktail of anger and confusion. Panic, at knowing I'd taken something from him, but he'd never know what.

People around us were beginning to take notice, and it was becoming increasingly difficult to slip away.

I should have never come here. It was obviously a mistake.

"Let go," I grunted and kicked at his shin, causing him to double over. The crowd murmured as I tried to shove through. It made me think of the back freezer of what used to be Red's Butcher Shop before he ran out of livestock, all the meat hanging meekly from the ceiling with steel hooks through their snouts. They were heavy and nearly immovable. Though, I suppose, it was almost the same thing; just sacks of meat.

Someone yelled out. For a second, I thought it might've been me, but I realized it came from behind. I'd made it past the front few people when the first shot rings out.

The herd began to frantically clamber over each other in a desperate shove for the exit. A shot went whizzing by my ear and pierced the glass in front of me, exploding the window. I tumbled forward, rapping my knees hard against the floor.

With ears still ringing, I swiveled the top half of my body. The Enforcer had a pellet gun above his head and fired rounds off into the ceiling, sending shards of the hanging lights propelling to the floor at warp speed. The poison had consumed him quickly and without front, submitting him to a fever that would eventually lead the way into hysteria and mania. I knew I had pushed him too far, damn it. I should've trusted that instinct.

Swiftly, the bartender that had been eyeing me earlier artfully grabbed hold of the gunman's arm, cracking it in one surgical motion, and kicked the gun towards the bar once it smacked the ground—Guardsmen training. My eye twitched as I scrambled back to my feet. They were all a part of it. The staff...

Sirens began to wail in the distance, their cries matching the agonized sobs of the terrified strewn along the sidewalk.

I never should've come here.

I took off running, leaving the others in my wake. It made me sick like someone had plunged a long-taloned hand into my gut and twisted my intestines around each knuckle. How could I ever think I could be normal?

Look what I'd done. *Idiot.*

I veered left, sprinting along one of the residential side streets adjacent to the Strip. I'd wanted for a day. One fucking day for myself, and I'd ruined everything.

Why don't you ever think?

The stars, subtle and infinite from the other side of the cover, wink at me from the blanketed sky as I followed the moon.

The sirens continued to wail, the noise winding through the streets and chasing my footsteps as quickly as I left them. The Centre was closed for hours now, and I had to take the side streets all the way down to the blue.

Harris was right, of course. I should've gone straight home. I chastised myself for it the entire journey, mentally preparing for what would be said and done upon my arrival.

When I reached our street, I was surprised to see the house as quiet as the streets, the lights long burned out, and the air still. Even my presence wasn't enough to stir the calm as I glided along our front path and stepped softly onto the porch. I pushed the door open, half expecting to see Harris on her old rocking chair across the foyer with knitting needles in hand, but the usually occupied seat was empty. Okay, I thought to myself. She must not care, then.

The old floor groaned loudly beneath me, even despite the thick, scratchy carpet. We'd started getting some rot spreading across the main ground before it got put in. The ugly thing helped, certainly a little, to prevent the continued wear and tear on the planks, but you could still hear the muffled screams of sinking wood. The rug merely delayed the inevitable.

If I recalled correctly, it was a boy who found it in the dump by a City construction site a few years back. Brought it over in tow and politely asked Harris if it would cover his fee for me to kill his father.

The memory made me frown softly to myself. Harris had been running this business long before me, and I imagined she'd run it until she was thrown to the waste bin and shot out into oblivion.

I left my hand limp on the railing and started up the stairs, careful to avoid the weakest spots in the wood. I'd like to think I was more than a pawn, but I was at least on the board even in the best case. She knew the game. But hopefully, so did I.

I stared at her door at the end of the hallway, my eyes tracing the faint indent of the deadbolt on the other side.

To keep people out? I crossed to my room and slipped the key into the lock, giving it a shove with my shoulder. No, just me.

I threw myself onto the bed and kicked my shoes off on the land.

She wanted to keep me out.

Everyone was afraid of death, in the end.

With visions of chess pieces swirling in my buzzed brain, I drifted off to sleep, tangled in the cotton sheet.

7

Leaving, Again

Heavy smoke was burning the inside of my nose. I wanted to brush it out of my gaze, clear my lungs, my vision, but everything was raw with each breath. My eyes stung from the heat and dropped fat, ugly tears down my face, leaving streaks in the soot. I was collapsed on the floor of a square room, my limbs crumpled and unnaturally bent beneath me.

Shadows of humanoid creatures crept along the corners of the room, long, thin smiles stretched across their empty faces. Their cackles echoed in my ears.

"No," I croaked out, "Please,"

One of the shadow men parted from the rest and glided toward me. I tried to scramble back, but I couldn't move my limbs.

"You..." it said in a gravelly baritone. I fought to catch my breath as the head bobbed over to mine. "...are one of us."

I shook my head numbly. "No,"

"Yes," it insisted. You are."

With a painstakingly slow meld, he drifted into me, separating my atoms to make a doorway for his.

"Look."

I was spinning again, sickness lurching in my stomach. I landed, hard, on my back in a clearing with my head swirling.

"Cia? You alright?"

My tongue swelled. I turned my head to the side and met Caleb's eyes- beautiful, soft brown eyes. Home.

The sunlight beamed behind him, creating a sweet golden halo around his head.

"What's the matter?"

The pain is swift and hot. I tried to speak, but my tongue floundered thickly in my mouth.

My quiet whimpers only drew more concern into Caleb's face, knitting his brow together seriously.

"Are you okay?" He laid a hand on my forehead and rubbed a thumb against my temple. "Hey, I'm here. I'm right here. It's okay." My head rolled to the side. "Look at me."

I blinked slowly and rotated back to him. He continued stroking in small, sublime circles with the pad of his thumb that spread warmth in my brain.

"Thank you," I murmured.

His cheeky smile burst across his face in the firecracker style I was so used to and lit a twinkling in his eyes.

"I was just thinking-" he coughed once, then again. "I was-." The coughing continued, and it was the sound of war.

He dropped his hand to his knee beside his other, only raising it to his mouth when he coughed again. I could hear his lungs rattling, and when he pulled his palm away from his mouth, it was speckled and marred with gobs of blood.

"What did you do?" Blood leaked from the corner of his mouth, the veins in his eyes quickly bursting and swallowing the white with the bleeding colour of rose petals. "What have you done?"

Then, screaming, *"What have you done? What have you done?"*

I woke up alone in my bed, gasping for air. My hands fisted in the sheet beneath me and a single bead of sweat trickled down my face.

The night ebbed on outside the window as I laid still, listening to the wind rattle our loose siding and toss our shutters to the air.

I closed my eyes again, raising my chest to meet the inhale and letting it fall. Caleb wasn't here.

I was alone. Of course I was.

"Okay," I muttered as my heart rate slowed. "It's okay."

It wasn't real. Cal wasn't even on the Plate. *Cal was gone.*

The clock ticked away at me from the nightstand, faded numbers pushed together to display

'4:24'.

I sat up, swinging my legs over the side of the bed, and scrubbed my face with my hands to rid myself of the sleepy grit that had caked itself on in the few hours of sleep. Dried blood flaked from beneath my fingernails and drifted listlessly onto my cheeks. The shudder was quick and involuntarily. Disgusting, I thought, pulling myself to my feet. I stepped lightly on the bare floor, careful not to trod too loudly, and maneuvered my way through the obstacles.

The bathroom lights flashed on with a familiar muted crackle and worked to illuminate the cramped space. Blearily shading my brow from the blare, I dragged my eyes up to meet my reflection in the mirror. God, it never got easier. I could swear I looked worse every time I caught a glimpse.

Sighing heavily, I dampened the washcloth hanging above the faucet and dropped my face into it. Images from the day before were flashing back and blurring together.

The strange bartender, staring with his stern and drawn face. I wiped beneath my eyes with the cloth, rinsing it again. The young Enforcer with the almost blue eyes and spiky hair.

Christian- his sister.

Collapsing on the ground.

Blood.

I dropped the cloth into the sink and let the water sputter onto it. A life, a death, what was it called if they happened at the same time?

I cranked the faucet off and dried my face, dabbing gently. Water dribbled down my forearm and dampened the cuff of my sleeve, darkening the colour from charcoal grey into a deep black. I had forgotten about my clothing. Stripping it off was the first thing I did when I returned from a job, with no exceptions. It was a vital service I paid to myself to separate myself from what I'd done. A small gesture, but a grand one for my conscious. Was it poetic, or merely lazy that I had forgotten to do so tonight? They hung limply from my frame and folded in wrinkles at the creases of my body. They were the same ones I always wore for my seeking, chosen for the deep hues of neutral greys that blended in with the shadows. The only part of the ensemble I had bothered to discard was my robe, which I had carelessly tossed over a wicker chair near my front door.

I was crossing back towards my bed when a sound from outside drew my attention. My immediate reaction was just one of confusion- it was much too late for anyone to be on the street and just shy of labor commencement. I wasn't scared. *I was never scared.*

It wasn't necessarily impossible for mild disturbances to occur, but the sound of muted voices and the buzz of engines drew me to the window. A faint clatter was one thing, but few would be so bold to make themselves known in such a blatant display.

Unless they were permitted to be here.

I used two fingers to pull the blinds' planks open, leaning a hip against the windowsill.

Two stories and four houses down from where I stood, a group of men milled outside of their armoured van. Each man wore a metal helmet that reflected the streetlights like a laser beam and created a bobble-head silhouette that teetered on alien. Raid uniforms. The breath caught in my throat.

Their radios lit up tiny blinking lights from their spot on the utility belt, making each figure easily traceable in the deep night.

One man returned from the house across the street, shaking his head and offering a flat gesture. The one who I assumed to be the driver stood near the front door and smacked the vehicle with a baton. Something from inside let out a high-pitched whimper that was dripping with desperation.

I swallowed thickly and dropped the blinds. Could they have followed me? No. I had been careful. It wasn't possible. My heart began to beat harder - loud, heavy bass.

I couldn't stay here. Someone would tell those Guards about the Harris house with the slightest bit of pressure. It wouldn't take long. People would sell us out in an instant if they thought their life was on the line. When it came down to it, the only thing people feared more than me was the Council. At least I might hesitate before taking everything from them.

With shaking hands, I grabbed my satchel and sloppily stuffed in an extra bundle of clothes and a smattering of items off the dresser. I didn't know when I'd be back. If I'd be back.

The thought was making me dizzy, so I forced myself into a cold focus. Blinking the stubborn sleep from my foggy mind, I dashed to the wicker chair, sidling up to where I had kicked my shoes beneath the night before. I was midway between putting on the second shoe when something thumped on the door. Hard.

I held my breath, waiting for it to sound again. When it didn't, I swung my cloak around my shoulders and dipped a hand in the pocket to reach for the gloves but paused. I had to go through whoever was out there. And that would be their problem. I stuffed the gloves in my bag and shifted grasp to the smooth doorknob, letting it warm before I turned it and undid the chain from the top.

It creaked with an old man's groan, opening the way to a hallway darker than the night outside. Even the emergency lights had gone out.

I glanced up at the ceiling now, squinting in the dark, attempting to make out the pathetic spheres in the shadows. The government generator for this block must've gone out. I'd never even seen them out before.

"Strange, isn't it?"

I startled, jumping back from the middle of the hallway and towards the walls. I had a foolish thought at first that the darkness itself had spoken to me, reminiscent of the heady nightmare I'd been submerged in just moments before.

The man pulled himself away from the wall, keeping most of his shape tucked in the shadows. He moved around me like smoke, drifting behind me before I've realized he'd even taken a step.

"I know all about you, you know." His voice was a hot breath against the back of my left ear. "'What you are." I flinched away, careful not to make a move. "Where you came from." Not yet.

I took a step towards the left, narrowly dodging his left arm and making a break for the staircase. I was nearly at the railing before he grabbed hold of my cape and gave it a hard tug.

I hissed at the unwanted force, toppling back as a direct result of the motion. I didn't want to kill anyone else today, damn it. I'd had enough of that. If I kept going...

I swiftly swiped a kick along the ground and came in contact with the back of his knees. He, infuriatingly, buckled but did not fall. I went in for a contact slam with my elbow to his nose, but he ducked out of the way and took the hit to the temple, reaching out and grabbing my bicep and sending me into the wall.

It barely seemed possible, but he was faster than I was. My head was still reeling from the impact of the siding when he spun me around, pressing his arm across my collarbones and shoving me against the wall. He splayed a hand on the space vacant beside my head, his own bowed as his chest heaved with effort. I resisted the childish urge to spit at him.

"Enough."

He raised his head to the light for the first time since I'd seen him in the hallway, and the reveal nearly inspired an exasperated chuckle. Should've really been warier of beautiful, dangerous men at the edges of bars. Turned out they follow you home. I strained forward, pushing my arms against his lean and wiry body.

Obviously infuriated by my unrelenting resistance, he dropped his hand from the wall and gripped mine, pinning it against the drywall. I stared at the skin to skin contact as it moved in the dark, waiting for the curse to consume him and the poison to spread. I could feel my skin wriggling towards him, like a hundred live wires reaching for an exit point- begging to be transferred out of my pores, poking against his for entry.

I stared at him, and he back at me.

With the illumination of the flashing lights, I could see the veins beneath his temples, pushing against the skin and worming about. His grip slackened, and he pitched forward but remained upright.

How could that be?

Impossible.

Inexplicably furious at the thought of someone being immune, I swung my elbow toward his jaw and connected with his softly bowed mouth. Using the moment of disorientation, I gave him a two-handed shove and sent him crashing into a narrow table, launching a vase to the floor. It shattered into hundreds of pieces, soft, plastic flowers ripped and torn alongside the shards of glass. It crunched beneath my shoes as I dashed for the stairs, nearly losing my balance but regaining it as I scrambled down the steps.

His warm skin against mine, his unwavering gaze, his-

Someone outside began banging on the front door and sent the thin walls rattling from the massive impact. Whatever they had, it was big.

I braced my hand against the top of my bag as my desperate clamber sent things spilling from the gaping mouth. From outside, I heard one of the officers yelling for residents to stay in their homes. The commotion must be drawing them out. I wouldn't make it past the lot of them, even in the dark. I rubbed my forehead against the stabbing pain of a tension headache that was growing and spreading across my skull. I'd have to go through the tunnels.

I hit the landing with force, scraping for the memory of Harris's emergency procedure she'd tried to browbeat me with during the early days. Because I was too frantic for conscious thought, I slowed myself down and closed my eyes, forcing deep breaths into my lungs. The banging continued, and I silently thanked my past self for locking both bolts.

Okay, Valencia, breathe. What did it look like?

It had been late morning when the sun was shining brightest through the window with thin beams that lit up the counter in stripes. I was sitting at the dining room table, one leg tucked beneath me, and the other propped up on a stool. I was wrapped neck to toe in thick, gauzy bandages like my entire body was a festering wound. I twirled the spoon in my tea, watching the ripples of the water chase after the rod. It made me think of the Spillout and the water tightening my chest. I had swallowed thickly and blinked away the memory.

"You're very kind to have me stay here," my voice was so small, so meek. Was that really how I used to sound? How I used to be?

"You'll pay your dues, girl. It isn't a handout." Harris offered me a thin smile, one of the only ones I had ever seen grace her tough and leathery face. "We both have something we need from each other."

I hadn't known what that meant at the time. I hadn't even known what I was, let alone what I'd be.

The images continued to come in flashes; the thin slice of toast on the chipped porcelain plate, the file of a man who went missing. No, that's not it.

The door began to crack from the top as the battering barrage continued. Fuck, Valencia.

What was it?

Harris' cane, her wobbly walk, her stubby hands, her scratchy scrawl- the envelope! My eyes flew open, and I sprinted into the kitchen, smashing my hip off the table as I whipped open the pantry. The shelves were vacant and sagging, covered with a thick layer of dust and cobwebs. Hastily, I used my fingernails to scratch the wallpaper behind the third shelf. The stiff material shredded my fingers as I peeled it back, revealing a slit in the drywall that held just one item- a slim, brown paper envelope held together with a thick wax seal.

Leaving drops of blood like a mouse trail, I hurried to the cellar door. My breathing was ragged and harsh, awkwardly clunking along and barely squeezing through my throat. I didn't know how much time I had, but I was sure it wasn't long. I spared a glance back towards the stairwell, remembering the man upstairs and the strange and inexplicable altercation. He should've been up by now. None of it made sense.

I didn't have time to worry about it. The cellar door was, as always, shut and soundly locked with a swinging padlock thudding against the planks with the shaking of the house. I fumbled clumsily to retrieve the key from my pocket lining and dropped it back into the cotton void before pulling it out with a trembling hand.

"It's going to give!" The man from outside yelled.

I dropped the key from palms slick with sweat and fell to a crouch to feel in the dark for it.

The door splintered and sounded like gunshots to my ears. I craned my neck around to see the blunt-faced cylinder making a sizeable hole of entry in the front door. Moving in the jagged tide of frustration, I blindly shoved the key into the bottom of the padlock and sighed in relief at the sound of the lock clicking its mechanical release. The door cracked again from behind, but I didn't bother to turn around. Either I would make it or I wouldn't. Looking wouldn't help me now.

I unhooked the coil and circled it into my hand, pulling the door open and tumbling through just as the sound of stampeding steps broke through the main hallway. Panting, I slammed it shut, frantically looping the cable through the latch and secured it once more with the padlock.

Chest still heaving, I surveyed the landing for anything I could jam the door with. If the cast iron battering ram could make it through the front, the measly cellar door would be no match for it. I could hear the men stirring about outside, aggressively dragging and tossing furniture, punctuating their violence with primal grunts that sounded like a clan of beasts. Sick, I pressed a hand against my stomach, willing it to unknot. I couldn't do this. I didn't know-

Count to ten, 'Cia. The memory whispered in my ear. *Then start again.*

8

The Station

Working only with the light streaming from the crack below the door, I collapsed to my knees to feel around for anything I could use to block the entrance. Finding only splinters, grimy beetle corpses, and the sound of my thundering heart, I remained frozen on the floor around the hole in the all-encompassing darkness.

"Take upstairs. Giles and I will take the front room." I heard the familiar whine of an opening drawer, the sound of papers rustling. I hoped they didn't find the files she had stashed about the Council. Shit like that would get you in serious trouble. I swallowed thickly. If she wasn't already in it.

The knocking against the bookcase kicked my cemented feet into gear and shocked me into a frenzied scramble into the tunnel entrance. I skipped the stairs entirely and thrust myself to the damp floor, landing in a crouch.

I had become comfortable post-mortem, and in that comfort grew foolish.

I crossed the ground with long-legged strides as I had just hours before, but I wasn't going to the City this time. No, not when a breach was happening. Not when I had so many people breathing down my neck, including the impossibly drifting man. I had to get as far away from here as possible. I had made such clumsy mistakes.

I had to receive atonement for them, wasn't that how it went? I shook my head. Of course, I had gotten greedy. Greedy and dissatisfied.

Winded, I slowed to a stop and leaned an outstretched hand against the wall of the tunnel. The surface was cold and wet against the pad of my hand, gathering drops beneath my fingerprints.

I spat the gooey saliva out at the ground in front of me, where it made a satisfying splat. *What an absolute idiot...* I began to move again, this time in a light jog.

My bag was heavy on my hip, and the repeated motion stripped the heels of my shoes down, the already pathetic rubber soles loosening from their cloth counterparts. My pace gradually slowed until I was merely walking, the quiet swish of my pants my only company in the musty cell.

Just to the left of the City Centre entrance, there was a ventilation system that let out into a shacked-out train station, a little further towards the Spillout. It was quick, cheap, and dirty, and precisely what I needed to get as far away as possible.

If I took it toward the south side, it could take me all the way to the Brink of our jurisdiction. The towns out there were nearly inhabitable, housing only the cheapest establishments by the sleaziest people. Brink was a last resort for most, pandering to those who clung onto the edges of the Plate in sheer desperation.

People only ended up there when they couldn't live near the City any longer, or when the City officials pushed them out. Rejects, drug addicts, the kooks. If the Council could push them all the way to the bottom of the Spillout, I bet they would. You weren't even required to have any licensing for Brink like you did when you were near the Blend. Once you're that far out, no one gave a damn about you anymore. Live or die, it's not their problem.

I squinted at the faded number as I passed. Two more rows to go, and I'd be there. Coughing, I pushed my spare clothing down in my bag and wrestled the zipper shut. Transient Subway had a hell of a lot of people with sticky fingers and seeing as everything I currently owned was in this bag, having it stolen would relieve me of what little luck I had left.

I wrapped my hair in around my hand and tucked it beneath my collar, securing my cloak around my neck. I was approaching PF-412 fast, the entrance signified by a blocked text in cracked yellow paint. Just past it was a rusted ladder with two of the metal rungs missing, leading up into a narrow, circular chamber above. Tentatively, I gripped the left-hand side and shook it weakly. The ladder squeaked back at me as the bolts rattled in their sockets.

There was nothing good about Transient, I thought as I clambered up the rungs. One step gave out beneath my weight, and my hands slipped from the side, rubbing the first layer of skin off.

Not a single fucking thing. My shoulders protested as I pulled myself past the missing ledges.

Unlike the City Centre entrance that made use of a handy rubber wheel, the access to Transient Subway was obscure, marked only with a small hook on either side. Opening it required the utmost balance and stability, forcing the user to teeter on the ladder and use both arms to push off and simultaneously prop it open. It was one of those things-theoretically simple until you were six feet in the air, balancing on a half-inch railing.

The first attempt was a mistrial, my clammy hands slipping off the thin hooks and almost sending me plummeting towards the ground. I brushed myself off and succeeded on the second, able to raise the cover enough for light to come streaming through the hole in the floor.

A toilet flushed, and a rush of choppy water gushed through the pipes closest to my ear. There was only one thing that would have the power to make the Transient Subway entrance any worse: it was a near-direct passage to the floor of the men's washroom.

I wiggled my hand through the opening and felt for the latch. I had time, arguably infinite amounts of it, as not many people would barge into the maintenance closet of a basement floor washroom with much enthusiasm. Without any hired help, the Transient Subway had been just another dismal building sentenced to a funeral from its grout. It was a marvel the damn thing was still standing at all.

I rapped my knuckle off the side of the metal clasp and hissed at the sharp jab. The pain relented quickly, but the warm trickle of moisture told me I'd nicked it good enough to draw blood. Moving in quick, methodical movements, it took just one quick flick to release the mechanism and free the tightly wound wire pressure, leaving the cover light enough to push it to the opposite side. The motion sent a thin layer of dust flying onto my face.

"Not a well-trodden path, then," I muttered indignantly, huffing out a breath to blow the residue away. I pulled the strap of my bag over my head and swung it into the room, sending it skidding across the ground. Raising my arms, I flanked both sides of the hole and wriggled my torso through after it. I kicked off from the ladder and let my body hang from the floor. With a low growl, I hurled myself into the room.

The shelves lowest to the floor clanked as I shook the foundation, causing the long-emptied bottles of cleaning solutions to jostle against each other. Knitting my brows in irritation, I drew myself to my feet. *The absolute worst.* A chain dangling from the light bulb bounced off my head when I rose, happily dawdling around to the side of my face before I batted it away. Everything about Transient was shitty. Even this little room was shitty. I kicked a rogue bottle further beneath a shelf and trotted to the small door, pressing my ear against the thin wall.

The murmurings of faint conversations came to a close with the punctuating slam of the bathroom door. Content with the implied vacancy, I angled my shoulder, turned the knob, and fell into the bathroom. A man, alone by the sink, gasped himself into a coughing fit, spraying flicks of water all over himself and the floor.

"What- wh- you-." he cleared his throat awkwardly and shook his head, wiping his hands on his jeans. The gesture brought attention to the heavy cloth pouch he had strapped to his waist. I tilted my head to the side and eyed the abundance.

"Alone in here, are you?" I eyed the swinging doors of the stalls, obviously emptied. "Well, isn't this a happy coincidence." I slunk to put myself between him and the door. He tried to shift past, but I had him blocked.

"You know, I was just thinking." I walked towards him, pushing the hood back and letting my tumbling curtains of hair frame my face. "About what I was going to do once I got here." I was close enough now to feel his breath on my cheek, a hot wind that reeked of spice and alcohol. Undeterred, I trailed my fingers up his chest, swirling around the buttons of his shirt. "You see, I haven't got any money." I reached his neck, tugged the collar back. "But you do."

"I- ah..." he stuttered, reaching up to grab my wrist. "Look, I'm not..."

Purposefully, I gently pressed my fingernails into the slope of his throat and held, waiting. It was no more than a pinch, a dull sting. I observed the flickers of his expression as he choked out a gasp and dropped his arms to his sides. Making a quiet noise, I released the sputtering man and let him fall. Carrying on a tune into a soft humming even as my hands shook, I unhooked the buckle and pulled the strap from beneath his massive, low-hanging gut. His wallet slid easily into my palm, and I graciously flipped it open to paw through it. Various identification cards broadcasted his round moon-face and thin-lipped smile, embellished with dull, person-less eyes. I glanced at the trembling man before me. He'd never be that way again, even if he recovered.

I took all the paper slips and tokens from his wallet and tossed it back down to him. Someone would find him here before long. He wouldn't be missed.

It wasn't until I crossed to the door that I spared him one last pitying look. Poor sap, I thought, before my roaming mind was shot off. There was no use fretting over it. I gave the door a hard pull and slipped into the hordes of people milling around the terminals.

There was no good or bad; there just was.

It took me what felt like hours to separate the mass of sweaty bodies and push my way through to the front. Even then, all of the automated token machines were booked up with lines intertwining with others, reaching the Far East end.

In the middle of it, all was a single open teller. One of the last employed from earlier and better years, I presumed. It had been a long time since the Council gave the Transient Subway any financial support. Judging by the heavy folds beneath her eyes, she'd probably started working here back when everything was just beginning to feel hopeful and new again. I bet people thought the Transient Subway was going to change everything. Everything was coming up for the underdogs. Long live the pioneers.

I studied the woman as I approached, careful to avoid the centre of her eyeline until I was ready to be seen. She was caught in an exchange with another patron, a tall and burly man with a shredded jacket and a dusty charcoal pack. He slid a handful of tokens across the counter, and she clicked her small machine to dispense a beige ticket after depositing the funds. I heard the clunk as the device dropped it into the bucket and wondered how often the Council collected.

"Next," she crackled out in a raspy tone. Since the other few people loitering around seemed otherwise occupied, I slipped in front of them and joined her at the counter.

"Yes," I said softly. Not quite a whisper, but somewhere halfway between it and a reasonable tone.

She chewed on the end of the gently maimed lead pencil and eyed me doubtfully.

"What can I do for you?" She asked, her fingers hovering precariously over the dingy keyboard that might have once been white.

"I need to get to the Brink," I said hurriedly, and then cringed at the lack of tact and social grace. I needed to blend in, not be the oddity of the night in this woman's memory. "Which is the first train leaving?"

She pinched her dry, purple lips into a well-defined pout and turned back to the machine, tapping out a complex array of numbers into the circuitry.

"We've got a train leaving for Klove Station in five minutes from terminal eleven." She leered at me, propping herself up with two equally bony elbows. "If you can make it there, It's an eight-hour ride. I don't know how prepared you are for that. It takes you as close to the Brink as you can get."

"That's fine."

The tapping resumed. I watched particles of dust fly from the keyboard.

"It'll be twenty-seven tokens." Her grin was plastic melting on hot pavement. My eyebrows raised before I caught myself. Granted, it had been a long time since I had taken any train, but I had no idea the prices had been hiked so high.

They really didn't want anyone going anywhere, not even to the one place that meant nothing.

"Do you have it?" She asked with a sneer as if expecting me to balk at the price and turn around, hat in hand. There must've been many who did.

I reached for the money in my pocket and tossed the differently shaped coins onto the counter. "There should be just over thirty's worth there. You can keep whatever else."

She sat in her booth with her jaw dangling slightly agape. "I can't- we can't take gratuities. It's against the law."

"I don't care what you do with it. I just need a ticket." I paused at length. "Please." I didn't want any of the dirty money on my person if I got stopped by a transit officer.

Nodding dumbly, she hit print and stapled the ticket with my receipt.

"Um, enjoy your trip. Thank you for choosing Transient."

As opposed to what, walking? I gave her a slight nod as I swiped the ticket from the counter and broke into a gliding run, submerging myself into the swimming crowd. The fuzzy speakers were blaring dialogue over the ancient PA system, "Now boarding, Route Eleven to Klove Station with no station stops, departing in five minutes."

I was sprinting towards the higher platform when I heard a shriek from behind me. I didn't need to question it to know someone had found old Bill crumpled on the floor.

"Someone call a Councilman!" Yelled a disembodied voice.

I blinked the light spots out of my vision and took the last flight of stairs two at a time.

There was no good or bad; there just was.

I allowed a small glance down as the sea of people migrated towards the tragedy like insects to a flame. It wasn't my fault. That's just the way it is. *There just was.*

The train behind me began to beep impatiently, giving out the final two-minute warning. I peeled my eyes away from the crowd and slipped anonymously into a car, avoiding the track guards that were directly employed by the Pod. I was pretty sure they didn't run along the straight and narrow, but you couldn't be too careful. Few would be willing to take on a route to the Brink. You had to be a particular kind of crazy.

The engine rumbled to life and shook the car walls around me, drawing my attention to the impending departure. I zeroed in on a faded blue seat far left of the carriage tucked slightly behind a metal panel. It didn't matter much, as the rest of the spots were empty, but I still walked to the cramped, shadowed seat.

Strained joints grumbled and groaned as I folded into the seat. I was settling in and leaning my head against the glass just as the train trembled to action.

Amidst the rumbling, thoughts of the lanky boy in the hallway with unruly hair and an apparent immunity surfaced again.

He had said something to me. I closed my eyes. What was it? Yes, that's right.

I know what you are.

I flexed my hand on my leg. How could he possibly know what I was when I hadn't the faintest idea? I balled it into a fist and dug my nails into my palm. I used to know what I was. Someone laughed, loudly, and a little hysterically from another train car. I used to be human.

I used to be human, and I used to be alive.

Whatever I was now was hollow and dark. I couldn't run from it. I couldn't control it.

It would follow me. It would always follow me.

I thought of the woman in Christian's apartment and squeezed my eyes tighter. People suffered around me. It's what they did- what I did. I curled my arms close to my chest. What the hell did he know?

There was no life away from this. Death was a part of me, whether I wanted it to be or not. That choice had been made for me.

It was one thing I would never outrun.

9

The Blind Leading The Blind

The old and crooked teller had been right about one thing- I was not prepared for a trip of this magnitude. It took only a few hours for restlessness to bite at me, and wandering the empty train car was the only outlet that I could comfortably do while trapped inside. There was nothing in the shuttle aside from a plastic sling hanging over the shifting door, pregnant with faded pamphlets and brochures that were left untouched and unclaimed. The abandoned promotional material had been left unchanged after the initial launch. Grand promises of a more luxurious and accessible trip had ended in beat-up tin cars rattling slowly over the cheapest set of tracks that looped lazily through parts of the city in the most inaccessible places imaginable. If it hadn't been in the contract, I doubt they'd have revamped the system at all. I picked a flyer out of the middle and flipped through. A conglomeration of smiling faces stared up at me; all of them dressed in clean, carefully pressed factory uniforms. All of this crap just to keep the masses at bay. It was novice, juvenile.

Pathetic.

It was impossible to keep my mind from wandering as time stretched and waned onward. Too stubborn to be controlled by will, my conscious thought twisted into an intense analysis of the events that had followed my mission- why hadn't I gone right back home? What was I searching for that I didn't have? I was asking questions I wasn't sure I wanted the answers for.

It wasn't hard to make the leap from my irresponsibility to Harris's disappearance, and it drew to me like smoke in a burning home. Had it been her in that van, I wondered, or just some unlucky bastard caught in the crosshairs?

The emotional turmoil brought me to a slumber full of dark, shifty dreams that made no sense. It broke later, when the train shifted awkwardly and tossed my head into the window.

Startled into immediate consciousness, I shook my head clear and blinked the remaining clouds from my eyes. I wasn't sure how long I had slept for, but it must've been a while. The view barreling past had been turned on its head, and for a moment, I was unsure if the train had somehow sent me to a different dimension.

What had been gritty, inner-city had shifted into a dusty, deserted mockery of what might've been, at one point, farmland. Vast fields, long since abandoned by their caretakers under the submission to modified food, were left dry and sparse. Any growth we might've managed at one point had been blocked by the plate, and there was no way to know if there was even anything left beneath it. Our life could just be teetering on a hunk of smouldering rock, and we'd be none the wiser.

The last of a few stubborn wildflowers bloomed from between thick thistles of dried grass, poking deceptively cheerful faces out of the brush.

It would've been beautiful here once, in this one spot. I imagined the settlers running with wheelbarrows full of the last fresh soil and planting seeds. Beautiful until the land insecurity struck- a certain instability in the ways of getting enough nutrients and the reality of what was needed to survive. Beautiful, maybe- but it must've been a variation of hell until Sustenance came to market.

I pressed a hand between my bosom and felt for the thready trembling of my heart. A lot of things here must've been hell. I'd say it still was if I had any idea what heaven looked like.

As if in testament to the notion, the gentle, sloping horizon was already blackening with shadows of buildings smudging charcoal fingertips above the grassy field. It was familiar, though I barely remembered anything about the Brink. I would've doubted I'd been there at all, if not for small memories, deeply seeded but never tended. Far away reminders whispered to me about the Great Wall and the weave of the web against the sky. I would've been young then. Before I had joined any gang. Nobody bothered coming this far out, not for anything. There wasn't even anything to steal down here.

After the Council took over, most viable people were pushed towards the city. Land and workers that could be monopolized were, and places that remained free from the Council government were far and few in between. A lawless land full of desperate, angry people wasn't much better than the inner one's capitalist exploitation.

At least you'd be less likely to get murdered or scalped outside your home downtown. I shuddered. No rules, no morals out here. I turned my attention back to the objects passing outside my window.

Outside, burnt down farms and barn houses crumbled in their commitment to decay, splintering what was left of life since forgotten.

We were getting close now; I could feel it. It was like a sickness in the air. Heavy. Oppressive.

We barrelled into town at full wobbling speed and sprayed up chunks of gravel that bounced off the medians. The track we slid on was flanked on either side by dirty grey buildings with faded, unintelligible signs and mud-splashed faces. A small group of men smoked fat, charcoal cigars on the cement steps of an abandoned factory, their hats pulled low over their stern, drawn faces.

The side that life forgot.

Feeling groggy, I reached for my bag beside me, quickly verifying its contents and slung the strap over my shoulder.

There was no time to be afraid.

There was no time to be anything, really. I swung the edges of the cloak shut and fastened the buttons rhythmically. The routine gave me a gentle sense of calm, reminiscent of the times Harris whisked me towards the downtown with envelopes tucked in the nook of my arm.

But all of that had now come to an end. I swallowed thickly when I thought of never seeing Harris again.

A friend? No. Of course not. But she was all I had.

Bracing myself for the plunge into the unknown, I swung in a flurry of cloth to the train door and waited for the shrill ding to sound.

Months ago, Harris had mentioned her cousin, Victor, to me for the first time. Described as a stout, bearded man with perpetually red-rimmed eyes and an ever-present pipe dangling from his lips, I was less than reassured by the notion I was insured by him.

He ran a business in the South of Brink, through a place that used to be called the Lighthouse Motel. I once asked her what it was he sold, but she only shook her head.

Some things are better not to know, she would mutter cryptically before hobbling away.

There was no good or bad. I rolled the words around again like they were the only thing keeping me sane. They might have been. *There just was.*

The plan itself was simple- I would exit the train at the Harbour station, locate Victor, and he would determine my next permitted move. There were two possible outcomes: I'd be released from my contract, or, in the event of Harris' passing, be passed right into another. Saved, but forever indebted.

The train puttered to a lengthy stop, and the brakes screamed as they scraped along the old tracks. I winced, resisting the urge to cover my ears like a child. Everything felt too much. Too loud. Too harsh. Too jagged.

The doors rattled open and invited the thick, smoggy air to fill the cabin. Instinctively, I used my draping sleeve to cover my mouth from the fumes. It did little to stop the rasping cough that shuddered in my chest. Wheezing and fighting my own irritation, I stepped down onto the curb.

The day was rapidly diminishing, using its last drips of light to paint shadows that stretched across lanes of abandoned street ways. It seemed despite the quickening of my pace, the darkness remained just one step ahead, swallowing the world before I could dip my toes in.

It was quiet - uncomfortably so, and God, the silence was as thick on my chest as the sickness was. The inherent sense of nothingness seemed to be the most disturbing, and although there were no real signs of danger, I found myself holding my breath in anticipation of it.

A rustle from an alleyway perked my ear, but I resisted turning. I knew enough to know that it could be considered a challenge to gaze upon someone's unsightly deeds.

The people here were often dead-eyed and angry, made more intimidating by the way the hollows of their cheeks jutted inwards and pulled tightly over the bone. I didn't want to look unless I had to, and even then. As if suddenly cluing into where I was, I slipped my bag beneath the billows of my cloak.

It sounded like the air grumbled an incoherent smattering of words that was almost English, but I doubted it was.

"If somebody's there, I'm really not in the mood," I said evenly, pausing in my rapid steps. "And I promise whatever you're planning will not end in your favour."

There was no reply this time, not even a whisper. I found myself missing the breathy mumble after another moment in the quiet. Brink Silence was not the calm silence of a foggy late-night drizzle or a park during Monday morning, but rather, a kind of silence that spoke of things stolen much too often and far too soon.

I rubbed the goosebumps off my biceps and hurried my pace. I still felt eyes on me, even though there was no evidence of any.

I headed toward the end of the main road, where a flat bungalow-style motel stood, marked by a burnt-out sign that fell crookedly over the front.

As I moved to cross the lawn, thick, opaque clouds opened a sprinkling of chilling rain and drooled into sludgy puddles along the muddy path. Grimacing, I used both hands to prop up my hood and shade from the unwanted shower and jogged to the front doors. The full glass panes, though dingy, made it easy to see into the front lobby. I took note of the several dead light bulbs strung from the ceiling and the dark and shadowy room. A large desk and a small box television with two skinny antennas faced each other in a broken relationship with each other, but little else.

I cupped my hands around my eyes and pressed them against the window, attempting to get rid of the glare from the outside lamp.

My heart thudded in my ribs as thunder rumbled in the sky. It sounded close- too close. I tried to look up at the stretch of the net, to comfort myself it was still there- that we were still protected- but was blinded by the onslaught of rain as it grew more burdensome and opaque.

An outburst of rain busting its way through the Net here, and there was one thing. This was an angry, wretched thing that if I didn't know any better, I might've said it felt alive.

Lightning flashed above in rapid flickering and illuminated the desk full of scattered papers in wild disarray. Someone must have been here not long ago- but where were they now?

I wrapped my hand around the handle and gave it two hard tugs, humbled by my futile efforts.

"Motherf-."

"Can I help you?"

I startled at the sound and rapped my knee against the tempered glass. Spinning despite the shock, I squinted into the eye of the storm but saw only rain.

"Who's there?"

"Are you... looking for something?" The voice from beside me was quiet and smooth, running over each consonant so gently it felt as if they were merely more gentle vowels. It sounded like a hissing whisper in my ear, though they stood a few feet away from me.

"I'm looking for someone," I said, hesitantly, turning to face them.

"Aren't we all," the person said softly. There was something haunted in the small phrase.

"Victor. Last name Harris. This is his inn. I have to see him." I felt as if I was shouting against the whipping winds.

They smiled, letting it inch across their face in haughty steps that hitched awkwardly at each visible wrinkle. They, too, wore a wide-brimmed hood that covered the top half of their face, leaving slimy tendrils of hair to creep out and cling to their temples like worms.

"I can think of a few others who share such a sentiment."

Confused by the vague and near irrelevant statement, I stood back on my haunches and tried my best to keep out of the rising water.

"Is he not here?"

"Victor is no longer with us, unfortunately." They leered towards me with a hand in their pocket. I flinched and pulled myself back until I am flat against the window. Seemingly amused by my evident and pathetic discomfort, they took their hand from its cocoon and waved a brass key in my face. "Let's take this inside, shall we?"

Obediently, I padded softly behind them, watching them as they retrieve matches from behind the desk. They trotted around the room, lighting the wicks in lanterns that hung from the ceiling.

With the warm glow of flame, the room seemed just marginally more inviting, but compared to what we had just left outside, I felt as if I'd just wandered into someone's home. The weathered rug and faded wallpaper had a rustic, rescued vibe about it that boldly sang, "remember me?". Opposite the desk, a circle of mismatched chairs was placed around a broad blue trunk.

"Tea?"

"What?"

"Would you like tea, something warm?"

"I don't..."

They waved a hand dismissively, clicking their mouth from beneath the cloak. "No trouble, it's no trouble at all. Have a seat, make yourself comfortable."

Comfortable. I stared at the flat pillows that slouched like servants on the back of a chair and squashed them down as I lowered myself into it.

Not quite there, I drummed my fingers on the arm of the chair as the shadows flickered and danced on the wall. A grandfather clock, easily the most admirable piece in the place, was parallel to me, a massive pendulum swinging between two generous planks. It was the only item in the lobby that stunk of higher wealth, boldly stating the fact with its gleaming knobs and golden hands. The base was carved into an intricate story of triumph, a masked woman holding a vase above her head in glory. I was mystified by the gouges that created depth in her hair, tangled, and weaving through the wood. I couldn't help but wonder how no one had stolen it yet.

"It's a beautiful piece, isn't it?"

I turned and saw my hooded comrade had returned, a china cup rattling in their hands.

"It's something, all right." Gracious because I had no other option, I took the cup from them. They hobbled to the rocking chair with a defined hitch in their step, leaning to feel the ridges before sitting.

"You can call me the Caretaker. What are you called?"

The way the question was phrased made me uneasy.

"It depends who's calling me."

They laughed, a warbling chuckle from the deep well of their throat that slowly turned into an eerie song.

Lost in the surrealness of the moment- and I wasn't certain that I wasn't dreaming, at this point- I leaned back in the chair and crossed my legs.

Continuing to hum the same note, the Caretaker dropped their hood. I was unable to contain the sharp inhale that whistled the air out of the room and cut through my lungs like a hard-edged sword.

Where their eyes should've been, where they must've used to be, were marked with thick angry scars that gouged deep in bruised sockets. Fatty folds of skin overlapped around the crest of temples, licking at the wiry eyebrows that bent at every possible angle.

I swallowed thickly, fighting against the bile that threatened to overflow from the depths of my stomach.

"Are you afraid, nameless? I imagine it would be quite the sight, though, of course, I've never seen it myself. I do apologize for unsettling you."

It took me a few moments to find any words to speak, so we sat in silence for those few beats.

"Why?" I asked evenly, even as I gulped the bile down. "Why would they do this?" I took in the twisted monstrosity. It was a kind of outright sadistic violence I was unaccustomed to. Downtown, you could cut off a finger or carve something into a spine, but you didn't dare do anything to a face. The Council would track them down and then take you too. It was too bad for morale to see that kind of blatant torture in the open. It would ruin their whole 'it's great out here you don't need to get inside' thing they pushed so hard.

The Caretaker knitted their hands carefully together on their lap and clasped them carefully together.

"When you're a servant, people forget about you." They began to rock slowly, the wooden chair creaking beneath the weight. "They forget you see things one might wish they didn't. They forget until someone has the presence of mind to notice the nosy child in the corner with the broomstick." They laughed. "I was never nosy again after that. There is no quicker way to learn to mind your business."

I didn't reply, solemnly building a picture in my head of the shifty person that sat before me.

"You needn't have pity at all, child. It was a long time ago. There are worse fates than mine around these parts."

It wasn't worth explaining that the feeling I felt wasn't quite pity, but something closer to discomfort.

The wind outside howled and rattled the windows. Dismayed by the sound, the Caretaker drew their shawl closed across their chest.

"It is getting worse out here, you know. No one from the mainland knows. But it will reach you there, too. One day."

"The weather?"

They waved their hand dismissively. "Dark and moody and dangerous. Tossing things about. Losing things. Lost things." They rambled.

"Who are you?" I finally asked. The whimsical back and forth had gone on long enough. "I need some information. What do you know?"

They continued to rock steadily, unperturbed by my demanding tone.

"I know that I know just enough, and not too much. Would you like to know where Victor is? How the Council found you?" The rocking stopped. "Or what's happened to your Harris?"

My hands were shaking, so I fisted them and pressed them to the sides of my thighs. My words came out rougher from the cage of my teeth as they gritted together. "Where are you getting your information?"

They tutted at me, shaking their large and oddly visually disembodied head.

"If you'll sit back down and be polite, perhaps I'll have something useful to say." They paused. "Your tea's getting cold."

I clenched my jaw and shifted in the seat, my innate rebellion whispering to disobey their every command. I sucked in a deep breath and pulled myself rigid and attentive at the edge of the ripped embroidered cushion.

"I need answers. To anything." It was uncharacteristic of me to beg, but I forced the words past my stiff lips. "Please."

A smile crept across the Caretaker's weathered face and puckered their greying cheeks.

"Yes. I'm sure you do. No one's ever told you a thing, have they?"

I sneered at the thought. "Not particularly. What's happened to Victor?"

They held up a hand to halt me. "One might say he got what he deserved." Looping a finger through the handle of their chipped china cup, they brought it to their mouth and took a careful sip. I respected them for not wincing since I was sure the mixture was about as sour as it smelt. "Victor is a man of many things, but not one of those things holds even an ounce of loyalty, dignity, or integrity."

The image of the stocky, nervous man reappeared in my brain. I could believe that.

"He's been in the business of people for a very long time."

"Meaning what?"

The Caretaker cleared their throat awkwardly in the first sign of discomfort I'd seen from them.

"This world is not a good one, child. He was a collector first and a man second, with no preference for the things he gathered- fine art, antiquities. Human beings. Whatever it was, he would sell to the highest bidder. He never cared much about what happened after. Though, what happened after had a great deal to do with why he disappeared." Another painstakingly, slow sip. "Some humans he traded were for people in the Pod. The Council used them to staff certain disposal units and the garbage dumps. Grimy jobs. It wasn't long until someone on the inside got sick from one of the slaves from the outside."

I raised my eyebrows in genuine surprise. "An illness? In the Pod? I thought they had a vaccine for just about everything."

"It was unlike anything they'd seen before. It progressed quickly, and the Senator deteriorated almost immediately. He survived the illness, but not the penance. Once you get sick like that, there's no going back inside. They burned his body and the one of the slave. After that, the Council launched the investigation that led them right to Victor's door." They chuckled bitterly. "That's the thing about burning all your bridges. No one cares much about protecting the island."

"The Council did his review?"

"Yes. And Victor, for all his integrity and strength, cracked almost immediately. He agreed to make a deal to skip the penalty. The deal included names of the Slum Militia."

The grimace was quick and unscripted. "That's how they found Harris."

The Caretaker nodded grimly. "He was quick to sell out his own blood."

"How do you know all of this?"

"People might've taken my eyes, but it does not mean I cannot see." They tapped the crest of their skull with a crooked index finger. "There are other ways to know if you pay attention."

"Right," I fidgeted nervously, "What's happened to them now then?"

"Oh... won't be bothered with them again. The Council deals in rapid and merciless life disposal." They gestured with a tough and weathered hand behind them. "Victor is here, in the garden, right where they left him."

My stomach rolled as I gazed out the back window, grateful the visibility was low.

"They don't usually leave bodies lying around."

The Caretaker laughed. "Maybe not where you're from. Here, the bodies stay where they lay. Sometimes we use them as fertilizer to try to grow on what little land is left, but if no one collects them, they don't move." A cloud fell over their face. "But if they stay long enough, there are certain parties that don't have any bias against what might sustain them."

Their phrasing was odd, and it took me longer than a few seconds to fully comprehend the meaning. Sustain them. I swallowed the rise of bile in my throat, tried to focus on the air I was pulling in through my nose. That couldn't be real. Could it? Were there people here, in the Brink, that would eat other human beings? I shivered, resenting that it surprised me. There was a part of me, however small, that took pleasure in select ignorance, and the jarring information was enough to make me feel like I was precisely as stupid and cowardly as Cal always made it seem like I was. *You've just got to be braver, 'Cia. It's a simple thing. Use your goddamn head.*

"And Harris?" I asked the question without thinking. Impulsivity. The fool's vice.

"I imagine she'll either be kept inside the gates for information or transferred out."

Transferral was the only official way off the plate, through two smoldering ovens and a compactor before being spat out into No Man's Land, besides the overflow from the Spillout. I didn't even want to know what it looked like on the other side of that door.

I felt remorse for Harris, and that surprised me. I had wanted to believe that I was without attachment, but it was strange how human nature was to find one wherever they could.

Habit, normalcy. Comfort. Somehow the brain could trick anything into feeling like home. Even if the house was as cold and unwelcoming as Harris had been.

"Are you alright?"

I had paused long enough that I heard the question in the Caretaker's voice. '*Is she, you know... all there? I think there's something wrong with her.*' I rubbed my knuckles across the side of my legs. It was a tone I'd heard many times. Before the Institute. Before everything. Before I was this. And if they had known me now, they would know that I would never betray a weakness. I had thought that they had known who I was, but it was now clear they knew only the things they knew and nothing more. I opened my mouth, but I didn't have time to figure out what I was about to say before the sound of distant scratching from outside started on the side windows. It scurried around to the front door, where they began to rattle the doorknob. The Caretaker sighed heavily. "Always want in. Everyone always wants in. It pours and slides, and everyone wants in," they mumbled. "It's best if you go now."

"Go?" I said aloud, surprised. Were they mad? "I have nowhere to go."

"Doesn't matter to me. Lots of people have got nowhere to go. You stay here, other people think they can stay here. Free, free, freeloaders."

"I've got money."

They scoffed at me, turning up their nose. "Your money's no good here. Currency is only as good as what it's worth to those who take it."

"What can I do?"

They shifted, furrowing their sparse brow. "Favours."

"You want me to do you a favour?"

They shook their head. "Not today. One day."

I raised an eyebrow, knowing they could not see the juvenile and dismissive gesture. "Sure."

"I hear the doubt in your tone, young one. But remember, there are other ways to see. I will make this alliance with you in the hope that a year from now, you will return and help me."

Dubious, but tired, I agreed. There was no way for them to know whether I would or wouldn't be back.

They brought steady hands back up to their mouth and downed another sip.

"Then, for tonight, you will stay. Tomorrow you must depart. People hear of Victor's passing, and they will not respect this place with the reverence as they once did. I, too, will leave this place one day soon. You must not overstay."

Since I hadn't been planning on staying longer than the night, I had no qualms about agreeing to the terms. "That's fine."

They held out their hand. "Do we have a deal?"

I stared at their outstretched hand, and the absurdity of the situation nearly made me laugh. Handshakes. Asking a carrier of death for a handshake. Still smiling tightly, I crossed to them and slid my gloved hand into theirs, careful not to squeeze too tightly. Wet fibers were thinner fibers, and I didn't want to take any risks. "Yes."

They rubbed a short thumb over the length of my hand, their thumbnail catching in loose threads. "Who did you say you were again?"

If the Caretaker didn't know who I was yet, there was no need to divulge it to them. A name was the first of many breadcrumbs, and if you followed enough of them, you'd find me at the end.

Seemed like an easy way to get professional disposal.

"I didn't," I said flatly, taking my hand back. The words hung in the air after they left my lips, partner only to the loud clicking of the clock and the slurp of boiling tea.

"If that is how you wish it to be. Remember, no one cares about the end of an island they've never reached." The Caretaker raised a wrist and jangled the strap, sending a wild array of keys bouncing off each other. "Retrieve your luggage. When you have, follow me to the main hallway."

I dropped back, wondering if I should tell them I hadn't any at all. Instead, I stayed standing and crossed to the front doors to stare out into the street. The rain continued to assault the blistered asphalt in a torrential downpour, filling the cement cracks with pools of dirty water.

By the time I'd turned back, the Caretaker had disappeared from the seat without so much as a whisper, the teacup still sitting steaming where they left it. They were terribly agile for someone with no eyes. I shuddered, thinking of it.

Believing I'd given it enough time, I skirted my way around the receptionist's desk and yanked the door open into the main hallway. The lanterns outside were few- one at the mouth of the entrance and one at the end- ensuring most of the trek would be done in the shadows. The doors along the sides were marked with metal-plated numbers glued haphazardly below single peepholes in the middle of the doors. I tried the handle of the first door but failed.

"After me, please."

I jumped as I had the first time they'd snuck up on me, though I managed to avoid the injury this time. From only a foot away, the hood had been reinstated and covered the horrific scene of tight seams and scars that creased the upper half of their face. Somehow knowing it was there but not being able to see it made it worse. In the shadows. Just like me.

"Some of the rooms haven't been taken appropriate care of once Victor was apprehended. I was the only one who stayed amongst the crew. You'll likely be the last guest."

"You knew, then? What he was doing?" I might not have been the most appropriate judge of morale, but something about it didn't sit well with me.

The Caretaker slipped a key into its door. "It is the world."

My own words from earlier echoed again in my ears; *no good or bad- there just was.*

"It was a pleasure to meet you," they crooned, nudging the door open with a stiff toe. "I will remember our deal, and I will find you to claim my prize."

I blinked- just once, quickly- but in that moment, they were gone. What a strange way to word it, I thought, frozen in spot. And just what had I agreed to do?

Lightning crackled outside and lit up the strange little room. The bed took up most of the space, even though it was small. A thick quilted blanket was tossed over a deep blue comforter, embroidered with something that might've been a floral pattern but greatly missed the mark.

I dropped onto the bed and unwrapped the tie of my cape from my neck.

"Holy shit," I muttered into the room and fell onto my back. I repeated it twice more before squeezing my eyes shut.

The anxiety I had tried to smother for the entirety of the day had risen to a feverish peak. The things I didn't understand significantly tipped the scale in its favour against the things I did, and it was infuriating.

I had spent month after month post reawakening seeking a new identity that would fit the monstrous being I had become, and Harris had offered me one. It seemed as quickly as that life had flared, it had burned out just as quick.

A tear slipped from my eye, drawing a warm river along the crest of my cheek and into the hollow of my neck. I dashed it away, aggravated and humiliated by the offending admission of weakness.

I was grieving, not just for Ms. Harris, but for the loss of my life, and everything I felt I had only just come to comfort with. I rolled onto my side and curled into a ball, pressing my hands on either side of my head.

Where did I go now? Was I destined to live a life like the Caretaker? Cold and alone, with my eyes gouged out? Would that be the only way I could stop hurting people? Locked up somewhere, left just to waste away while the world forgot about me?

All I ever did was...

The man. My eyes flew open and I stared at the shadowed ceiling. In the numb confusion, I had almost forgotten.

He had gripped me, fiercely, and I him, and he had survived. *Or maybe he just took longer to die*, a small voice inside of me whispered.

I sat back up, rubbing away the moisture from my cheeks. Whether any of it was true or not, I had to find out. If he had lived, perhaps there was an existence for me.

There had to be.

There had to be.

There had to...

At the edge of the bed, I dropped my face into my hands and tangled my fingers in my hairline. The slow, steady breaths I sucked in attempting to halt the panic proved to be in vain as my pulse continued to throb angrily. "You're *just a coward, 'Cia. You're holding me back," Cal said when I wouldn't give him the Firestarter.*

I stood restlessly, untying the string from my cloak and desperately tearing it off of myself, discarding it over the back of a torn vinyl chair. Still feeling the utter claustrophobia from being wrapped tightly in my clothes, I shed them in a frenzy onto my floor, kicking them out of my path. Clad only in my cropped undergarments, I fisted my hands aggressively in my hair.

I had sentenced Caleb, and now I'd done the same to Harris.

I had as good as killed the only people that had ever cared for me, and it was my fault.

In a fit, I threw a pillow across the room.

Everything was my fucking fault.

The pillow smacked a painting ajar as thunder rumbled ominously outside. Something was brewing inside of me, and it was darker than anything the night could dream up.

It crackled and raged against my intestines, pressing against my ribs as I tore through the room. Snarls ripped from my throat and burst into the air like warriors, dicing their way towards the ceiling. Furious, I kicked and screamed like a tyrant in the deepest whirlwind of a tantrum, flipping chairs and sending lamps into the wall. In the swell of the uncontrollable rage, I tore a drawer out from the old plastic dresser and dropped it to the ground, dumping its contents across the carpet.

Panting, I stared at the carnage around the room and took in the destruction, my chest heaving.

Something on the floor glinted at me beneath the moonlight, its shape a long claw slit in the carpet. Hypnotized, I bent to grip the strange knife, curling my fingers around the handle. I stood with it my hand for more than a moment, the lightning flashing through the window twice before dimming down. Violence. The sweet tang of it. Entirely and fundamentally unnecessary and indulgent. I tightened my fist against the blade and felt it pierce my skin. I squeezed harder. What good did it ever do? Destroying everything in the name of survival. Blur all the lines together until everything is just grey. Blur all the lines together until everything is gone.

Until there's *nothing* left.

I opened my fist and dropped the curved weapon. Blood had beaded up like the ruby-red flowers in the park and dripped down my hand, wrapping like vines around my wrist.

Blood didn't run from the dead: only the wicked and the living.

Exhausted from the explosive burst of energy, I collapsed onto the bed and let the blood trickle from my arm and patter onto the sheets, watching silhouettes of the raindrops projected onto the bumpy ceiling.

There was no good or bad.

There just was.

10

The Ghost with All the Questions

A dark winding tunnel twisted around me as I swirled and spiraled into the gaping mouth of a cave. Dropping, dropping, dropping, as the heaviness of my limbs dragged me into the void. I tried to call out, but my voice was but a puff of smoke in the crisp dark air.

My eyes flew open, and, desperate for relief, I wiped at the sweat that had beaded on my forehead. I was still sprawled in the dingy motel room with the sheets tangled around my bare legs, the old cotton rubbing against my skin. Panting, I sat up, pushing the hair from my face and rolled my neck back. Bile was a sour taste in the back of my throat. I didn't want to be sick. Fuck.

"Bad dream?"

Reflexively, even in my groggy state, my head snapped towards the voice. A dark silhouette of a man was sprawled in the chair near the desk I had but a foggy recollection of tearing apart. Though softly spoken, his words were tinged with the timbre of a man who knew power and who wasn't afraid to use it.

"You again," I said, mild fury seeping into my words like blood in cloth. Incensed that he was able to find me with such casual ease a second time in twenty-four hours, I glanced to where the blade had fallen. I didn't need an extra weapon, yet, but I eyed him owlishly. Did I imagine his immunity, I wondered, or would he fall victim to it if we fought again?

"Yes," he leaned forward into the thin stream of sunlight peering through the curtains and flashed a smile, his canines scraping his bottom lip. "Me."

"You're following me."

"Yes," he replied smoothly, his voice still infuriatingly mild and pleasant. "But I wouldn't have to if you didn't keep running away."

"That seems like a rather weak argument." His eyes glittered at me in the early sunshine. Something was mesmerizing about them- not quite brown, not quite yellow, they stayed sharp and focused like a hungry cat with a cool, steady gaze. "Why aren't you dead?" I blurted out before he could muster up a retort.

"That's a bizarre thing to ask someone." He leaned back in the seat, crossing his arms over his chest.

"It's what I want to know. And if you can't tell me what I want to know, then..." I trailed off, leaving the threat open. "I don't usually take kindly to being followed." My voice was hot and frigid at the same time, probing for holes in his exterior to find a weak spot.

He held up a hand in interruption, waving off my emotional offense. "I just want to know how you got here."

"To the Brink?" I asked.

"Not exactly." He dropped his expression into a grim line. "Don't you know who I am?"

"Should I?"

"I'm hurt." He pulled the chair up closer to the edge of the bed and balanced his elbows on his knees, dangling long-fingered hands loosely. I studied his angular face, the gentle dip in his top lip, and the long dark eyelashes. The glossy black curls that fell over his left eye in one gentle wave, breaking apart the sea of creamy tan skin. I had thought before that he wasn't quite beautiful, but here, I could see that that wasn't true in the soft morning light. He was so grossly beautiful, it should've been against the law. Any law. Every law.

Then it dawned on me.

"Oh."

He sat back, gesturing his palms towards the sky and cocking his head to the side. "Hey?"

"You were Richie's roommate. At the Institute."

A shadow fell over his face now, adding an edge to the mischievous charisma. It was quickly veiled by a quick grin.

"Sometimes. Elijah. Eli."

"Yes," I said thoughtfully, though no less cautiously. "That's right. What do you want, Eli?"

And what are you doing out here? That was the unspoken question floating between us. Could it be that Eli, the Institute's golden boy, had been rejected too? That would be a shame. I picked at a fuzz in the blanket. What did that say about the people they kept?

"I need your help," he responded earnestly, his eyes never leaving my face. He kept staring as if he expected to see something that I wasn't showing him- like if he stared long enough, he could pull the splinters of my secrets from rosy flesh and leave nothing but rotted pockmarks behind. I made appearances of mulling it over, but I kept my body tense and my arms stiff at my sides.

"Why would I want to help you?"

"Because I can help you right back. You want answers, right? I can get all your answers for you."

"That's an awfully grand promise. Why should I believe you? How can I believe you're trustworthy?" Despite my reservations, I scooted towards the edge of the bed, tugging the frustrating tangle of hair around my shoulder. "Why aren't you at the Institute anymore?"

His smile was slow and deliberate as he leaned forward, bringing his face inches from mine. I curled my lip at the proximity even as the pulse drummed in my throat.

"Why aren't you?"

"You can't respond to every question with a question. That barely counts as conversation, let alone answers. You're not making a strong case for yourself."

"I'll give you your answers," he said, rising to his feet. "But not here. You'd be surprised who's listening."

He flipped a cigarette out of a pack tucked in his back pocket and dangled it in between his curved lips, unlit. "You might want to get dressed before we go," He muttered through the filter, his eyes half-lidded and deceptively lazy, "But it's up to you."

Horrified that I had forgotten my state of undress, I gathered the throw from the foot of the bed and pulled it to my breast, heat spreading through my body. The effort proved to be in vain, as he had already crossed the threshold into the courtyard and was happily puffing on his cig, oblivious to the state I was in. For the first time in over a year, I felt the itch to take it up again, drag that poison into my lungs. It had a way of numbing things, just enough to feel disconnected from your tether to the earth.

Jeez. I raked a hand through my hair, blinking the last ebbs of fatigue from my eyes. If I was going up against a man like this- a man of smoke and shadows- I'd need to have my wits about me. I shot him another glance, studying his rangy build and apparent cavalier attitude. Something told me that the answers he'd give would only conjure up more questions, but the pull was there, present and strong in my chest. Perhaps it was the fact my newest life had disintegrated into ash, dusting the back corners of my brain as it began to slip and pull from my catacombs, but I made the decision to go with him in an instant, despite my pitching stomach. Two predators in play now, I thought as I pulled my hair back into a loose tie. I guess it'd come down to who had the sharper teeth.

~~~~~~~~~~~

Muddled and distracted, I rummaged roughly for my clothes in the debris, kicking aside the clutter from my earlier rampage. I no longer bothered with the throw, but I still kept my eyes trained on Eli's figure while I shimmied into the wrinkled clothes.

He didn't turn around- which was appreciated. At the very least, I knew he wasn't a pervert. And if he was, I wasn't his type. I might've given a brief thought to what his type might be, but it died as soon as it hit consciousness. I didn't think about things like that. Ever.

I was caught off guard, that's all.

To ease the strangely churning thoughts, I took extra time to pull the pants over my hips and secure them with the button
~~~~~~~~~~~

top. Composure seemed to be a very distant and unattainable thing, and I hated being out of the control seat.

Shaking it off, I turned to reach for the door, flipping the key between my index and my thumb.

I was halfway there when I realized I'd almost forgotten my gloves, and subsequently felt a shudder ripple through me. One person didn't shrivel up and die, and I'd already forgotten the darkness that followed me in an ever-present affliction. Shaking my head in disapproval at myself, I pulled the gloves over shaking hands. Where the fuck was my head at? These last few days had been a fucking mess. If Harris could see me now... I winced, almost immediately, because she wouldn't be seeing me at all.

I was reaching for the handle simultaneously as Eli, but he was faster, sliding it open in a gesture far too grand for context. He gave me a quick scan, pausing only slightly at the tattered gloves, my high collar.

"Nice outfit."

I cocked an eyebrow. "It serves its purpose."

His face creased in puzzlement. Relief mingled with disappointment as the realization sunk in. He didn't know what I was- what I could do. And I shouldn't be mad at that. I was supposed to be a secret. Supposed to be a ghost. I anxiously rubbed my palms along the sides of my thighs again, already returning to my childhood mannerisms. The same mannerisms that bought me the stinging label of *coward*.

I dropped my hands, started forward. Felt something on my neck.

"I wish you wouldn't do this," he added, tugging at the ponytail that sat on the nape of my neck. "You've got such beautiful hair, Valencia."

It was the first time he'd used my name, and I was surprised he'd remembered it at all. Through the haze of pleasure, logic prevailed, and I realized he'd probably looked into it before following me. Feeling the inklings of irritation rising again, I swatted his hand away. "Keep your hands to yourself."

"Just some constructive advice, darling."

"No," I said firmly, "None of that either." When he only smirked, the anger flared. "I am agreeing to speak with you, and that's it. I haven't decided to help you, nor have I decided to be your friend. When and if those decisions are made, you'll know."

The smirk was still on his face, calm and unshakable. "Sure thing."

"Great," I commented, banking my emotions and smoothing the front of my shirt. "So, where are we going?" I surveyed the empty lot. In the light of the day and without the dense formidable rain, the Brink was less impressive but no less foreboding. "I don't think we can get more private than this."

"It's an illusion," he said curtly, cuffing the sleeve of his shirt. "If there's no one else around, your voice is going to be the loudest."

"So, where are we going? Somewhere... loud?" I could barely help the sneer. He spoke in that deliberate way men do when they're trying to teach you something. Like they think you're so much less educated than them.

"Yes," he flashed a quick, genuine smile. "And somewhere with food."

I folded my arms across my chest and watched him as he walked towards the street. No, 'walk' didn't suit the way he moved.

Dancer's grace, I thought. Fluidity. "Was there no instance while watching me sleep that you thought to grab something to eat?" I called out to him.

"Hey, now." He glanced at me over his shoulder, shooting me a quick and mischievous grin. "I wasn't watching you. I had almost just gotten there. It's not the easiest place in the world to follow someone to."

He waited at the curb for me, adjusting his gait to match my pace.

"Sorry to have put you out," I said with about as much apology as a rabid cat, "Not that it's any business of yours, but I was supposed to be meeting someone." I wrapped my arms around my body beneath the cloak.

He squinted at me, his hands tucked in the pockets of his jeans. "How'd that turn out for you?"

"Yeah, not great. They're dead."

"Huh." He pushed a hand through the mop of hair and clicked his tongue.

Irritated that the statement had neither surprised him nor shaken his impenetrable cool, I diverted my attention to the buildings that surrounded the cracked sidewalks. The concrete structures stretched high into the sky, marked by the chunks missing from the upper floors where they'd been scorched and blackened into oblivion. The doors swung open and shut in the wind with quiet thuds that echoed through the narrow alleys.

Glass crunched loudly beneath my feet, and I spared it a glance, but somehow, I'd missed Eli slinking away. I looked up to an empty winding street. The breeze lifted the tail of my coat and sent it swirling around my knees, wrapping in a loose knot.

Within seconds, I briefly contemplated using the opportunity to take off. If he wanted to play games, I didn't want to be a part of it.

Heaving a sigh, I dismissed that thought. Realistically, he'd probably just find me all over again like a damn transmitter. I eyed the thin scratch on my palm that had already begun to close up. It wasn't as if I had anything to lose, anyway.

I had meant what I said. He was far from a friend, but he did fall somewhere in the air of companionability. Without Harris, my allies were few. I'd be a fool to waste a chance to foster a new tie. What was that the Caretaker had said?

Burn all your bridges, and no one cares about the fate of the island?

Something crashed in the building next to me, the loud bang kicking up dust that billowed out from the permanently agape windows. Curious, I followed the noise, picking my way through the debris. The building's courtyard was cluttered with metal beams and bent frames, creating unintentionally haunting structures that twisted like skeletons.

"Eli," I called out when I reached the door. When I was met with no response, I braced a hand on the doorframe and took a hesitant step over the stoop. Unexpectedly, my shoe caught on a crooked nail and yanked my foot out from beneath me. I swung my arms in a full, circular motion in an attempt to regain my balance but with my foot still caught, gravity was void of mercy.

A lean, muscled arm wrapped around my waist and pulled me back, leaving me dangling slightly in the air. I tensed, though I was already sure of its owner.

"What are you doing? You're going to hurt yourself." Eli said with slight disapproval in his tone as if I was a small child who ignored direction. The stubble on his face rubbed against the nape of my neck as he curled me against him. Because we fit together like a screw and bolt, I pulled my foot free and pushed him off of me, shaking out the folds where my cloak had bunched during the fall. Scowling still, with humiliation burning my cheeks, I shoved by him back onto the street. No one touched me.

"You disappeared. I was looking for you," I spat out.

He fell back in step with me with ease, his eyes suddenly cloudy and dark. "I didn't go anywhere."

The equal pulls of needing to be right and not wanting to engage in an argument had me simmering until I relented, blurting out, "You did. Then I heard a sound."

"Lots of things make sounds around here. I'm not sure you want to mingle with any one of them."

"Yet here we are, roaming around this barren wasteland full of crawlers," I said dryly.

"It's daytime," he retorted, flicking me a glance. "No one's going to bother us."

I said nothing, knowing that taking safety as a given was a massive risk in itself.

The street got thinner the further we walked, the buildings leaning towards each other to create a pyramid-shaped corridor. The sun broke past the clouds and beamed through broken windowpanes, dancing along the old weeds that poked out from beneath crumbling stone.

"Where are we headed? Somewhere you've been before? You don't seem like someone who'd frequent the Brink." It was true. He had none of the distant, shrouded markings of the people who dwelled here. He was, I thought reluctantly, too good-looking and well preserved for this area, despite all of his rugged edges.

Eli stretched his arms above him in a grand gesture and rolled his shoulders. "Don't you trust me, Valencia?" He drew out the last three syllables into their own hissing, winding word.

I wrinkled my nose at the continued use of my full name. "Val," I corrected, but that was the only response I had.

His eyes twinkled playfully; the shadows gone from his face. "Sure, Val. We're taking a right here."

Already hating having someone else in charge, I begrudgingly traipsed after him into the slight stretch of pavement between two unmarked buildings. My sour expression was wasted on the slope of his muscular back, the alley far too narrow for the two of us to fall into step together. Feeling more agitated by the minute, I scratched anxiously at the dry skin of my forearm.

Christ, there was barely any air down here. I tugged at my collar. It was stale. Artificial. Despite the onslaught of rain from the night before, the heat was persistent and merciless. I shaded my eyes from the ebb of the sun and looked to the sky, attempting to make out the tendrils of the net amongst the clouds.

It was a simple system, and, in theory, made sense; the net could deflect most extreme weather conditions from the old world, and the netting left space to release some of the pressure and let in a bout of moisture and relief for small crops and the people who lived among the streets.

It was an adequate system, in theory. But lately, it seemed all the rain did was cause torrential destruction and leave the air just as dry as before it rolled in.

Eli exited the path a few steps ahead of me, gliding in his effortless way into the open road. I followed shortly after, kicking up dust that settled uncomfortably in the ankle of my shoe. I was too aware of the silence and the way it had started to press uncomfortably into my chest. It was odd to walk in tandem with another person when I was so used to being on my own.

"So-"

Eli held up a hand, cutting me off before I even had a chance to speak.

"This is it."

"This?" I poked my head around his shoulder and surveyed the land. Unimpressed by the barren city, I rocked back on my heels. "Think you might've cracked a little."

He scoffed at me and gestured towards a broad, square building that bore a stark difference from the rest. While others were tall and slender, this one was squat and fat, with tiny windows and no door. I moved forward suspiciously, keeping my arms close to my body. Eli made a note of the shift in my energy with a surveying glance.

"You recognize it?"

I shook my head, unable to explain the feeling of dread that had spread into my throat at the sight of it. It wasn't the building itself, but the way the air seemed to ripple around it, shaking and shimmering with untold stories of the worst kind.

A sloped driveway came into view as we approached the building. The ramp led down beneath the structure, blocked off midway by a large, cast-iron gate that stretched across the entrance's mouth.

We entered from below, swinging open the rusted gate that squealed upon entry. If the occupants hadn't already known we were there, they certainly did now. Something scurried along the walls, and the sound of long toenails scratching against the stone etched itself deep into my brain.

"Are you scared?" Eli whispered from beside me, laughter in his voice.

I wasn't. I was by far the most dangerous thing in these tunnels. I looked over at him but could only make out the faint outline of his profile. Except maybe to him.

I thought about the way his veins shifted and bubbled beneath his skin when he grabbed hold of me, but yet he stood next to me as if it had never happened. I knew that his body had a reaction- but why didn't it hurt him? Why was he still so flippant and nonchalant?

The lights blazed on in a flash of crimson fury, and both Eli and I flinched against the optical assault.

"What is that?" I hissed, bowing my head and crossing a forearm in front of my face.

"It's just a defense tactic," Eli said coolly. "If they deemed us a threat, the lights would disorient us long enough for them to slit our throats."

In response, my own started to itch. The lights felt warmer and warmer as they sat against the surface of my skin.

Understanding the precedent, but still annoyed being in the midst of it, I hiked my hood over my brow. "The element of surprise is a cheap way to get your kicks," I muttered. Eli either didn't hear me or pretended not to. The lights shut off, and the building groaned with a final creak.

"Is this good or bad?" I asked into the dark. He left me again without a response, in the way I was beginning to get used to, but not grow fond of. "Eli."

"Shut up," his muttered from in front of me. Minutes pulled by like hot rubber, a steady dripping our only company in the damp cave.

A door at the end of the hall opened into a pulsing white light. Eli took two quick steps and was swallowed by the glow. It took me all but a moment in the suffocating darkness to decide to traipse after him. As much as I hated it, without Victor, following him around was about all the direction I had.

I shielded my eyes with little success as I sidled over the threshold, wincing as the beams seemed to blaze right through the cloth of my sleeve.

The voices began as whispers, then grew into a barrage of overlapping chatter as I stumbled through the doorway. My eyes needed time to adjust from the vibrant flickering, so I squeeze them shut and pressed myself against the wall closest to the door.

"First time?" a gruff voice asked. I peeled my eyelids open. The man across from me was broad- broad face, broad shoulders, broad arms. His wiry beard was separated into three wide and equally stiff braids that twisted together into a stubby ponytail at the bottom, all the colour of burnt wood. A long-barrelled pipe hung sloppily between chapped lips, puffing out gusts of smoke alongside breaths. Because the stink of old tobacco was burning the inside of my nose, I turned to the side, deftly casting the arm of my robe over my mouth.

"Crossing over, I mean." He smiled, but it wasn't friendly, showing off rows of crooked yellow teeth. "Ain't no one has it easy."

A shudder lightly ripped its way through my body. I open my mouth to reply, but Eli slipped seamlessly between the two of us and wrapped a proprietary hand around my arm. "Just get back to your drink, man."

He grumbled out a reply and waved his meaty hand dismissively behind him, swiveling on the stool.

"You come here a lot?" I asked Eli as we skirted our way around the patrons seated at the circular tables.

"No. Just remember things from when I do."

He chose a booth against the east wall, each bench wrapped in an old vinyl that cracked at each crease of where bodies had been before. Waiting for me to be seated, or perhaps guarding me- from others or from escape- he leaned on one hip casually. Obliging, I slid across the seats and winced as the ripped fabric snagged on my pant legs.

"He wasn't really causing me trouble."

Across the table, Eli slid into his respective seat and shot me a dubious look. "The people here aren't the type you want to be socializing with. Just trust me."

"How many times are you going to tell me to trust you before this is over?" I asked, gingerly poking at the menu that was left sitting on the table in front of me.

"As many times as it takes for you to do so."

The snort I let out caused a haggard woman at a neighbouring table to glare at us, clearly annoyed by the interruption to her conversation. Eli offered me a crooked half-smile and leaned against the backboard. "I enjoy you, you know. And your table manners."

Deliberately ignoring both comments and his mockery, I flipped the crinkled menu to its opposite side. A few items were listed in royal blue block letters, their description scrawled in shorthand beneath them. The one thing they lacked, however, were prices.

"How much is this going to be? You know you're paying, right?" I'd used up nearly all the coin I'd gotten from that chump at the train station before I'd even got to the Brink.

He eyed me quizzically, touching his tongue briefly to the head of his canine.

"You really don't get out of the middle city much, do you?"

"I'm not even from the middle city," I said through my teeth. The middle city, where Harris was from, was the most densely populated and easiest navigated. But I wasn't *from* there. Surely, he should know that. I was opening my mouth to argue when my blossoming was rant nipped short by a waitress slipping to our table and greeting us both.

"Hi, I'm Suis, and I'll be taking care of you today." Her cheery smile dropped into a small 'o' upon seeing Eli. It was indubitably a place he frequented, though he might've denied it.

"Oh my god! Eli! Hi! It's been a while. What can I get for you and your friend?"

I curled my lip at the way her voice hitched over the word. Don't worry, Suis, nothing to be jealous of here. I had done little more than decide to tolerate him.

"Just waters and a couple rounds of waffles, for now, thanks," Eli said. Waffles. I furrowed my brow and scanned my brain for any knowledge I had of the silly-sounding meal. I pulled it out from some corner I didn't know I had—thin pastries with little holes for syrup. Celebrating my own private victory, I looked back at them. He had yet to look over to see if I agreed, and I was beginning to doubt I had any say in the matter. Truthfully, I wondered if I had any say in any case at all. I tapped my finger on the table in a slow, monotonous beat.

This isn't forever, I told myself. You're just here to hear what he has to say. And if you decide you don't like it, you can leave. You can just disappear. You can be on your own again.

All I had to do was wait for this incredibly friendly woman to take a hike.

Suis' doe eyes were still bearing into Eli's, her back angled slightly away from me in an unconscious movement that cut me from the conversation. Her cheeks bloomed a tart pink beneath her skin while her eyelashes fluttered like wings. I seethed in annoyance at her softness- the blatant and unconscious display of being 'alive'. You don't belong here, the voice cooed in my mind. Monster.

"You're sure that's everything?" she asked hopefully. Eli pulled the corners of his mouth down and raised his eyebrows at me in a curious expression as if to ask, "not for me, what about you?".

Oh, he was including me now. How nice. I shook my head and leaned back in the booth, waiting for Suis to curl back into whatever bizarre kitchen she had crawled out of.

"So, what brings you all the way out here?"

I let out a low growl in my throat that Eli pretended not to hear. I hated chitchat. Stewing in silent resentment of both the buzzing, cherub-faced brunette, and Eli's apparent enjoyment in human connection, I crossed my legs beneath the table.

"Just visiting an old comrade of mine. It didn't go well."

My reaction was quick and unintentional, scrunching my face into an expression vaguely reminiscent of crumpled paper in a bin. There sure was an old comrade tied up and beat in the garden shed, but it hadn't been his.

Suis the Friendly whispered something unintelligible to Eli and placed a delicate hand gently on his shoulder. The moment dragged on until she finally trotted away, her prim white shoes not even drumming up a squeak on the way. Making a little 'hmm' noise in my throat, I returned my attention to the table and caught Eli staring at me with his ever-present expression of mild interest. It made me feel like a smear on a slide.

I laid the paper menu flat on the table and folded my hands carefully on top of it, interlocking my fingers tightly like the teeth of a zipper. Eli leaned forward onto the table, bringing his face closer to mine. I could smell the sweet mint of what I assumed to be what he used for aftershave, though from the scruff of hair on his jaw, I doubted he'd done so in a few days.

"You jealous?" His tone was buttery smooth, a quiet whisper against the commotion behind him. He flicked his eyes at my mouth. Good-looking men were truly good for nothing.

I intentionally leaned further away from him and re-crossed my arms over my chest, creasing my brow.

"Do you need a reminder that this isn't a social call?"

"Here I thought I might've been growing on you." The wry smile returned as he straightened. "But don't worry, I can play nice."

"Can you?"

"No. Probably not." He shoved his hand through the mop of curls and briefly left it there, tangled in the tendrils like wires around a house. "I can try, though."

"Thought it was a pretty juvenile concept, learning how to play with others."

His eyes twinkled. "I like to think I play just fine."

Despite my better interest, I smirked in response. "You toy with people. I think that's a bit different."

"What is it that you do then, Valencia, if not toy?"

Uncomfortable from how his face fell shadowed, I glanced around the restaurant as if expecting to see the patrons gazing at me. What is it you do, Valencia? I thought of the man crumpled in the station's bathroom. What is it you do?

"It's okay if you don't have a proper answer," he said, in an almost overly casual way that made me think he'd asked something he hadn't planned to and was deliberately trying to back away from the edge. Too bad you can't snatch words back once they were out. Something I learned way too late. I pulled on my earlobe, avoided his eyes.

Suis slipped back to the table unannounced, sliding drinks in front of us. She mumbled something under her breath about food being on the way but seemed disheartened by Eli's lack of interest. If I thought it was my business, I would've told her not to waste her time on someone like him. There was something... off about him.

I looked at him now, across the table where he was leaning in the booth. Even relaxed, the energy crackled off of him like jagged ripples. No, Suis, I thought gently as she turned back to the kitchen. This wasn't a man you wanted to swim with. I stared defiantly as his unreadable cat-like eyes flicked over the length of my cloak. You might drown.

After Suis was out of earshot, I returned to the exchange. "What would be a proper answer?"

"For what?"

Frustrated, I blew hot air indignantly from my nose. "The proper answer on how to play with others."

"I imagine if we had normal socialization, we'd have the definition on hand. But then again, the Institute didn't waste all that time constructing us to make us good at parties and gracious goodwill."

Constructed? I fought the urge to cringe against the slight. "I'd like to think I'm my own person," I said slowly, the words sounding like a lie as they came off my tongue.

"Ah, come on now. You're smart enough to know the second we walked into the Institute, we were just a couple of test subjects."

I was immediately edgy- anxious at what that suggested and irritated that the thought had crossed my mind too. Caleb and I had talked about it sparingly before we'd been taken. We always used to say we'd die before the Council got their hands on us for that reason. We used to say a lot of things.

"Vaccination and immunization isn't an unusual practice, from even before the Plate," I said slowly, "It's always been that way. If you want to get into the Pod, you have to have a clean bill of health. That's just the way it is. Everyone has to go through it. Even the people that were originally there."

It felt as if I was reading from a script, pulling lectures from my memory as if I was sitting back at that desk in the Institute.

Eli's eyes sharpened as he stared out into the restaurant.

"You know, that's actually what-"

"Hey, guys! Look what I've got!" Suis' good temper had returned as she glided towards our table with two plates of waffles in tow, balancing them on the balls of her hands. Saliva pooled in my mouth at the sight of the creamy stacks the instant she set them down in front of me. I couldn't remember the last time I'd had anything other than Sustenance slop.

Foolishly hypnotized, I stared the syrup swimming in the delicate pools that dipped the surface of the dough and dripped over the crust in sticky dollops. I swiped a finger along the side of my plate and brought the stinging sweetness to my mouth, sucking gently on the tip.

The taste exploded like firecrackers on my tongue, slithering down my throat and leaving a devastatingly sweet trail where it disappeared. Captivated and entranced, I greedily reach for a fork, only to realize I hadn't one.

"Looking for this?" Eli asked, waving a tightly wrapped utensil pair in his hand. Blinking slowly, I extended my hand and left it hovering near his end of the table.

"Come on now, what do you say?"

I rolled my neck to the side, sparing a quick glance to be sure Suis had scurried away and was not to hear my begging.

"Please," I hissed.

Chuckling, he pressed it into my palm and began to unwrap his own. "I didn't expect you to be capable of such wonder, Valencia. You surprise me."

Refusing to allow his words to embarrass me, I carefully removed both of the simple elastic ties from my set and stabbed the fork into the waffle. I spied the engraving in the plastic as I lifted a bite to my mouth. Council licensed. I cocked an eyebrow. Someone was smuggling.

"You don't know me that well," I tossed back. Carefully, I twisted my fork into the side of the waffle. "I've never had any of this before. Waffles." I said, practicing the word that felt so awkward in my mouth.

"Really?" He chewed in thoughtful consideration. "That's not unusual, I suppose. You can't get them in many places out here. This could very well be one of the last places still open."

"There were others?" I asked through a mouthful.

"Sure, yeah. All over the county. Before the Council seized control, a lot of this stuff was pretty readily available."

"So, they were bringing it from the old world." I poked at the slop on my plate.

"Sure, yeah. In the beginning."

"And the others ran out." I was already mulling over the probability of how these strange dough discs managed to still exist when so many other things had gone extinct.

He rolled a shoulder in a shrug. "That's one interpretation."

"And the other? How would they make more beneath the net? The only factory developments we even have are damn near touching the Pod, and everything goes through the Council before we get a slice of it." I was too busy thinking out loud to remember my vow to keep myself reserved. "How would a scummy little place like this get something so unrestricted and decadent? It's ludicrous."

"Sure," he nodded soberly, "It is, isn't it? So that raises the question then. Where does a scummy little place like this," he paused, leaning closer to me pointedly, "Get waffles like these?"

I mulled the question over around the shapes and bends of my brain, tossing it in the gelatinous stretch and pulling it back out until the words were merely images of what they might've meant. I could tell Eli was trying to lead me something-leading me to my own conclusion, so when I arrived upon it, it would seem less jarring, less confusing, less...

"They made them. Out of nothing. Just like sustenance." The words jumped out instantaneously as the wires connected. "Right? That's what you're getting at."

He smiled at me, the grin inching across his face as if I had just mastered a new trick.

"You're getting it."

Intrigued, though not entirely convinced, I tapped my fork against the plate. The different plastics made a dull thud against each other.

"So they're genetically engineered waffles?" I asked wryly.

Eli let out a soft laugh, acknowledging the absurdity of the conversation.

"It's not about the waffles, necessarily. The waffles are just a part of a larger whole. The Council runs a monopoly on genetically altered slop. They wouldn't dare let on to the broader, outside community that they could, in theory, recreate any kind of food. The slop is part of our tragic brand."

"Our... brand." I drew it out, dubious. The words, strung together, made sense, but it was hard for me to move away from the fact we were debating waffle politics in a hidey-hole. "Why would we have a brand?'

"They tell us that it's all there is, so we feel less bad about not being able to have more. We think that wanting more, inherently, makes us greedy, gluttonous, and unemployable. Nobody wants someone who's always begging for more, so they say. So, they give us the bottom of the barrel- the scraps of whatever food they're processing for people on the inside- and we thank them for being so gracious and giving us any in the first place."

"I could see that," I amended, but was finding the food on my plate dramatically less appetizing.

"So, underground in the market, if you've got the right kind of stuff to offer, then you can end up with waffles in a place like this."

"Okay."

He watched me from over the rim of his glass as he sipped.

"I take it this is supposed to be a metaphor. About the Council keeping all of us down, but we all know that already. Nobody on any part of the Plate thinks that they've got it good. The only hope any of us hold onto is that one day we'll get scouted."

The last consonant swayed gently in the stale air as if to say, but we did get scouted. Look at us now. His eyes bore steadily into mine.

"You know, I saw you that day. Downtown. At Ed's place."

I swallowed thickly at the swift change in conversation and reached for my own glass. "What?"

"Just before there was that big security sweep. You were downtown, in the open, with all those uniforms."

I swished the water around in my mouth, chilling the back of my teeth. "I went in to do a job. I was being careful."

"I didn't see much work or caution," he replied softly. "You went and sat in a booth for hours without concern."

"So what?" I shot back, inexplicably annoyed at the sudden chastising.

"You think it's a coincidence that the first night you spent warming up a bar stool in a heavily monitored energy hub is the night we have the biggest security sweep of the decade? If I saw you, they saw you."

My stomach pitched at the idea. I had been a dead man far too long to walk now. "I had my cloak on. There's no way they could've known. I look nothing like I used to."

Eli shook his head. "That doesn't matter. They know. They just know. Your nice waitress probably sent a snapshot the second she walked up to your table. Run that through the facial recognition database, and you're done."

"They had no reason to run me. I paid my due. I could've just as easily been some ex-institute kid that was expelled and tossed back to the streets." I was working myself into a lather, and I tossed the utensils onto the uneaten waffle half. "It shouldn't be the end of the world just to relax a bit. You were doing a pretty good job of mimicking it yourself."

The table shook as Eli started to bounce his leg anxiously.

"Don't be ridiculous. I was involved in deeper matters than that."

"Like what, Eli?" I aimed narrowed eyes at him. "What was it exactly that you were doing?"

He was clearly annoyed, whether it was with me or the confrontational turn of the conversation. Eli dabbed at the corner of his mouth with a napkin before tossing it back down indignantly.

"Small details. It isn't of any vital interest to you just yet."

"Oh, no. Quite the contrary. Go on, big man. Validate your day drinking."

Simmering, he took a couple of silent, angry bites, but I knew I'd hit a nerve. He'd share, whether he was ready to or not.

"I was doing research," he said carefully.

"On what?"

Eli glanced around the room, distrustfully and eyed the fellow customers closest to us. Once satisfied that they were immersed in their own passionate discussion, he leaned toward me and dropped his voice low, but steady.

"Things are worse than people think they are. A lot worse. The whole damn system. I've been looking into the Institute, for starters..."

Curious by his drop off, I stirred my straw idly and watched the ice cubes clumsily clink off one another.

"The Institute's fucked up, everyone knows that. Squeezing a bunch of poor kids in with the vague promise of a better life and then give it to a fifth of them. Toss the others back out to the streets with nothing more than the clothes on their back." I shook my head disapprovingly. "It's sad."

"That's just the thing. I don't think that one fifth makes it through." He held up a hand when I opened my mouth to comment. "I don't think the others get tossed out, either. Valencia... I don't think anybody makes it out at all."

11

The Vicious and The Foe

His statement rang in my ears. My mind went right to Caleb, his screaming face behind the wires of the Outdoors' Area. Nausea reared in my throat, ruining my appetite. Not that there was much to lose- the waffles were already falling out of form, melting into a small pile of mush in front of me. I pushed them away to the farthest edge of the table.

"I don't-."

"Just hear me out." His eyes lit afire with passion, he leaned toward me again. "How many times have you met someone that came back from the Institute? Or even heard of one, for that matter?"

Pausing in consideration, I rolled the napkin into a ball in my hand. I'd met an older boy near the Beamline when I was a child who had claimed as such. I couldn't quite remember his face, but he was thin and tall, like a weed, with dark hair and a scar across his shoulder. Last I saw of him, he had taken up residence with the Moore family, who everyone blessed their hearts for being so generous. After that... I furrowed my brow. Didn't see much of any of them after that.

Eli noticed the quick change in my facial expression.

"No more than one or two, right?"

I nod numbly, thinking it couldn't possibly be true... there must've been others. Surely, I would've noticed. But in the deep and formidable catacombs of my memory, I reached in and pulled out only a handful of dust.

"I started asking around, looking for anyone who knew about any kids that were enrolled. The problem is, they had no family or involvement in the community. Nobody knows anything about these kids."

No, I thought as my stomach rolled with nausea. Nobody knew anything about them. Nobody cared. Nobody would notice if they just...

"The program's been in play for decades, Eli. You can't just steal kids and have no one go looking for them. It's not plausible."

"Theoretically, no. But with the right amount of variables in place, Christ, you can get away with whatever you want. The Council has enough power that anyone who did notice would be too scared to open their mouths. Fuck, even asking the question had people looking at me like I was about to pistol-whip them and drag them to disposal."

Sweat beaded on my forehead in gentle droplets, doing little to cool the fever that rose with the anxious tide. Where was Caleb, then, if not there? The panic threatened to swamp me.

"They couldn't get away with that. The kids. They would know."

His expression warped into one of sharp disapproval. "And what if they did, Val? Some kid in the third quadrant figures out he's about to be taken out the next day, and not in the way he thought. Maybe he winds up bent and broken. Maybe they say he did it to himself. Maybe they say he went nuts."

Richie. The memory was tossed to the surface as if it had been sitting there the whole time.

"Lives aren't just disposable," I muttered, then realized the hypocrisy of the statement when it left stale chalk in my mouth.

"They are when you stop seeing them as what they are."

Knowing Eli knew little of my true vocation gave me small relief from his statement, but my mind became static as I struggled to move past the overwhelming guilt and shame.

I wasn't the same as them.

I wasn't. The soggy napkin crumpled in my hand.

"There isn't any proof they're doing any of this. Maybe when they release the kids, they just let them out with a contracted job, and none of them return to where they came from. All you have is a bunch of scared people who are just as confused as you are, and a bunch of kids too embarrassed to admit that they failed out."

Clearly irritated with my unwillingness to participate, he crossed his arms over his chest, flexing the muscles in his forearm in tension.

"Look, I just want a chance. You don't have to believe me yet. But I need someone else on this. I can't just leave all those kids in there."

"You don't even know that they're as stuck in there as you think they are," my soft mouth set in a stubborn grim line. "You got out, didn't you?"

Steady as a still, calm lake, Eli stared unblinkingly at me. Similarly, darkness simmered below the surface.

"In a way."

I didn't like how he spoke when he said it as if each word was too big, too awkward coming out of his mouth.

"Which way?" I asked, despite myself.

"Well, that's just the thing." Eli offered me his open palms on the table. "I had to die."

The brief statement landed a heavy-handed punch to the softest part of my gut, forcing all my air out into the atmosphere.

"Die," I repeated quietly. I was plagued with the feeling of my body hitting the water as if it was concrete, my bones shattering on impact. Waking up, cold, wet. Alone.

Dead.

"Yes." He said shortly, rising to his feet. "I wasn't, of course. They just started to misread what it means to be alive. That's the problem with science like that. Spend so much time looking at the facts, and you'll miss the miracles." Sensing something amiss with my long pause, he slung his bag over his shoulder. "I have to settle this in the back if you want to stay here."

He waited a while longer, but then, just like smoke, he was gone. Alone at the table, I clasped my hands tightly together until perspiration soaked my palms. He couldn't have been right, because that would mean that Caleb was still in there, or Caleb was dead, and I couldn't accept either of those things. I forcibly swallowed the lump in my throat, but I could still feel the pressure of it in my esophagus.

And if what he was saying was correct... how was I supposed to fix this? I couldn't. This wasn't my fight. I didn't know what he thought I could do. All I did now was ruin things. People. Ruin people. I didn't make things better. I couldn't.

Suis' tinkling wind-chime giggle lifted above the noise of the room and carried over to me.

Fuck it. Eli could deal with it himself. I was out.

Tingling, I propelled myself out of the booth, bashing my thighs against the rugged underbelly of the table. The plate I had pushed to the side clattered to the floor, splattering the chemical sludge onto the floor and bringing the attention of the room onto me. The incessant chatter faded into a curious silence, and they all leered towards me with dark, opaque eyes. I parted my lips as if to speak, but instead, made a dash towards the high bar and the glowing EXIT sign. The man who had greeted me earlier stood from his seat as I passed, shifting his drinking hand to accommodate for my awkward, jerking movements.

I had to get out of here. With my heart pounding wildly in my chest and my mouth drying into a paste, I pushed on the slim handle and burst back into the shadowed tunnel.

The noises did little to unsettle me now, the hissing whispers and scratching nails acting as a soundtrack to my unfortunate retreat. I started to run, the cloak flying behind me like a cape, kicking up gravel as I went. My legs ached as I hurdled over the upward ramp, and I pushed until I chased the paper-thin beams of sunlight working their way through the clouds.

I slowed down now that I had put a block between me and that strange building, but my breath continued to wheeze out in near painful pumps.

Nobody gets out.

I curled my arms around my chest and dug my fingers into the spaces in between my ribs.

Why would the Council even take all those children in? Why spend all that money on training them, feeding them, medicating? It would be a waste of time and energy to take care of and teach all the residents.

I stopped walking suddenly, alone in between two narrow rectangular buildings. The wind whistled and rattled a series of fire escapes that lined the sides of the buildings and sent a cardboard box tumbling across the alley in front of me.

Damn it. It was weird.

I should go back. I glanced back at the street I had come from. The interest in abandoned kids was, actually, abnormally high for such a reputably narcissistic government system. It didn't make any sense that they would care so much for the little guy without any funding and no personal gain.

Making my decision, I took my first two steps back toward the restaurant when my legs were deftly knocked from beneath me. I had just enough time to utter a crisp 'motherfu-' before my chin rapped off the ground. My teeth smashed together in a resounding crash that shook my brain against my skull.

"Hey, sweet little thing," a man said from behind me.

Fucking men. It was always men. I spat blood out of my mouth and gingerly poked at my canine with my tongue. It was loose, and that pissed me off.

A second man rounded in front of me and pressed the toes of his boots down on my fingers while a third man whistled from further away.

"What's good, darling? Didn't anyone ever tell you not to wander 'round these streets alone? Where's your handsome friend?"

Handsome friend? I craned my neck to source the first man, and his face swam into view. Motherfucker. It was the man from the bar.

"Idiot," I muttered at myself, already scolding myself for not paying more attention to the present threats. Observation was your most potent weapon out here, everyone knew that. You had to be able to see trouble before it happened to have the slimmest chance to avoid it.

"What you say, girl?"

The man with his boots on my fingers scratched at his groin, drawing my attention to a fat copper ring on his pinky finger. A 'V' was carved into the face of it, the flesh of his finger being squeezed through the narrow lines. All thoughts of a tactful and respectful escape flew out the window. These guys were professionals. Victor might have been dead, but something told me his trade was good and kickin'.

"I'm going to give you a chance to back off, right now, and we all just forget about this whole thing," I said calmly, starting to feel the pressure from where the steel toes of his boots hit my knuckles.

There was a stunned silence before both men burst into boisterous laughter that bounced off the brick walls and headed towards the sky.

"You hear that, Buck? I think she's trying to threaten us. Now, little filly, I don't think you're in any position at all to be doing so." He crouched beside me and pulled me up by a handful of hair. "Pretty little thing, too. I bet you'd get us fed real good for the next quarter." He flipped a thin metal blade out of its holder and pressed it against the exposed skin of my neck. "Creamier skin, too. Could be lighter, but not one of those burnt breeds. The genetics paid you a favor, didn't they?" He licked his lips as if thinking about how I would taste on them. "You mixed in a real nice batch."

Irritated, I twitched my fingers below the boots. It wasn't the first time my complexion drew the attention of the wrong sort.

"I'm telling you, asshole, pick someone else."

He rocked back onto his heels and dropped the knife slightly away from my throat. Rage flooded his eyes, eating up the slimy grin with a sinister ferocity. "Are you psychotic, bitch? Here's what's gonna happen. You're going to give me whatever you've got on ya' and that stupid little purse. After that, we gon' take you down to the warehouse, and you're going to shut the fuck up." He bashed the sheath of the knife against the back of my head and forced me forward again, bringing my face into the dirt. "Got it?"

God. I wasn't in the mood for this. I spat another gob of gooey saliva and chunky sand back out towards the ground. It leaked a crimson red into the dusty grey earth.

"Cat got your tongue now, huh?" The man pinning my hands shifted his body slightly to adjust for a view of my face. I'd bet it was hard to see past his bulbous stomach, and the shift managed to accidentally relieve the pressure off one of my hands. I yanked it free from confinement.

In a flash, I shoved my hand beneath his pant leg and wrapped my fingers around his ankle. His blood pulsed through delicate blue veins that snaked beneath the stretch of his skin and throbbed against my palm. The world became muted as I dug my nails into the slightly risen bump of his ankle bone.

He had just enough presence of mind left to thrash his leg to free himself from my grasp, but it was too late. He was patting his leg down, panicking, as if trying to put out a fire. He stumbled backward and fell against a dumpster, sliding meekly down with his back against the rusted steel. The man from the bar quickly pressed a knee into my spine to keep me on the ground—definitely professionals.

"What did you do to Buck? You gonna pay for that."

The feet of the third man crossed my vision path as he briskly jogged to where Buck had begun to seize wildly.

"Jack, he ain't looking too good, we gotta get him back. He's foamin', and his eyes are all foggy."

"Shut up, Carl."

The man on top of me- Jack- shifted his weight from my spine and gripped my bicep in an aggressive vise. "Poison? Did you poison my man? Is he gonna die?"

I couldn't help the smile, though I knew my teeth were stained and bloody. "The only weird thing about this is that he isn't dead yet."

He tossed me like a rag doll onto my back, as of yet unaware that he had just signed his death certificate.

I had yet to lift my eyelids fully when Jack wrapped a rough and weathered hand around my throat.

"Shame we gotta do this," he began, but his thought was never finished. Jack's hard amber eyes met mine from over his dusty bandana, and his grip went slack. "What... wh..." He blubbered like a baby, falling onto his butt and clutching at his chest, trying to locate an injury that was not there. That was the poetry of it, I thought to myself as his face turned blue and swollen. How powerful a mind has to be.

How weak a body.

It took Jack seven seconds to die.

Carl, who had been trying his damnedest to resuscitate Buck, turned and caught the last of Jack's slumping body. Already halfway to my feet, I sprung from my crouching position and loped across the alleyway. Carl fumbled with his gun, but before he could get a clean shot, I had him herded up against the wall.

"Y-you're making enemies you don't want." Sweat bubbled on his brow as he fumbled with the chamber. He managed to land a pellet in my shoulder before I made contact.

Hissing, I shot a hand out and firmly gripped his chin, leading his gaze to mine. "Don't ever fucking shoot me." I spat out at him, aware that the words would only hang in the air for the next five seconds before the wind carried them away with his ghost.

A squeak escaped his thin lips, mingling with the air in a whimper before his eyes glazed over, and he dropped.

Jesus, I shuddered as I looked down at him. With those looks, hell, he was a dead ringer for someone from the Pod. The broad, eclipsed forehead and the pale alabaster skin combined with the narrow, streamlined nose screamed aristocrat.

I was speculating on the origins of his weapon when the wave of dizziness hit me like a freight train. I braced a hand on the dumpster and tried to breathe through it, blood dripping off my face.

"Valencia?"

I whirled around at the sound of Eli's horrified voice. He was standing at the mouth of the alley with his bag casually thrown over his shoulder. His eyes rapidly danced around the three men, settling on me.

"What happened?"

Exhausted, I took a step then stumble sideways, holding a hand against the blossoming wound on my shoulder. Fucking dart guns. Pussy weapons. Good for... good for...

"What exactly did you see, Eli?" I muttered through clenched teeth.

"You touched them and..." he gestured at Carl's corpse. The look on his face was reminiscent of the one the young woman had at Christian Diern's house yesterday. Horror. Monster

I let my eyelids drift shut, swaying in the wind. "You were right, Eli."

He said something back to me, but I was already hollowing. "There's something wrong. Something's crooked. It's all..."

The darkness was inviting me, coaxing me towards it. Embracing me. I could no longer fight it. The ground was a hard bed beneath me, but I was relaxed and unfeeling, too far gone to be tethered.

12

Conversations Not To Have Sober (Or At All)

I woke up to the steady rocking of an engine vibrating. Beneath me, the seat was uncomfortably warm and stiff. The texture was unfamiliar to me, and it creaked beneath my weight.

Baffled, I opened my eyes and squinted wearily at the driver. It was only Eli, I noted with some relief.

I turned my gaze to the windshield and the acres of open fields that flanked the sides of the road and stretched far beyond the glass barrier. We were leaving the Brink. Grateful, I felt the weight creeping off my chest.

"Eli, where-." I began softly, but he shook his head.

"Just don't, Valencia."

I lapsed into silence as we whipped around the sharp curves at a hundred miles an hour, the wind howling through the open windows. The strange dial on the dash clicked along mercilessly, mile after mile, a mechanical cackle in the face of silence. I wanted to ask him how we were even in an independently owned vehicle, and why he wasn't worried about being on BirdsEye, but because I could feel the tension simmering off of him, I held the questions in with my breath.

After a while, he punched a few buttons on the dash and summoned the sound of instruments through the speakers. It was only marginally better than silence.

"You know, I remember when it happened."

I was just beginning to get used to the noises when he spoke, and I was surprised to hear his voice accompanying the wailing violin and the dull throb of bass but was careful not to discourage it. I opted to say nothing at all.

"I was in Physical, at Warehouse 7. They came and got Lieutenant Warby right in the middle of class. Peter Griswald overheard that someone from Sector 7 had made a run for it." He shifted his jaw, running a hand through the floppy bangs. "We all gathered around the skinny barred window, waiting to catch a glimpse of the action."

I closed my eyes against the dull ache that worked its way into my breastbone every time I thought of that day. The terror. The sickness.

The grief.

"You came running around the dirt path after mostly everyone stopped watching. Scrambling on those skinny legs, kicking up dirt. They were firing shots at you.

I remember thinking to myself, Eli, you're not going to let them kill her, are you? But I didn't do anything. I watched all of you as you rounded the corner and disappeared into the main channel, then went back to the weights so Warby wouldn't reprimand me. I heard the crash just minutes later." He pressed his foot down on the gas pedal harder, and the engine growled in response.

"Okay," I said, confused.

We entered a sparse valley of dead lights that hung over the cracked and forgotten highway, weeds sprouting up from in between the flats of cement.

"I should've done something," he said, but his voice was uncharacteristically shaky, "Instead, I let you die and turn into..." Eli trailed off helplessly, keeping his eyes on the road.

"Into what?" I asked softly, twisting my fingers together. "A monster? Is that what you were going to say?" I told myself I wouldn't blame him for his answer, but I knew that was a lie even then.

"No. I just... I should've done something. It shouldn't be like this."

"No, I don't suppose it should be." I leaned my cheek against the cold glass and waned, desperately, to be out of the jostling box. It stank of class. Of everything they had, but we didn't. "But sometimes the things that are decided for you shouldn't be what they are."

"You don't think that you had any choice?"

Tears gathered at the corner of my eyes, and I blinked furiously at them. This wasn't a conversation I wanted to have, not in a stolen car with a near stranger and a split lip. I felt hysteria nagging at my throat.

"Please, none of us do. Look around you," I gestured at the road stretched in front of us. It was even drier and more desolate than the core of Brink. The beams along the route were rusted and peeling, leaning precariously as the plate pushed against their buried root. "Nothing lives out here. How are we any different?"

A mound of garbage blocked the roadway, and Eli was forced to deftly twist the wheel to the shoulder to avoid the impending collision. The vehicle trembled violently as the uneven ground sent the wheels wobbling in their wheel hulls.

"We don't have lives out here," I said softly. "We call this a life because our hearts beat and our heads hurt, but at the end of the day, it's just a bunch of prisoners and a wall."

"Is that how you justify what it is you do?" Eli asked, but his tone wasn't sharp. In any case, he was right. I couldn't blame him if he were judgemental. I wasn't a good person, though I might've been once. But that didn't mean anything anymore.

"I don't know if I justify it," I said quietly. Lord, was I tired. My head was pounding in a clear indication that I had pushed my body to its capacity. "I don't believe it is a righteous act. It is just something that is."

He mulled over my statement, dropping the engine to a low hum as we broke into a clearing. A BirdsEye drone flew above our car and blinked a quick double shutter. I shadowed my face with a strategically placed arm. "When I woke up again, I just felt lost," I continued, though he hadn't prompted me, "I didn't know who I was anymore. I had nothing. I was scared, lost, and confused. I needed a purpose, and it was handed to me."

"And now?"

"Now what?"

"What is your purpose? Is it the same?" He spared me a flicking glance, the intensity of his eyes burning alight, "Is your life's purpose taking that of another's?"

I curled my hands on my lap, burrowing them between my thighs. The curse was still there, as it always was. Wriggling. Waiting. *I'm hungry*, it breathed into me. *I want to consume*, it said.

"I don't think you understand it as well as you think you do. It's not that simple."

"What's not to understand? You take the lives of others, with little to no care for what they leave behind. I understand that perfectly."

"Not everyone deserves to live," I hissed back and surprised myself with the venom that leaked into the words. "Those men back there had no value for my life or any of the other girls they had taken. Why is it my duty to spare them when they haven't done the same? Why is my duty to be good when others fail to be?"

He contorted his face as if thoughtfully mashing words in his tight jaw, but I no longer cared for his opinion.

"There is no longer a single definition of anything in this world, Eli. Some moments seem beautiful and pure, but even those are burnt and tinged with madness. A mother, laughing with her child, is pretending her stomach isn't hollow, and her heart doesn't ache for the father the Council stole away."

"You argue those moments don't have merit? That you can't find happiness in the face of all of this?" Eli spat back. It was the most genuine I had seen him. "Hopelessness is a coward's way out, Valencia. Saying the world is too far gone, so you might as well be is just you admitting you quit."

"I didn't choose this," I barked out, my throat raw and sore, "I didn't want this. I don't know why it happened to me." I stared angrily at my hands, picking apart the way the scars marred the purple skin. "It's inside of me. Not a weapon, not a choice, but who I am." I dropped off briefly, fiercely staring forward, "Do you know what that feels like? Knowing that there is a sickness that lives inside of you that fundamentally destroys people? One touch, and it tears them apart from the inside out."

He was the first person I'd spoken about it since it happened. It was a conversation I'd avoided having for so long as if somehow expressing my dismay out loud made it all exceedingly real. I squeezed my eyes shut as tears forced their way to the forefront, fuelled by exhaustion and mania. I had been a child when Harris had found me, but a child I no longer was.

"Do you see it as a power? A gift?"

I peeled my eyes open and directed the gaze towards him, trying to decipher if he was making a mockery or not.

"It's not a power. It's a curse if anything." I rubbed the bridge of my nose at the absurdity of the situation. My chest felt full and heavy, but thankfully the tears had receded. "I find it hard to believe myself, sometimes. Often, if I go too long between jobs, I begin to question the plausibility of it all, and if I'd imagined the whole thing."

"And you realized that you haven't," he commented with an air of resignation. There was something in his tone that I couldn't put a finger on. Why it bothered me, I didn't know.

"I'm not crazy, Eli. I've picked this apart and turned it upside down, and I have yet to find a true answer." I held a hand up against the light streaming through the windshield. "All I know is it's something I carry, like a virus. I touch people, and something happens to them, but it doesn't, not really. They're just alive one second, dead the next."

"So why am I still here?"

I stared forward, twisting the hem of my shirt in my hand.

"I don't know."

He sighed and leaned his head in the crook of his left hand. "Well, shit, Val."

It was one of the few times he would refer to me with my nickname.

We entered a crossroad beneath an overpass, and the shadows flickered strangely over his face, casting silhouettes over his smooth skin. The skin around his eyes was darkened and bruised, making his face appear even sharper and gaunt. He was exhausted, I noted.

"I can't explain any of it. I've never even tried to," I said hurriedly, "I didn't have to because as soon as it was my reality, I had someone ready to swoop in a put a price tag on it." I couldn't stop the words as they rushed out, "I didn't even have a chance to think about how it worked or the repercussions of any of it because that strange skill was the only thing keeping me off the streets and out of the Council's hands. I don't need you making me feel bad for something I felt like I didn't have a choice in."

My rant hung heavy in the air for the remainder of the song until the final chords ring out, and silence floods the cabin.

It was all truth- both sides of it, his and mine- I was as everyone had already labeled it, a murderer. I could make excuses for myself - no one in this age was void of sins; by twelve, most of us had blood on our hands of some form- but in the end, I was what I was. Regardless of the innocence these people did or didn't have, I had taken their life, and in that, lost what was left of my own.

After what felt like an eternity, Eli finally relaxed his hands on the wheel and offered a small, crooked smile.

"I'm sorry."

My heart did a small roll in my chest, so I turned away and curled my arms across it.

"I don't mean to be obtuse. I had an idea of what you were going into all of this, but just a different interpretation. It's not always easy to accept that others are... incredible," his voice was uncomfortably soft, his eyes dry with secrets. There was something about how he said it that made me wonder how deep the things he was hiding from me genuinely went.

"Everything was once unexplained," I bit back, his even tone making my skin crawl, "This isn't necessarily a stretch of reality, just not yet figured out."

Still, he appeared relatively unshaken with only a slight ghostly sadness clouding his eyes.

"Sure, but those are just words. The unknown is always hard to accept," Eli said casually, lifting a shoulder in a shrug, "It changes the story slightly, but it doesn't change that you and I are the only surviving alumni of the Institute."

"That's why you didn't leave me back there. Camaraderie?"

"Sure. If that's what you'd like to believe." His eyes were soft when he looked at me. "We need each other, Valencia. More than you think."

"You still think I can help you?"

"I'm asking you to," he said unambiguously.

I twisted my mouth in quiet contemplation.

"You still want to risk being around me?"

He looked at me doubtfully, raising a brow, "I'm trusting you won't try to kill me in my sleep."

I smiled, though it felt strange on my face. "Don't take that camaraderie too far now, Eli."

"No, I wouldn't dare." We were zipping along the side road, pushing further to the west of downtown. "It's a dog eat dog world. You just happen to be higher on the food chain. I wouldn't be likely to forget that."

"It should be a consolation that you seem to be immune to whatever it is I do."

"I wouldn't say that."

My head swiveled to attention, and I shifted in my seat.

"It had an effect on you?" My pulse thrummed. "You can feel it?"

He dragged a hand over his mouth and rubbed at the stubble poking through his tender skin.

"Yeah. I mean, it didn't curdle my blood or tear any organs from where they sat, but I could tell there's something about you. Like static electricity. It kind of hums on the skin. Makes every hair stand up."

"Does it hurt?" I questioned.

"Not really. Just feels a little weird." He smiled at me, this time more genuine. "As for right now, I'm not all that afraid of you."

"Well, that underestimate may work in my favour if we ever get into hand to hand combat again."

He thoughtfully ran a thumb across the scabbed cut on his bottom lip. "You did okay, even without your magic."

"So maybe you should be afraid of me after all."

"I'll just bank on the fact that I won't give you reason enough to attack me."

"Might not be the safest bet to place your money. I'm still on the fence about it."

"Again- you're my only hope. I'd rather take a risk than have nothing at all."

I snorted. "Bravery in the face of adversity. What an admiral trait to have."

He chuckled, catching wind of the faint sarcasm drying my tone.

"It's all part of my master plan to make you like me. How's it going?"

I snorted, angling my knees towards him. "Could use some work. I guess you'll need some help with that too."

He paused before slipping his sunglasses slightly down the bridge of his nose and peering down at me. "Did you just make a joke?"

I scoffed and folded my legs onto the seat beneath me. "I do try to keep some semblance of good humour."

"If you asked me ten hours ago, I'd have said you failed on that front, but you continue to surprise me."

A few grey buildings were breaching the horizon, seemingly abandoned by the spray paint's aggressive nature and the broken windows. We were headed somewhere, but where I wasn't sure.

"I'm full of surprises," I said softly, "Want to hear another one?"

"Sure."

I leaned towards him and gently laid my hand on his exposed forearm. The hair prickled against my palm, and the flesh warmed beneath my skin, but he remained steady on the wheel. No curse. My heart rammed into my throat. It was a perverse and unholy thing to be able to lay these broken, twisted hands on a living person and leave them intact.

It was an even darker thing to hate the moment for taking the one thing I lacked even further out of reach...

Life.

I swallowed thickly against the feelings and brought my mouth close to his ear, feeling his muscles tense under my hand.

"I have an unfortunately shit temperament and very little patience, and if you don't tell me what's actually going on and where we're going, I'm going to split the other side of your lip and send your ass back from where you came from," I whispered, but felt the threat lacked conviction. I wasn't nearly as angry as I thought I might've been, being touted around in a car with a stranger.

Clearly unconvinced himself, he chuckled and pulled his arm out of my grip.

"Just when I was starting to think we'd gotten past this inherent aggression. You disappoint me."

"You've stalked me halfway across the plate and given me little information what you need me for or any steps in your process," I pointed out, "All I've got to go off of is some half-baked theory, speculations, and an imposed sense of companionship."

"It's by no intention, really. Scatterbrained, that's all." He took an exit aptly called 'exit 43', a road marked only with a sign that had long fallen on its side in the dusty gravel. "It all began on admittance day. Do you remember what happened when we got there?"

I furrowed my brow in thoughtful recollection. Of course, I did. There was no forgetting. There was no forgetting any of it, no matter how far away it had become.

"Sure. They stripped us of our clothes, hosed us down, and shaved our heads. Trying to create blank canvases."

He waved a hand in a dismissive gesture as if my slowness was a mild irritant, like a buzzing fly.

"After that."

"Ah..." I tucked a stray strand of hair behind my ear.

"Here," Eli said, rolling up the sleeve of his jacket. "This will jog your memory."

I stared at the smooth tanned skin, dark hair curling softly at the ridge of his muscles. It was unmarked save for the thin scar that ran just below the crease of his inner elbow.

"The implants."

"Yes. The implants."

I began to piece what he was saying together. "The cataloging. You think the Council's still got tabs on the kids."

"Now you're catching on."

I pushed a hand through the unruly waves that tumbled into my face. That was nearly a hundred years of kids in the system. Jesus, there would be thousands of them.

"So if we get into the system, we could find the resident trail. Prove or disprove your theory."

"In short, yeah."

"Seems easier said than done."

He shrugged, keeping his eye on the road.

"You got a plan?"

He winces. "That's the thing. You're not going to like it."

I had a feeling I wasn't going to like any of it. "It's risky?"

The expression that clouded Eli's face more than answered my question, but he replied anyway. "Yeah."

"Do we have an access point?" I had learned a few things over my time under Harris' particular direction, and one of the biggest was that nothing could be left up to chance.

"City Centre."

I squinted at him, dubious. The City Centres were always easy to access. Every house from here to Aras had a course to the place. "What's the catch?"

"Ah," he said, rubbing the back of his neck. "We've gotta get through to the fourth floor."

I swore then, dropping my back against the seat.

Plate residents only had approved access to the first floor, whereas engineers and composition faculty members were granted the second and third. Anything above the third floor required Council level clearance.

"That's impossible. Just getting up to the fourth floor is half a battle on its own, let alone making it into the surveillance room. You'd get caught."

"Maybe. But I've seen you slither around like smoke. People don't see you until it's too late."

I thought of all the times I'd screwed up in the last three days. "I'm not sure about that."

He brushed me off again. "You don't slip up when you're working. I was trying to pin you down for a while. You slip up when you're off a job because you relax. But when you're on, you're on. Untouchable."

Untouchable, unreachable. Uncatchable. "On my playing field. I have no idea what it would take to take on an army." My voice shook on the last word, and I was annoyed by it. He didn't need to know I was afraid.

"You wouldn't have to take them on if they didn't know you were there. You break in, you make it by, start a distraction, I'm behind you the whole time."

"I'm your errand boy," I said, irritated. That hardly took any skill at all. "So you can sit back on your haunches and wait for me to clear a path."

He pursed his lips at me, furrowing his brow. "Not exactly. I've got to be close enough to the action to sync the computer, but not close enough to get caught. You've just got to make it to the surveillance room."

I crossed my arms, weighing my options. "I'm not committing to this just yet."

He sighed, "I knew you wouldn't just jump on board. I'm not a total idiot. I've got other stuff to show you. Probably the stuff you care about."

"Blueprints? Outlines? Tangible information?"

The grin was quick and wicked as it creased his face. "Yeah, all that boring stuff."

We rattled past a rickety board that advertised 'engine stop' in sloppy charcoal that smeared around the letters like a grim shadow. Eli made the turn and followed the street, but the feeling of dread was hitting me again, in the same way it had at the restaurant. That feeling of wrongness.

"I didn't know that citizens had access to any type of vehicular transport," I commented. I'd ridden by car exactly twice before. Once, when Caleb and I were still young and foolish, and we'd clung to the back of a patrol van for the laughs. We'd won five food tokens from an old man with a pension for bets on that one. The second was when we had been taken to the Institution. I didn't remember much of that one and didn't care to.

Eli scratched the shadow of a beard around his mouth. "We aren't supposed to."

"Then how'd you fuck around and get one for yourself?"

"There's a lot of things we all do that we aren't supposed to," he said flippantly.

"Wouldn't it ping on BirdsEye?" I asked, scanning the sky for a drone now, but there weren't any.

"Might've, but they don't send too many out this way, and the ones they do barely make a blip on the report. Things more centralized attract a lot more attention. They don't worry too much about people this far out. Sometimes they'll send a low-level guard with a rifle and pick some of us off, but for the most part, they leave us be."

"Why is that?" I scanned the land around the strip of road. Vacant, vacant, vacant.

"Everyone dies out here, Valencia," he said quietly, "Slowly and painfully. They make it so unless you buy their food, you don't have food. Same with medicine, same with anything. If you're not close to the Centre, they don't bother with you as much. Figure you'll be dead by the end of the year, anyhow. It's easier just to drag people to them and pick them off from a big lot, then spend money and time chasing a few dirt crawlers around the edges."

Eli drove the car into a fluid deceleration onto the dirt shoulder, gently easing off the gas pedal until we pulled into an oval lot, fringed by dusty, blowing fields of tall burnt grass. In the middle of the lot stood a single oxidized pump, the long hose wrapped around its trunk several times before pooling onto the ground. A thick, heavy chain had it tethered to a single wooden shack at the back of the lot.

"Pull you in with what they promise," I muttered.

"Give you what you need to live just to steal your entire life," he finished, clicking his seatbelt off and sent it snapping back into its compartment. "Ironic, isn't it?"

He was reaching for the door handle when I felt a sudden wave of apprehension at the abandoned space.

"You're really going out there?"

He smirked at me, popping open his car door.

"Not as if I pulled over for kicks."

"You can't honestly think that old-"

With a wink, he hopped out and slammed the door smartly behind him, leaving me blinking in shock alone in my seat. In front of the car, Eli was already slipping a faded gold lighter from the pocket of his jacket and lighting a dangling cigarette.

The grass shifted in the wind, creating a quiet swishing while Eli untangled the old rubber pump and fumbled it into the tank. I listened to him rattle outside for a few more moments, then pushed my door open.

"It's not going to work," I said, "It's abandoned."

He stubbornly wrapped a ringed hand tighter around it and squeezed the handle again. It hissed but did little to spurt out any semblance of liquid.

"It will," he insisted. "Just needs a second to warm up."

The grass shifted again; only this time, a shadow fell into the lot before swiftly disappearing behind the shack.

"Did you see that?"

Eli looked up from the mouth of the tank and turned to face the grasslands. "See what?"

"Someone's over there."

Lifting an eyebrow, he took a final drag from the cigarette before dropping it and crushing it beneath his boot.

"Could be. You want to get out and come hold this for me?"

I didn't, not particularly, but since the engine was teetering on empty and we were in the middle of nowhere, I grudgingly lifted myself from my perch and wandered a few feet to the pump. Seamlessly, Eli dropped it into my hand and molded my fingers with his around the handle.

"Keep trying it," he said flippantly, cuffing the sleeves of his jacket as he walks to the outskirts.

"Keep trying," I mimicked quietly, releasing the handle before squeezing it again. It spat at me and sputtered out only droplets.

Rolling my eyes, I turned to look for Eli, but the lot had been vacated. "Great, the disappearing act again," I muttered. "He's awfully fucking good at that."

The stale breeze lifted dried dirt from a mound and sent it spinning in a slow cyclone. Using the back of my hand to wipe off the grime that had blown into my face, I squinted into the grass. It was hard to be sure, but it seemed as if the blades on the North side were shifting in the opposite direction than the wind. As if something I couldn't see was moving through them. I took a step away from the car, still clutching the pump.

"Eli?"

The rustling halted at the sound of my voice.

"For God's sake..." I tightened my grip on the pump and pivoted back to the car, slamming solidly into the body I had sensed. I cast my gaze lower than the ghoulish company, staring into the eyes of a wobbly-lined serpent tattoo that wound around his thick neck.

"You trying to steal my engine spit, lady?"

"I'm pretty sure it's called gasoline," I said coolly, "And I wasn't stealing anything. There was a sign advertising this place about a mile back."

My entire body was on high alert. *Wrong*.

"It ain't gonna work unless you pay. Only I got the know-how about turning it on." He crossed beefy arms across an equally broad and muscled chest. There were patches of his skin that were peeling and scaly, lighter in colour than his regular complexion. "So you pay, or you get the hell off my land."

Torn between my initial impulse to meet his fabricated attitude of authority with aggression and the desire to get back to familiarity, I waffled silently. Taking advantage of my hesitation, he reached out to grab the pump from me. I immediately dropped it, snaking my hand into my pocket. If he were cursed, we wouldn't get our gas, and Eli- wherever he'd gone- would be a colossal pain in the ass to deal with when he returned.

"How much, then?"

"Not a matter of how much, but what you got to offer. Always looking for stuff that's easy to sell; supplies, water, clothing. But if you got somethin' cool, I'll take it." He took a toothpick from his pocket and began to wiggle it between his gapped teeth. With his other hand, he held the pump behind him, afraid I was going to attempt to snatch it back. "Pretty spiffy vehicle you got there." He pronounced 'vehicle' as if every syllable were its own word. "Probably got some pretty spiffy stuff in the boot."

Might've, but there was no way to know what Eli kept in his stolen machinery. If he was even half-smart, he wouldn't hold anything worth anything in there. "You wanna go 'head and pop that for me, pretty girl?"

I snorted, but obliged, driven by my own curiosity more so than obedience. I reached through the front window and sent the trunk popping open. Surprisingly, the Serpent waited for me to meet him at the back.

It was sparse but not empty, hosting only a large black duffel bag and what looked to be an old, ratty quilt. Acting with the assumption the quilt was worth nothing in its current state, I unzipped the bag hastily. The contents, though shadowed by the high canvas walls, were all Council-lead items. Curious, I pinched a pack of liquid between my thumb and my index and raised it from the bag. It moved against me as if it was alive, the material whispering against the zipper.

"What are you doing?" Eli asked.

I lurched guiltily, dropping the unidentified item back into the bag. Distracted by the discovery, I hadn't noticed Eli coming to lean against the side of the car.

"I'm looking for something to pay the guy for his goddamn gasoline," I said through gritted teeth.

He shook his head and gestured with two fingers for me to follow him. With a resigned sigh, I shut the trunk and stalked to the passenger door, where Eli was bent over and digging through a small compartment. Re-emerging with a small container, he flipped the hair out of his eyes and left the door open. "Get in."

"You know manners exist, right?" I retorted.

He scowled at me, his eyes darkening. "Would you please get in?"

Wondering what had caused the stormy attitude, I folded into the seat, yanking the door from beneath his hand and slamming it shut. He crossed to the man and said something inaudible through the thick glass pane. After a moment of apparent disagreement, the container quickly exchanges hands. The gas attendant turned his back to me while he opened it, hiding it from view. His fingers took something out and rubbed at a small spot on his elbow, massaging it in. Apparently appeased, he nodded and passed Eli the pump before disappearing back into the folds of grass. The car shifted as it clunked back into the mouth of the gas tank, heavy and awkward. Restless in my seat, I kept an eye on Eli's frame in the rearview mirror and flipped the handle of the glove compartment up. It popped open with a loud snap.

Directing my attention to its contents, I grabbed a stack of papers from inside. Each was stamped with the Council's official emblem: a broad, hollow thin-stroked circle, a thicker, smaller black one in the centre, with the outline of a triangle reaching just outside the borders of the larger circle, crossing over the black centre dot.

I had always known this car didn't belong to Eli, but this discovery brought up a latent concern for precisely who it did belong to- and if they'd be needing it back in any sort of hurry.

Digging deeper, I found a box of matches- which I tucked in my pocket- a pair of gloves and an empty cigar case. All very cold and very dusty.

The driver's door swung open, and Eli slid into the seat. I made no effort to hide my scavenging and leave the compartment door hanging ajar.

He glanced casually at me before reclining in the seat and turning the key in the ignition.

"Looking for something?"

"This isn't a regular guardsmen's car."

"Didn't say it was," he said calmly, pulling back onto the street.

I held the fistful of papers at eye level and waved them at him.

"Then whose is it? This has high-level Council shit in it, man. The car's going to be tracked."

"No," he said firmly, "No one's looking for it."

"Oh, yeah? Why not?" I stuffed the papers back in the drawer. "It's a nice car."

"No one knows it's missing yet."

Mulling that over, I sat back and closed my eyes. A pressure was brewing somewhere deep in my temples.

"Is there a reason for that too?"

"Isn't there for everything?"

I scoffed and rubbed a hand over my gritty face. "How about you give me a straight answer for once?"

"Are we done with good humour, then?" He smirked at me and tugged at his hair. The gesture was one that survived the transition from nervous boy to hardened man, "It belonged to a doctor at the Institute. He was dishonourably discharged due to some, ah, unsavoury outsourcing, so to speak. The car was left to be impounded. So I took it."

Unsure of whether I believed him, I bit my tongue and lapsed into silence, flicking the music back on to compensate.

Something moody and melodic filled the car, inspiring some deep swelling feeling inside of me that fought to the surface. Though I was aware of the manipulated origin, it still led me to gaze upon the deserted fields and crumbling houses with a sense of romanticism for the way things must've once been. Free. Beautiful.

Hopeful.

13

A Tentative Truce

We reached the outskirts of the South in the evening when the sun was winding down from its highest point. Clouds of smog billowed from the factory structures five times the size of ones near the middle city, though they were unable to smother the stubborn sunbeams despite their best and most desperate effort. I craned my neck at the towering eyesores and tried to make out the details of the strange and crooked buildings, but the sun blinded me.

"Production facilities," Eli said, answering a question I had yet to ask.

"Yeah, but..." I peered closer, taking in the blank, blackened face of the building. There were no visible windows or doors, though people were lined up outside. "Production of what?"

"Mostly sustenance capsules, I'd say," He leaned towards me to look at my window. "Maybe a few housing material development places? I know there's been a huge surge again for plastics in the last little while now most of the old world stuff is biting the dust."

"But those specifically," I commented, watching the black smoke puff from crudely built chimneys. "Why is it so dirty? I don't remember it being like that."

"Maybe you just weren't paying attention?" He offered me a puzzled smile, "It's not clean work, making something out of nothing."

Granted, I had been relatively young when our group had made our way around South, busking for spare tokens and hitting up the workers on their way home. Perhaps I really had been too self-involved to notice the dark stains on their clothes and singed eyebrows. Still, I eyed the smoke cloud dubiously as we left it behind us.

"Is this where you're from?" I asked casually, attempting to mask my probing with the guise of an idle conversation.

"I wouldn't say I'm really from anywhere."

"Your parents, then. Were they from here?" I paused. "Did you know them?'

It wasn't uncommon for babies to be abandoned at various drop points around the plate. It was damn near impossible to live an honest life feeding and taking care of just yourself, let alone a wailing child.

Eli looked at me, apprehensively. "Knew my dad around for a bit," he said carefully. "Lost him when I was about seven. He worked mostly grunt stuff. Helped fix repairs in the wall more than once. Took me down with him until I was old enough to make my own choices. Probably wished I made different ones, but hey."

"Council got hold of you, anyway," I murmured.

He laughed in his sad and haunted way. "Yeah, in a way. Probably had a mark on us before we'd even lost all our baby teeth."

We whistled into a residential area, drawing attention to the black sedan as it spat up gravel and squealed against the plate surface. A skinny pin of a woman clutched her boy against her hip at our dark omen, attempting to shield his face with the sleeve of her tattered blouse.

That isn't going to help, lady, I thought bitterly. If the Council wanted to take your kid, they're taking your kid. You don't have a choice.

"Worried about the attention?" Eli asked, dropping the speed to a more acceptable pace.

I shook my head.

"Not worried. Just thinking about what seeing these cars usually mean to the people here. How crazy it is that something inanimate can incite so much fear." Another family scurried inside a bent sheet-metal hut.

"We'll drop it off soon," he replied, calm and steady. "I've driven through here many times before."

"And I'm sure they were scared every time before," I quipped back.

"Train doesn't come out this way," Eli offered me another nonchalant shrug and took a slow left turn. "Only way to get this far off Centre is walking. And that's a good and easy way to get yourself killed."

I rubbed my forearm where gooseflesh has risen on my skin. It was colder here than it had been at the Brink. "I thought you said the Council didn't watch this place as much."

"Ah," he said noncommittally. "That doesn't mean not at all. I'm just saying, a single civilian, walking alone? Breaching conduct? Passing borders? Pretty easy to pick them off." He mimicked a shooting gesture. "Blast them through export, and you'd never even know they were missing."

"So why hadn't that gasoline man been picked off? That was isolation if I'd ever seen it."

"Please, Valencia," He twisted the wheel and took a sharp right turn. I slid off the edge of the seat and pressed against the door. "You're not that naive."

"What is that supposed to mean?" It came out jagged. Humiliation stung.

"I'm not stupid," I'd whined plaintively at Cal, who'd only shaken his head at me, his body angled away from me like it was

an embarrassment to be seen with me. "I'm not stupid," I insisted, pleading.

"It means," he said patiently, ignoring the outburst, "That he wasn't just allowed to be there, he was supposed to be there."

"Like he was working for the Council?" I thought about his sloppy gut and boil-covered face. "Doesn't quite fit the image."

He clicked his tongue softly, pulling the car into a narrow canopy, maneuvering around a fallen barrel. "Guess you don't know much about civilian hires, then."

I didn't, but I didn't want to admit it. "So man's paid to be an informant."

Eli pulled the brake and cut the engine. "Well, that, too. But they probably let him operate there under the understanding they get the majority of whatever he gets from it."

"He was asking for scraps," I said, grabbing my bag from where it had fallen to my feet.

"And all those scraps go back into the belly of the beast, wet with information," Eli said dryly, "Gasoline Guy makes his report, gets his sustenance capsules for the week and maybe even a buck or two on the side."

"And you're not worried about him reporting us? Describing us?"

"I took care of it."

I raised an eyebrow. Somehow Eli's version of 'taking care of things' didn't seem to ease my mind.

"With the container," I said, rolling my head to my shoulder and looking at him from beneath my lashes.

"Yes, Valencia," he snapped off his seatbelt, pausing with his hand on the door handle, "With the container."

I huffed out a small puff of frustration. It was like trying to lift moisture from a brick wall. "What was in it?"

The stare he offered was blank and steady as he popped the door open. "Enough to mean something to a broken man."

The car creaked as he lifted his lanky weight off the bearings. "How could you have something-."

The door slammed shut in the middle of my sentence, leaving my mouth hanging open in the empty space. I fisted my hands and pressed the knuckles into the bridge of my thigh. The absolute nerve...

The passenger side door opened, letting in a blast of wind that lifted the ends of my hair into a spinning disarray.

"Are you getting out, or are you planning on hanging out in here all day?" Eli's tone was playful, matched by the twinkle in his eye.

"Why do I feel like you hide more things than you let on?"

He leaned against the side of the car, resting his hip against the open door frame. "Just trust that I tell you what's necessary and hold back what's not."

Incensed, I pulled myself to my feet, narrowly missing his head with mine. "How do you decide what's necessary for me to know and what isn't?" I cocked my chin, bringing my gaze firmly to his.

"To ask you to be my partner in this is to take responsibility for your safety," he gestured for me to move away from the car and shut the door. "There are things I must keep to myself as the knowledge may put you in a position you don't have to be in."

The car alarm made a soft beep as he bumped the door in and flicked the lock.

"I can handle myself," I said to his turned back and watched the muscles in his shoulders ripple as he tossed a braided rope over the roof of the car.

"Maybe. But you don't need the weight of my secrets on top of yours, Valencia," Eli wiped the sweat of effort off his brow with the back of his hand. "There is a level of accountability in the things we keep hidden. More often than not, it's for a reason."

I chewed on his statement, considering all the things I'd done that I'd kept close to my breast. Stealing fruit from the marketplace, burning down an old house, setting someone up for arrest.

Leaving Caleb.

Catching a whisper of the strange expression on my face, Eli thoughtfully wrapped the winding rope around his knuckles, pushing the blood to the tips of his fingers in a burst of purple. "Care to give me a hand?"

The wind whistled beneath the canopy.

"How?"

Eli shifted the rope to one hand and pulled a sheet from the side of the tunnel, holding it out to me. "We've got to get the car covered."

I rubbed the tarp between my fingers, testing the texture against my skin. It was damp and cold, yet scratchy and illogically patched. "I thought you said no one paid mind."

"The Council won't bust us if we don't push our luck, and most civilians will likely avoid a parked government car," he paused to grab the other side of the tarp. "But we've got scavengers down here. Slip around like shadows. They'll take whatever."

I clicked my tongue and followed his lead to the back of the vehicle, draping the material carefully over my end. I knew much too well about the scavenger life.

"Got bold people out here to fuck with stuff like this. Even scavengers know enough to have a code of conduct," I commented, earning a quick glance from Eli.

"It's a pre-emptive measure. Haven't you ever heard the phrase 'better safe than sorry'?"

The snort I made was brash and unrefined. "Not from anyone born in the last fifty years."

His head snapped up, and the corners of his mouth pulled into a slight frown. "Sentiment withstands time."

"So do cockroaches and garbage," I conceded, allowing myself a small smile. "Doesn't mean it's a measure of their validity."

"I'd say cockroaches are a refined insect for their ability to survive," he tossed back. "Are we not the same as them, pushing onward even though our world had become uninhabitable?"

I chuckled and finished fastening the back clasps of the cover. "I'm not sure Jebediah would much care for that comparison."

The noise Eli made was close to that of a hissing cobra. "Jebediah called himself a pioneer, but all he had was money and a false sense of elitism. It is as if no one bothered to tell him that once the world around him crumbled, money would have no relevance."

"Money has meaning when we let it," I said quietly, pulling the front of my cloak closed as a frigid wind began to rear its ugly head. "We still have to earn tokens to get food and pay for shelter."

"It is not the same," his voice was colder than the wind could ever dream of being. "When the world fell, the system did the same. Anyone should've been able to get in that Pod," he spat out. "Anyone. We should have all saved each other."

"Should've," I said. "But didn't."

The end of my statement was almost lost to a horn that sounded from just beyond our hideaway. It was unfamiliar to me, but I picked up on the tension that raised Eli's shoulders.

"That's bad?" It was almost not worth asking, since his entire demeanour had changed, but I did anyway. Moving to the small split in the cave's walls where we had entered, I peered out but saw nothing beyond the bleakly empty street and rattling shutters.

"Just a warning."

"For council officials?"

"Not this time," he commented, tilting his head to the side as if in wait. "Weather warning. We've got about thirty minutes before we're as good as dead out here." He glanced at a slim, understated watch I'd scarcely noticed on his wrist. "We've got to move."

"The clouds can't nearly be dark enough to be a serious threat."

The sun was still pushing through.

"How many times do I have to tell you this isn't Downtown crap anymore?" Eli flipped a cigarette into his mouth and struck a match, burning the tip into a pulsing red glow. "You guys are safest down there because that's where the net is strongest; over the Pod. That's not the case down here, not in a million years."

"It's the same fucking system, Eli. Stop acting like I'm some cushy Patron. I lived on the Fringe for years."

"And how long ago was that? About ten years, isn't it? Things change. Things change, and nobody pays mind because it happens so slowly."

A shudder vibrated its way through my body. Could it really have gotten worse in the time I'd been away?

"Why would they change?" I asked, but he was already slinking away, his long legs eating up the sidewalk. I clambered after him, feeling clumsy in my flimsy shoes. "Wasn't the net built to be a sustainable system?" There was fear in my voice, edging on hysteria.

"I don't know," Eli retorted, his eyes glimmering as he puffed. "Was it?"

"If it hadn't been, the settlers would have never agreed to it. It has to be sustainable."

"Look," he took a deep drag of the cigarette, scratching at the thickening beard on his neck. "A lot of us look at that moment as a triumph. As if we won because we got what we wanted. We 'won' because they wanted us to."

"To have workers."

"Sure, and whatever suited them to have. It's having a kennel full of subjects and a gloved hand at the ready to pick one up. If the kennel is kept subdued, the power remains in the gloved hand's favour. It's harder to control people who resent they're being controlled."

"What does any of this have to do with the net?"

He sighed and flicked the butt of his cigarette to the ground, where it quickly ashed itself out against the dry dirt.

"They don't actually give a shit about us out here. Not really. It's not like the Council wants us having kids and populating and trying to live actual lives. Why do you think they did that emergency sterilization in Courtside? It doesn't have anything to do with our health. It's population control. They just want the ones that are useful and necessary."

"Like engineers," I added, "And scientists."

Eli nodded. "That's why they keep the good ones Downtown. It's by deliberate intention that they're safer up there than we are down here."

"Because grunt workers are replaceable," I said, then cringed when I remembered his father. Luckily Eli doesn't even seem to be affected by the comment, keeping his steady but fast pace.

"Easier to find a citizen with muscle than it is to find someone who can create food from a plate of nothing."

The first drops of rain splattered onto my forehead, splashing dirty, cold water into my eyes. "So, we're unsafe out here." My tongue dashed out and moistened my lips. "On purpose."

Eli sent me a weak smile- the first semblance of softness I had seen grace his face in what felt like a lifetime. "Yes. On purpose."

14

The Academia of Eli Manning

There was something familiar about the houses built in the City that stayed constant no matter which direction you faced: the flat-faced buildings were always poorly assembled and angled way too close together. Typically tucked so close to each other, there was less than an inch of space between the outside walls, the yards themselves had just enough room for a disposal unit and half a walkway. The only homey addition to any residence were the porches, jutting out a meter from the door and sagging in the middle. It was a whisper of the hopeful symbolism the houses once held.

Eli's house was nothing like I had ever seen before. It was narrow, as was expected, but it stretched higher into the sky than the ones beside him, tapering off into a thin point that looked like an antenna. The sharpness of the top was offset only by the rounded windows of mismatched sizes, framed by clumsy shutters powerless against the wind.

"It's so..." I touched the tip of a post on the iron gate, and flakes of rust drifted up to my hand, eager to greet their new host. "Why is it like this?"

There were so many things to consider on the plate- zoning laws, height restrictions, property guidelines- and it seemed that this particular house fit none of them.

"You mean stylistically?" He knocked the gate open with his foot, "I suppose it's a little unusual, but it's just one of those things." Eli offered one of the rolling shoulder shrugs that fell effortlessly off of him, "The house has always been like this."

He spoke of the place with such casual intimacy that it made me wonder if it had been his home, even in youth. I tried to pull up the image of the rangy, challenging man before me as a small child, but failed. It was hard to even imagine him as the adolescent at the Senator's side.

"Was this your father's home?" I prodded.

He nodded curtly, standing in the pathway with his hand lazily resting on the gate. "Some would say it has been in the family for years." The way he said it was distracted, casual even, but there was an edge behind his words.

"Wow," I responded, pressing my tongue to the roof of my mouth. It was a lackluster response, at best, but the reveal left me with little to say. "Mighty odd to have yourself a multi-generational residence."

He grunted in response, offering little to the conversation. Eli had his eyes trained on the darkening sky, ignoring the few droplets spattering on the pavement in front of him.

Keeping a house for any duration of time in itself was a victory. Housing in lower neighbourhoods was something less based on assignment and more on a 'first come, first serve' basis, and even once you had it, protecting your belongings and artifacts took a lot of brawn. It all came down to who had the most guard dogs and the most power. It was a weak system, based on respect- an alpha/beta playing field. You could stay somewhere only for as long as people feared or respected you. I glanced at Eli's drawn face. Just which of those things did he fall under?

"You live here alone?"

He huffed, impatiently darting his eyes back to mine. "Yes. Just me."

Who had kept to the house while he had been away? He had been in the Institute as long as I, probably more. I sized him up, taking in the scruff of a few days of beard and the muscles that pushed against the skin of his forearm. He was at least a couple of years my senior but had remained in the Institute even longer than I had. I shuddered. It'd have been years.

"Did you-."

"Valencia," he said tightly, reigning in frustration, "We need to go inside."

I hadn't realized I'd stopped dead. The rain was picking up now, the wind wielding a pointed sword to blur my vision and dull my ears.

I had been frozen at the gate, paralyzed by questions, and doubting my choice to follow Eli anywhere. What did I even know about him?

The sky rumbled a deep and throaty growl that I felt in the soles of my shoes. Eli lurched forward and took hold of my arm, angrily pulling me onto the porch beneath the overhang. He fumbled his keys from his pocket and unlocked the front door, shoving me inside just as the flow of rain became a barrage. The door slammed behind us, blocking the worst of the storm from the room.

"Fuck," Eli said, running a jerking hand through his hair, "It's getting worse."

I backed out of his way as he stalked to the shaking window. The glass looked like it would give out any second.

"The weather?"

"Yes," he spat out, dropping a tarp over the glass. "The goddamn weather."

"I didn't know it was like this," I said softly, barely loud enough to make out above the thumping storm. "We've barely had anything like this near the Harris house." The closest I'd seen of this magnitude was in the Brink the night before, but even that torrent paled in comparison.

Eli grunted at me as he pushed a desk in front of the rattling door. "Wind might blow it in."

Had I been blind? I cupped my elbows with my hands. Had living with Harris for the last two years made me ignorant? She hadn't lived in the best neighbourhood, but I'd never had to cover windows frantically or barricade doors. We were so close to the Centre that I hadn't stopped to think about what it might've been like for people who weren't. Of course, the Council would protect the downtowns first. If the net was failing, the first thing they'd do is make sure the Pod was safe. I guess Auntie had been right, rest her soul, with all her ramblings. The Council never gave a shit what happened to any of us as long as it didn't affect any of them on the inside.

"Did you need any help?" Seeing Eli agitated was making my skin itch. Something prickly had overcome his warm nature, now ebbing off of him in icy waves.

He swung his gaze to mine, his eyes the same golden irises framed by soft lashes, but all wrong. There was something slick across them that made me think of the reflective surface of a still pond. Glassy and empty.

"What?" He asked, his tone distant.

"Did you... want any help?" I kept my back to the wall, carefully skirting to where he stood.

"Oh, no." He shook his head, and some of the life came back into his body. "It should be fine now. Just keep your shoes on when you're in this room. You never know when the glass might go."

We stood in the room quietly with the storm raging on outside for a minute or two. Eli leaning against the desk, his chest heaving, and me, awkward and out of place in the dusty living room. Finding myself feeling discomfort in the silence though it was a place I'd drawn such a home in, I shifted my focus from the sweaty, shifty man in front of me to the sprawling room. The sky had considerably darkened since we'd left the car, the storm clouds masking the rest of the sun's weakening rays as it slipped beyond the horizon. The result left Eli's house looking like something out of a child's nightmare. All shapes and shadows that jutted out from unsuspecting angles, crammed against each other in a fight for space as they leered towards you.

"Is there a light in here?" I asked, keeping my voice light and steady. I only liked being surrounded by shadows if I was one too.

"Might not work, but you can try it. There's a lamp behind you, by the big chair. If you flip the little switch, it should puff out a flame or so."

I could barely make out the big chair from the sea of shadowed lumps, but I stroked my hand across the table until I settled on something that felt compact and mechanical beneath my hand. After a few seconds of awkwardly fingering the cylinder, the flame burst out of the funnel and into the glass bulb, illuminating the room with a dull orange glow.

"Well, that's something," I said.

Eli offered a shy smile and one of his smooth shrugs. "Sorry. It is what it is. I'm not here all that often, anyway."

"Right," I said, but the furniture was catching my eye. "Traveller's life."

"Yes," he said calmly, but his eyes twinkled as if he was enjoying his own private joke. "Always out looking for something."

"Trouble?" I asked with a half-smile, feeling a warmth in my breastbone when Eli let out a short, rumbling laugh.

"You're not wrong." He shook the raindrops from his hair. "But I'd say most of the time trouble comes looking for me."

I trailed a finger over the backing of one of the chairs, tracing my nail around the grooves of the rich, glimmering material. "This is beautiful," I said breathlessly, forgetting to be reserved and dispassionate. "The detail is incredible." I crouched to bring myself closer and get a better view of it in the low light. "How did they get such patterns into it?" I rubbed my hand over the thick material. "It doesn't feel like polythorane."

"It's not," he said, and when I looked over to him, I realized he'd taken off his shirt.

"Why are you undressing?"

"It's wet, Val. Don't be such a prude." He tossed the shirt at me teasingly, and it missed by a meter, landing next to my feet with a definite 'whap.'

"So's mine, but you don't see me stripping."

"You say that like it's a good thing."

"It is to me." I stared back at the chair, forcibly turning my attention to it instead of his bare and muscled chest. There were scars zigzagged across his chest, and it looked like smaller ones on his shoulders. Who had hurt him? And why? I cleared my throat, unblinking until my eyes burned, and gestured at the piece of furniture. "What is this made out of?"

"Oh, it's old."

"How old?" I pressed.

"It's an antique."

I sucked in a sharp breath, not faking as I stroked the edges with both hands in reverence. "Solid wood?" I said my voice barely above a whisper.

"Yeah," Eli said casually, passing by me to walk towards the other room.

"Do you realize how amazing that is?" I whistled softly, running my hands over the length of the chair as if it was a lover. "It's in such incredible shape."

There were bits and pieces of wood around the plate, spread out in a sporadic distribution that spoke of carelessness. It was true- wood was a dying industry long before humans were, but in the ghost town of what used to be, it lived on. Still fascinated, I gave it a final rub.

It was hard to imagine a tree big enough to make something out of it. Most people on the plate had a vague enough understanding of the concept of vegetation, and we'd managed a few sprouts in the few inches of soil here and there, but nothing to the enormity of a full tree, or forbid, a forest.

"Yeah, and now we're in a plastic incubator," Eli said with an unreadable expression. "Oxygen filtering into the atmosphere from what? A scientifically enhanced net?" He shook his head at it. "All of this stuff just depresses me when I think about it."

I straightened, becoming embarrassed by my outright awe. "Well, at least we're still alive. If we were off the plate and beyond the wall, we would've gotten sucked in the ground like everything else."

"Yeah," he offered another shrug, which I was beginning to hate. "But would that be worse than the fate they've offered here?"

The annoyance was quick and sharp, but I held my tongue back from the lashing it wished to give out. I couldn't very well alienate the only ally I had. Even I knew that was a stupid move. "I'd like to use your washing room," I said stiffly, effectively ending the conversation.

Unbothered, Eli gestured vaguely to his left, pointing down a dark hallway. "It's on the right. You'll have to crank the faucet a few times to get any water out of it. Good luck."

It shouldn't have bothered me as much as it did. It wasn't as if I disagreed with any of it, not really, but even after Eli turned and left the room, the anger whirred in my chest. Nobody wanted to end up doing a tap-dance on a metal disk, balanced on whatever's left of the earth, breathing in modified chemical compounds, and consuming mush. I unclipped the neck of my cloak, swinging it in a broad circle before tossing it over my bent elbow. It was infuriating. How could someone care so much and so little at the same time?

I stumbled into the hallway, tripping over the drooping fabric of my cloak. Of course, it was shitty. It was all shitty: the air, the food, the economy. The entire system was awful for everyone, except for the handful of people that lived in the Pod, enjoying a blissful lifestyle that didn't include a rickety plate, a weak net, and a continued threat to survival. But the fact was, if the earth imploded on itself, we'd all be dead. Cushy egg or not. I imagined they just liked to tell themselves that it didn't affect them because they were rich and 'pure,' like any of that would make a difference to the unseen forces of deliverance.

I pushed the door of the washing room open, surprised that the light was already buzzing and illuminating the room. I wasn't mad at Eli. Not really. It was a pretty horrid deal, and maybe the people that fell victim to the Reckoning did end up getting the better side of things. It just rubbed me the wrong way.

I pulled the lever on the faucet, and, just as Eli had warned, it took at least a few cranks for water to start spurting out. I splashed the chilled water onto my face, blissful at the flecks of grime and dirt that finally flew out with it.

I was reaching up to dry my face off with a towel when I noticed the bloomed crimson stain on my left bicep. Curiously, I pressed the spot gently, remembering the alley fight and the man with a gun. I couldn't really be still bleeding, could I? That was supposed to be one of the perks of being an honorary member of the deceased.

Quickly and competently, I peeled the shirt off. Standing half-naked in the flickering light, I was able to see the full extent of my injuries. My ribs were speckled with spots of purple, black and blue, framing a particularly nasty vision of a boot-print across the length of my torso. It made me glad for my predominantly unresponsive nerve endings.

I turned to the side, pulling at the skin of my arm until the wound was visible. The hiss of air I let out was one out of shock.

The wound was the size of a token coin, maybe less, with a near-perfect symmetry between each side. The skin around it was crackled and split, with crooked lines of blue pushing towards the edge of my shoulder. It oozed thick, goopy blood that didn't drip but glugged out, sending a lump down my arm.

"Gross," I said aloud, propping the limb over the sink and shaking until the chunk fell in a black smudge against the cracked porcelain. It was odd, but I didn't want to focus on it. It could just be a change of environment. Maybe I'd picked up an infection. No big deal. It was fine. I was fine. Nothing to worry about. It'd be gone within the next couple of days. They always were.

I splashed water onto the gash and rubbed it with a spot of soap until the memory of sludge disappeared, and all the was left was a perfect, fleshy hole at the top of my bicep. Since it was still open, I tore a piece of cloth from the hanging towel and tied it tightly against the wound.

Satisfied with the temporary solution, I slipped back into my damp shirt- which, thankfully, was nowhere near the sopping mess Eli's had been- and slicked the sides of my hair down from where they had frizzed up. God, I was a mess. I offered my reflection a weak smile and gently gave my face a couple of light taps, hoping the blood rush would make me seem less ghoulish, before admitting defeat and leaving the washing room only slightly sloppier than I had been greeted with.

Without the light from the bathroom to guide me, I carried my wet cloak and heavy bag back towards the living room, carefully stepping though there were no obstacles in the narrow strip. I was debating calling for Eli when he popped his head from the doorway on the other side.

"I want to show you something."

He'd put on another shirt, which should have relieved me for the cloth barrier now set between us, but oddly enough, I found myself regretting the distance. The soft green shirt was trim and tight, the texture moving with his body more than the monochromatic standard could manage. "Nice shirt."

"Oh, this?" He pulled at the hem, lifting it a fraction of an inch to show off a deeply tanned torso and a tapering of his muscles that disappeared below his belt. He grinned when he saw my eyes flick to the exposed flesh, and though it had been more instinctual than primal, I flushed and looked away.

"Yeah. It's an interesting colour."

"Finder's keepers," he said, the same hint of humour I'd spotted earlier making another appearance in his eyes.

"Was that what you wanted to show me?" I asked dryly, feigning ease though my heart was bumping uncomfortably in my throat.

"No, of course not. It just happened to take centre stage for the quick second." He gestured at a tall door on the other side of the kitchen. "It's in the study unless you wanted to relax a bit before diving in."

Did I want to relax? Yes. Could I? I rolled the question around, felt every nervous twitch in my body before dismissing the possibility. "No, I'm fine."

I wouldn't be able to relax in this house until I could gauge where I stood in it.

Eli pulled the keys out of his dark jeans, sifting through until he landed on one with a grey sticker.

"Do you lock every door in this place?"

"Only if the stuff inside is worth protecting. The bathroom wasn't locked," Eli said pointedly, taking my simple question as judgment.

"It doesn't seem like anyone messes with this house, anyway." I patiently waited as he unlocked it. "Despite the high crime rate. Makes you wonder."

"Wonder? Wonder about what?" He asked distractedly, pushing the door through the frame. It stuck a little and groaned, almost humanly, as it released itself into the air.

"Why no one fucks with it."

"Yeah." His response was flat. "Go on, then," he said, gesturing for me to start down the dark and narrow hallway.

"Any particular reason you want me to go first?"

"Ladies' honour?" His face split into another one of his dazzling grins that I just knew he used to get his way, way too often. And that it usually worked on everyone, which made it work significantly less on me.

"I'd rather follow," I said calmly. It was the first rule of living on the street. Don't let anyone get behind you.

Eli raised an eyebrow but slid ahead of me, eating up the short stretch of ground with legs that seemed impossibly long. I waited until the lights came on before I followed, pulling the door shut behind me. Since he'd shown up in my room for the first time, I'd found myself continually waiting for the other shoe to drop. I still half-expected a group of Councilmen to be waiting at the bottom, ready to grab me and drag me away.

However, it was not the case, and instead of men with loaded guns, the room at the end of the hall bore only books and documents stuffed onto shelves too small.

"What's all this?" I lifted a paper off the middle table, gingerly pinching it between my thumb and my forefinger. It was covered with jolting black scrawl and a photo of a map.

"Information."

Not all his, from what I could gather. The papers across the table were speckled with different fonts of different colors, marked with retractions and smudged with additions until the sheets were nearly just a barrage of scribbles.

"This is... a lot." I pulled a thin folder from the shelf and idly leafed through it, skimming the words on the pages.

Experiments... children... nuclear testing. "What is all of this about?"

"What isn't it about? This is our life." Eli gestured at the wall of books. "This is the truth, the woman behind the veil. It's past, present." He picked up a book, labeled 'The Logical Deductive Progression of Events,' and waved it at me. "The future."

"People here wrote these? On the plate?" I picked up a note that looked like it was written on a napkin. Some of the writing smudged off on my finger from the acrylic. I wondered what they might've been like; what kind of lives they led.

"Yeah." Eli re-shelved the book he had waved at me, stroking the binding like the cheek of a lover. "People know more than they want to, I think. As much as we try to ignore the things that are happening, people know. In their hearts, they know. It can be drawn out."

"You met these people?" I dropped onto a stool that was sitting ajar from the table and started organizing the papers into neat stacks. "What were they like? Hopeful? Or afraid?"

"Probably a little bit of both, but no, I didn't meet them."

His voice was low, dripping with melancholy.

"What happened to them?"

Eli sighed, raking his hands through his hair. "Vanished."

"They just disappeared?" I flipped the paper I was holding over and glanced for a name. It was untitled. "They disappeared, but their stuff didn't? Wouldn't this be the first thing the Council destroyed? It's proof."

Eli reached and snatched the page from my tight grip, saving it from the crinkle that had been forming on the side. "What it is is saved conjecture. We need actual solutions. Testimonies from a bunch of outcasts long-since stamped with the brand of 'crazy' and exiled from their communities aren't going to change anything."

The stool groaned as I shifted it back to give myself a more extensive gauge of the room. On the shelf adjacent to me was a small, delicately bound book labeled 'interviews.'

"What's this, then?" I pulled it off the shelf, clumsily, letting another book fall flat on the plank.

"A lot of dead ends." Eli dropped into a seat at the other side of the table. "Sometimes, I think I'm almost breaking through, but then they close up."

I flipped to the middle of the book, pausing at a line that stuck out at me.

"But you've found where they're missing from? Where are their families?" I flipped the sheet back over, looking for a quadrant. This one was three.

"Some. But there's just too many kids. Many of them are just off the street, so few can say for certain if they knew them at all. With such a high number of people in every quadrant and drifters being so common, there's an overwhelming amount of people you'd have to speak with to track any of these damn kids."

"Ah," I said, pressing my tongue to the roof of my mouth, "A feat too big for even the best."

The statement obviously miffed him- as if the hint of being taunted was something he'd experienced little during his life.

"I could find them," he responded coolly, "it would just take an absurdly long time."

"Eli," I started, but paused when he angled his gaze at me.

"What?"

"Do you even care about these kids? Really?" I stared at the papers scattered on the table and felt sick. "Do you want to find them because you're worried, or is it because you can't stand the thought of there being something you can't do?"

The air swelled, then dropped, leaving the room feeling empty though we were rhythmically taking breaths in tandem.

"I care." He said firmly, but I could hear his secrets haunting the edges of his "I hope you never ask me such a thing again."

I grunted in acknowledgment and skimmed the paper I held once more. I could tell I had pressed on one of his secrets again; one of the things I wasn't allowed to see, for my safety.

On the second run-through of the interrogation of a woman named Bethesda, the format stood out for being incredibly thorough and well documented. Stilted. Professional. I slid him a look. He was hiding something, here, in this room. "How old are you, Eli?"

His eyebrows raised, and his fingers halted amid the incessant tapping upon the table he had taken to. "How old am I?"

I leaned to the back of the stool, delicately balancing to keep myself in place. "Yes. As in- how long since you were birthed."

The smile etched itself with fine lines into his face. "Somewhere around two decades ago. Maybe more. Probably not less."

"Okay," I said quietly, dropping the paper into the stack before picking up another.

Eli stared at me patiently from across the table. I could feel his eyes burning into my skin, but I said nothing.

"Valencia," his voice was low and drawn out, but not altogether unkind, "Why do you ask?"

"Trivialities relax people. Distracts them from being grouchy. And partial curiosity because this," I waved the paper at him, "is meticulous study at its finest. Obviously, you were able to learn something at the Institute." I started to wonder why such a proficient candidate never graduated, then I remembered, with a thickness in my throat, he had vanished the same as I had.

The laugh caught me off guard, as it often did. When Eli laughed, it was as if the room laughed with him.

"You're the strangest kind of girl."

"But one that can effectively alter your moods," I said pointedly, referring to the way he would blow hot, then cold at the drop of a dime.

"I really just..." Eli raised his hands helplessly and let them fall into his lap, "I haven't much experience socializing, especially not lately."

"You seemed to do okay with what I saw at the bar."

"Ah, so you were paying attention to me." He played with the corner of a file that was in front of him. "I was working. In my occupation, you have to have a decent amount of charm to get what you want. It's acting."

"I wasn't paying attention to you," I retorted, latching onto his first comment with revolt. The scowl was quick and unprecedented. "And if I was, I was just gauging whether or not you were a threat."

"I'm flattered." He spun a pen idly between two fingers, watching it fly. "Is that a practice you entertain often, or did something about me strike you as dangerous?"

"Oh, Eli," I said mockingly in his signature drawl, "You've got danger written all over you."

"Hey, now, might I remind you one of us here is a known assailant, and I'm pretty sure I'd know if it was me."

"Known?" I leaned towards him on the table, feeling my eyes blaze. "Known by who, exactly?"

Without so much rousing himself from his perch, he swiveled and selected a smooth Manila envelope from the stack, studying its face only briefly before dropping it in front of me. "Me."

Because I took an interest in all things' me'- an admittedly narcissistic trait for the dead- I pulled it close to me, digging my fingers greedily beneath the front flap. My name, Valencia, seemed strangely foreign now. Harris had almost exclusively referred to me as 'girl' and little else. A file. An entire file. I shuddered. She would have been furious. I would've earned that cane to my back at least thirty times.

Sucking air through the gap between my front teeth, I tossed it open.

Valencia stared at me, narrow-faced and unsmiling, from the photo square on the ID. I, the girl, stared back. She was a stranger, who might have once been cute, in a haunting sort of way. Her fuzz of dark hair lightly framed a sharp face, highlighting her dark, almond-shaped eyes and the set of the deep Cupid's bow of her lips, supple and pressed together. The plastic card was dingy and waterlogged at the corners, causing the paper inside to curl against itself and ripple. Suddenly offended by its very presence, I pulled it free of the paperclips. "Where did you get this?"

"Right where you left it." He had his feet kicked up on the table now, his boots almost scuffing the papers. "At the bottom of the Spillout."

"Took up snorkeling, did you?" I sneered.

"I happened upon it in my own way," Eli worked out another cigarette from the pack but merely held it in between his fingers. I knew enough to know that he wouldn't risk lighting up around his extensive work. "In my own time."

I snapped the card back onto the table with a loud crack, making sure that Valencia's face was hidden against the table.

All the better that intense, burning gaze was aimed directly into the tabletop.

The file was fuller than I would've liked to admit, primarily since I had been confident in my ability to fly well below the radar. Frowning thoughtfully, I shuffled through some crudely printed photos. Most were blurry shots at best, from cameras along the wall or dining establishments.

"I was able to get into security systems. Council doesn't care to have as tight a reign on that technology," he answered before I asked.

Any place making money had to have cameras, I knew that. I just hadn't expected anyone to be looking for me. Of course, Eli was. I flipped them over and scanned them for the dates.

Cursed with an unflinchingly honest memory, I remembered the victims as if their faces had been seared in my brain. A horribly beautifully wretched thing it was to watch someone die.

Since my stomach was turning, I dropped the photos of the blurred cloaked girl and rifled through until I find a map, dotted sporadically with multicoloured dots. "This." I slapped my hand on it. "How did you know where I had been?"

Eli chuckled softly and massaged the back of his neck. "Rumors, really. Strange deaths. Some of them were less than accurate." He dropped his feet and folded towards me, reaching his arm out to the map. "Some turned out to be, well, rather ordinary."

"All worked out for you in the end," I murmured, rubbing the edge of the paper between my forefinger and thumb.

"There was a point I thought people had really just been off their rocker the entire time. I was getting so unbearably frustrated. Every time I got close to you, you would just wisp away. It was like chasing a ghost."

I didn't think the reality was much further than that, but I didn't say it. The thought of being seen made me queasy.

"I was in that bar for the better part of a week waiting for you to show up. I'd gotten a tip you'd be on a hit near there. On the last day, I said to myself, Eli, if she doesn't come in, you go home, and you give up. But you did."

"Huh," I said, no longer interested in the writing on the pages. Nervousness was fluttering around my heart like a flock of birds. I closed it and pushed it back to Eli. "Seems like an awful lot of trouble."

"No one else would suit what I want. They wouldn't have been nearly as remarkable as you," he replied in his puzzling sort of way where I couldn't tell if he was making a pass at me, and I couldn't tell if I wanted him too. He might've been joking, too, but that was even harder to decipher. Shifting uncomfortably in the hard seat, I struggled to find the apathetic nerve I'd acquired in the last couple of years.

Damn it, he unnerved me.

I didn't like to be unnerved.

"Tell me, Elijah," The deliberate use of his name caused him to lift an already impossibly arched eyebrow- "Do you allow yourself such unshakeable certainty in me because you truly believe I am destined to help you." I paused, wetting my lips. "Or is it because you're so desperately afraid of being wrong?"

He was a man that found great entertainment in being challenged, apparent now that I could see his bemused expression. I suddenly felt like I was a rat coming face to face with an incredibly sinister cat.

I was used to being the cat.

"You wouldn't be trying to use word weaving to scare me, would you now?" Eli had dropped back into his lazy, languid state as if my bad attitude had somehow relaxed him. His shoulders sat less rigid but did little to make him less intimidating. "Because I should tell you, I'm not afraid of anything."

I scoffed, picking at a small chip on the surface of the table. "People who say that are usually more afraid than most."

"Those people must not be like me," he said calmly.

"I don't think anyone is," I muttered shortly, feeling sour.

Disheartened from feeling too small in the face of evils that were too big and being asked to change things that seemed unchangeable, I felt myself fizzing out.

Eli was wrong.

I was not incredibly powerful- neither in life nor death. Cowardly in different ways, but a coward, nonetheless. Always hiding in shadows and feeding off of other people.

Killing people did not mean I was brave.

"Valencia?" He waited until I look at him, the glow from the light highlighting the peaks of his face. "I don't think anyone's much like you either."

I had said mine like an insult and him as a compliment, but somehow he seemed to irritate me more than mine had irritated him.

"Why are you trying to mess with me?" I asked tightly. I could have been nicer to him, but something in him made me think that if I gave him an inch, he'd take a mile.

It was a good thing I was never all that polite.

"Have people really never been genuinely kind to you?"

"Stop acting like that's what you're being," I said, clenching my fist into a tight ball beneath the table. "This was never about me. I'm of use to you, that's all." I pushed back at him as he waved on his high horse.

He rolled a sharp shoulder in a ragged jab. "Sure, but you care for what I'm trying to do too. So that makes it a common passion, does it not?"

I wanted to fight. Damn it, I missed the fight. I missed the swell in my chest, and the thundering of my heart dropped it. What were we even doing? Sitting here, stewing in hope, like any of it mattered. Like two idiot kids would be able to make a difference. Wouldn't it just be easier to accept the way things were? Keep our heads down, make a decent living? They had all the power, and us none, yet I was supposed to forge ahead into battle with a system so great it had swallowed all of us whole?

What if nothing changed?

Caleb's voice was a whisper. *Just because we're scared, Cia, it doesn't mean we can't try. We can always try.*

Always.

If it was all true, then Caleb was in trouble. Massively. And what kind of loyalty could I claim to have to someone if I couldn't even try to uncover the truth?

"So," I hesitated, swallowing thickly. "Where do we start?"

As if he'd merely been waiting for me to ask, he retrieved a sizeable charcoal-coloured binder from the second crate at his feet. It made a loud thud when it hit the table.

"Here."

15

Funeral For a Lost Boy

There was no appropriate alluding to Eli's abhorrent devotion to this task. He had mentioned his research with the same easy nature he'd approached nearly everything else- not quite laziness, but a sort of casualness that misled intention rather than adequately informed. I had been sucked into a whirlwind of his doing, surrounded now by books and studies on something I'd just began to peek at again myself. As I had often found myself doing in the last few days, I wondered what it would be like to believe in something with certainty and void of all doubt. I had once been like that, hadn't I? I rubbed my hand at the length of bone between my breasts, coaxing at the immovable pressure. Full of dreams, ideals.

Morals.

The thought had my jaw tightening in shame, but I was careful to mask it from Eli, turning my face down to the binder in front of me.

The book he'd plopped in front of me was a condensed version of, what I could gather, only the most essential information from the scraps of paper around the room. The chaotic organization that was Eli's apparent brand meant pages coordinated with obscurely marked tabs poking out from either side of the flaying sheets.

Eli drifted to my side of the table and took control of the binder, flipping right past the first section and diving into the second tab.

"The first part is mostly summarizing." He explained, even though I knew I'd end up leafing through it the second he left the room. "Shorthand for all the other notes I have, so I know what I'm missing."

"Obviously, because how could you tell otherwise?" I asked, but it came out sarcastic.

He sent me a quizzical expression, his ordinarily bright eyes fogged over. "Yeah. Sorry, I know everything's a little all over the place. I should've been more prepared to show this to you."

"Yeah." I nudged him gently, hoping to smooth the worry lines from the skin of his forehead. My sharpness up to this point had been unintentional, but it had thrown him off all the same, and I surprisingly felt a small rush of regret. A whispering voice at the back of my head asked, *'why do you care?'*, but I shoved it aside and treated him as though I would have treated Cal. "Get it together."

To my relief, the lines dissolved into his bronzed skin, offering me a weak smile. "Working on it. Remember- I haven't slept in two days. I've earned a certain level of fool status."

From Eli's place above me, the current topic of discussion, his head, was only a few inches above mine and less than a foot away, allowing me to study his face in more depth. Bent over the book, his eyelashes fluttered delicately over the angry purple smudges that shadowed his eyes. His cheeks were faint and drawn.

"Are you sure you don't want to sleep first? We can go over this after?"

He shook his head slowly, his brow already knitting itself back together. "It won't take long for me to show you, and then you can look through it over the next few days in preparation."

"Preparation?" I blinked slowly as if struggling for the definition of the word.

"Yeah. You didn't think we were just going to go running into the heart of hell on some whim, did you?"

I had indeed thought that, but I wasn't about to admit it now. If Caleb were here, he would have caught the falter and clucked at my impulsivity.

"I want you to get familiar with the personnel first." He continued briskly, his tongue sounding heavy with fatigue as it struggled to wind around the words. Using his middle finger and thumb, he pinched a tab and tossed it to the side, flipping open to a blurry photograph of a slim, white-haired man with hollow cheeks. "Everything in here has been pulled from around the downtown. Sorry about the shitty quality." He grimaced. "I've gotten ahold of a camera before, but without going through the Council, there's really no way to print photos, and this is just..." He gestured at the low-quality photograph. "It's easier. Beyond that, I don't think you really need me to spell this stuff out for you."

"No. Thanks," I said, tensing when Eli turned his face towards me. His breath feathered gently against my cheek. Heart suddenly throbbing, I turned back to the book just as he straightened upwards.

"Look, I need to grab some shut-eye. I'm not going to make it if I don't." Eli laughed breathlessly, tossing the hair from his eyes. "I'll be passed out in that corner before you make it to the second page." He twisted his head to his shoulder and cracked his neck with a quiet pop, massaging the tension from behind. "Can I trust you to not make a run for it this time?"

Pausing in consideration, I fluttered the pages absentmindedly. I felt the familiar kick of cowardice, but it subsided into background noise. "I think I'm in this for real now."

Intentionally, I made no promises. He could trust me to not run during this particular nap, but I wouldn't have recommended it carrying over. The sentiment seemed to work regardless, and relief flooded his dulled eyes.

"Okay. I'll be upstairs," Eli paused at the first step, "And, Valencia?"

"Yes," I replied with an uncharacteristic amount of patience.

"Don't go outside."

That inspired a quick wrinkling of my nose. I was on the verge of voicing my displeasure when, even in his exhausted state, he managed to disappear into the shadows of the old house.

Then it was me, the binder and the quiet rattling of the lights above, whirring in a sort of lost conversation. I usually didn't mind being alone- in fact, really, I'd come to prefer it- but there was something about this place that made the hair on my arms stand up.

Shaking it off as paranoia, I indulged Eli by diving into the assigned task and began leafing through Council personnel. Gripping the edge of a handful of papers, I let them go one by one and watched the faces in the pictures switch rapidly between each other. They all looked the same to me:

same build, same height. I paused on a group of snapshots of the Senators, letting the shiver run through my body. Now that was an unnerving sight. Same forehead dip, deep-set eyes, light hair, and skin. It was like they'd all been birthed from the same brood, like a damn litter of sociopathic generals. Could've made a general policy not to engage with any pasty men with angry eyes and saved a lot of trouble.

I flicked a glance at the hallway. I would've brought that up to Eli, had he still been here.

Sighing, I focused on the thick scrawl beneath each photo.

Two Senators stared at me from the page, listed with a garbled sort of tasks that seemed, even to me, mundane and average. Higher on the pole than guards, they handled all the details and would eagerly lay it out for their executioner when asked to present the facts. Usually too damn stuffy to get their hands dirty, they often left full disciplinary action to whatever branch of guards was at the ready. It was arrogance, I imagined, that kept them from stooping to the messy, often dangerous level we skulked on. Unfortunately, even arrogance and narcissism couldn't net the weight of the aggression they carried. They'd lay on the pressure, intimidate, threaten, but I'd never even seen one of them break a sweat. But, I supposed as I rubbed a finger against the face on the paper, they didn't need to break one to fire a gun.

Exhaustion ebbed over me, more profound than physical. But they weren't predictable. I would be foolish to think as much. Some of them were as cold and in control as they seemed, like Gideon. The shudder came before I could swallow it. He was evil, pure and liquid silver in his veins. He didn't chase. He maneuvered. I believed, to this day, that if he put a mark on you, he'd find a way to kill you—no matter where you went, what you did, or who you became.

I flipped the page. There was the rod straight back of one, gliding into one of those silver vans with his blond hair gleaming from where it lay flat on the scalp. I didn't need to see his face to recognize him.

Griggs.

The laugh that exploded out of my chest was breathless and humourless. Here he was, my killer, my murderer. He existed. This was proof. I'd spent the first year of my life shaken out of sleep by the image of his flint eyes and the smile that seemed so rabid, so inhuman I'd told myself I imagined it. But of course, I hadn't. Yes, I thought, laying my hand flat on the table. Madness was capable of infiltrating the most iron of minds. Senators were proof of that, no matter how contained they were.

There was no humanity in their eyes.

Eli had cataloged the probability of two of them just at the mouth of Circumvent, and at least a group of twenty or so surrounding guards.

How much would it drain me to kill all of them? Making a small tsk sound at the back of my throat, I dismissed the idea. I could do four, maybe five people in one burst, but I usually needed at least thirty minutes before I could do anything without passing out again, and thirty minutes was more than enough time for them to send back-up.

Maybe I did need preparation. What the fuck did Eli think I could even do here? I inhaled deeply. He was insane.

I flipped past the rest of the photos- confident in my ability to determine a Senator from a guard and both from a citizen- and settled on a large chart that marked small variances of 'regeneration' times between staff. From what I could gather, it was an allotted three to five minutes every five hours. There was a single metallic cube stapled in a small, clear bag, marked 'empty regeneration capsule, e.20'. I massaged it from outside, pushing it around the bag until it strained against the thin plastic.

Magnet Regeneration was only available for people on the Council, being as it was a significantly more sophisticated practice to our Sustenance. No matter how many tokens a plate resident managed to collect, they'd never be able to get some of those.

They were supposed to enhance performance by teasing the electrolytes in your brain using magnetic energy. Guards tossed it in their mouths like candy and left it clanking around against their teeth. I tried to stop hearing it, but it was thrust into my brain like a song that wouldn't end.

The memory started like an ebbing tide just below my ear, pressing until my eardrums were home to the sound of rushing water. Clack, clack, clack.

I dropped my face into my hands and closed my eyes as if slipping a veil over them could free me from what they'd already seen. It never worked.

Dirty grey pavement.

That was always the first thing I saw. I was crouched above a crack in the cement, poking a skinny coil down the middle when I heard the bang.

Panicked, I jumped to my feet, teetering on legs too gawky.

"Cal?" I whispered, forcing the name past frozen lips, "Cal, are you there?"

I was supposed to be the watch-out. The older kids never wanted me to go on a run with them. Not yet. I wasn't old enough, they said. Not experienced enough. It didn't matter I'd been to the deep downtown alone three times as many times as they had. I knew what it was really about. It's 'cause I was a girl.

Cal told me not to fight with them about it. We were lucky to have them.

We had needed a group since we lost the Cardinals. The Cardinals had been my favorite. I scowled as I thought of it, keeping my eyes on the barren, winding road in front of me. Stupid kids weren't quick enough, so Cal and I were on our own, again, until the Jockeys picked us up. But they were all old- Jeremy was almost fifteen- and boys! I liked the Cardinals better because Zoe and Jenu actually let me do stuff.

I rubbed at a scrape on my leg and accidentally pulled the side of a scab up, releasing a trickle of blood down my calf.

Oh, jeez. I tapped my pockets for the signature lump that meant stashed tissues, but they were empty. I wondered if Cal had any in his jacket. I wasn't confident enough to ask Jeremy or anything of the other boys, not yet.

"Cia! Cia!"

I turned my head towards the sound, unable to entirely make out what Caleb was screaming beside my name. He was the only one to ever call me that. I saw the two leaders rounding the corner before anything else. Their long, muscular legs tore up the dirt, leaving a cloud of dust and grime in the air. "Run!" The taller one screamed. I'd already forgotten his name. Robbie? Ruby? Reuben? "Run!"

I itched to make a run for it, but I couldn't leave without Cal. "Come on," I whispered, ignoring the two boys that motored by me with fierce determination. "Come on, Cal."

Cal rounded the corner, not a second later, thick coiled curls sticking to the dripping sweat on his forehead. He was dragging the smaller kid, Kairo, behind him, who was crying.

"Come on, guys!" I yelled, my voice trembling. They weren't far from the left alley now; we could dart in there and hide. Had they taken something from a merchant? I strained to see what was in the carry-out bag, but it was blocked by Cal's body. Idiots. If they had brought me in, we would've been in and out in a fraction of the time, and no one would have even noticed I was there. I resisted the urge to scowl as Cal neared me. "What did you do?" I asked incredulously.

He hooked his free arm around my waist and pulled me down with him behind a set of trash cans, desperately trying to shush Kairo, whose wails were becoming more pronounced with his heaving breaths.

"What the fuck?"

"Shut up," Cal warned, his eyes dark. He peered through a gap between the cans.

"I don't see anything," I said impatiently. I was always impatient. It was Cal's least favourite thing about me, he said. Always.

"Shut up, Valencia."

The use of my full name stuffed my throat. Cal never used it unless he was dead serious, like if I didn't stop what I was doing rightinthatinstant that something awful would happen. I lapsed into silence, pushing Cal's arm off of me to peer around the other side of the can.

We waited with bated breath for something to round the corner, our palms gathering sweat and our lungs tight, but nothing came.

"You think it's clear?" Kairo asked, his voice trembling. It was hard to believe he was only a year younger than me. I raised my upper lip in a sneer. Little Kairo Karmich couldn't handle anything worth a damn.

"Not yet," Cal said evenly, his tone never faltering. He always sounded so damn sure of himself. "They may be trying to trick us."

"They? As in who?" I asked, but I mostly already knew the answer.

"Council dudes," Cal said, pulling the zip tie shut on his pack. I caught a glimpse of a small, spherical container just before the gaping opening closed beneath his hand.

"Why are they chasing you, Cal? What did you do?" I reached over, ripping the bag from his grasp. He moved to protest, but I was faster.

I was always faster.

I wrenched the small container out of the hole, blocking Cal with my back, though he had stopped fighting for the evidence. "What the fuck is this?" I pushed the release mechanism, and the lid shot open. Inside, four metal cubes were sitting on a black plastic platform.

"Oh, Caleb," I breathed out, my chest tight. "How stupid are you?"

Irritated, Caleb snatched the container back from me. "You wouldn't understand."

"I wouldn't understand?" I spat the words out like they were foul in my mouth. "Why? Because I'm just some stupid girl?"

Caleb shrugged. Kairo wheezed.

"Don't be like that, Cia. You're good at like, other stuff."

"Other stuff?" I raised to my feet, incensed into stuffy anger. "Other stuff? What do you think we did for all that time before the stupid Jockey boys picked us up?"

"Keep your voice down," Cal hissed, but I did not want to be anywhere near him anymore.

He was supposed to be my friend. My family.

I shifted positions in the time it took Kairo to draw in another breath to cry again. I was moving across the road, low and quick when the van bulleted down the street. The windows were tinted nearly black, but I knew that the man behind the wheel had his gun out of his holster and his eyes set.

I somersaulted off the street, narrowly avoiding the collision. The brakes squealed as the guard pulled to a stop, and I could hear Kairo's growing whimpers from where I had wedged myself. Sandwiched in between two buildings, I was waving for Cal to cross behind the vehicle, knowing that if the two of them stayed low, they'd be out of the view of the mirrors hanging from the side of the doors.

He didn't look at me.

It took me less than a minute to figure out where his gaze had landed, and if I knew anything about anything, I knew Caleb. His dark eyes were trained on the back of the guard- some tall, wiry guy who couldn't have been all that much older than Jeremy- and his fists were clenching and unclenching as he pushed Kairo behind him. Caleb raised himself onto his haunches and set himself into a runner's stance, reaching behind him for the Swiss army knife he had tucked in his back pocket.

"No!" I yelled out, dragging myself into the view of the Councilman. My teeth smashed together as I barrelled forward, low and hard, and I tasted the grit and blood in my

mouth. He fired a shot and narrowly missed the back of my head. Caleb lunged, clinging to his back like a skinny monkey man, all elbows and knees and hard edges. The Councilman lifted his arms and struck a gnarly hand into Caleb's curls, fisting and twisting his beautiful hair around his knuckles until Cal's mouth twisted into anguish.

I danced in one spot, my feet itching to bolt. Coward.

I charged forward, leaping at the Councilman's lower half, fighting to keep his arms at his waist as his finger stretched for the trigger of the gun. I wrapped a thin arm around his elbow and strained for the sound of a crack, but his broad bicep was too strong for me, and he began to fire shots wildly while Cal struggles to nick his neck with the blade.

Sweat dripped into my eyes and my mouth, slipping sloppily into my mouth and leaving traces of salt on my cracked lips.

The gunshots were making my ears ring, and though my ears were not strangers to loud bangs and screaming fear, the sound was eating away at my sanity in steady bites. One, two, three, four. I saw the knife at the Councilman's throat-a fleeting opportunity of bare and white flesh exposed to the winking sunlight.

"Do it, Cal," I pushed my hand up against the bridge of the Councilman's nose, straightening the column of his throat.

Caleb's hand hesitated. Mystified, I gaped at his faltering face—Caleb the great, Caleb the brave. Caleb the- the Councilman wrenched free from my grasp, sending my body slamming into the dusty ground. The force of the impact rattled my bones and left me in shock.

Cal slid the knife across the length of his throat, but the weapon caught in the uneven flesh as the Councilman turned his head, breaking the stroke and knocking Cal off. Blood was spurting from the wound like water from a broken faucet, and the Councilman stumbled drunkenly, firing off a few more final shots before crumbling to the ground below him.

"Holy shit," I said finally, staring at the body in front of us.

"Yeah," Caleb replied, bracing himself on his straightened arms behind him. "Holy shit."

"That was insane." Terror was an all too unfriendly visitor pressing against my chest.

"Kai, did you friggin' see that?" Cal called out, his juvenile masculinity pulling ahead of his fright.

We both turned to look at Kairo at the same time, expecting to see our skinny, trembling friend with fat tears running down his face. There was no comparable feeling- none at all- to the sight of his limp, frail body bleeding red against the beige earth.

Kairo got hit.

Kairo got hit.

"Kai-ro," I stuttered out, his name falling just short of my lips. Kairo got hit. Kairo got hit.

Kairo laughing, Kairo with his trembling lip, Kairo chasing the train, Kairo catching moths. Kairo, Kairo, Kairo. Cal had leaped from his position and frantically pulled Kairo's clothes aside, ripping at the already torn fabric until his knuckles were dirtied with the innocent's fresh blood. I was staring at the metal cubes that had tumbled out of his tiny hand until my eyes started stinging.

"Fuck," I said, shaking my head and bringing myself back to the present world. The past was a whirlwind that did no good to stay in it. It would suck you under soon as you let it.

I pushed off from the table and began to pace, rubbing my hands on my scalp, but the harsh, gritty feeling was enough to drive me to the brink of sanity. If I had to look at one more page of text, my head was going to blow clean off.

What time was it? I glanced at the walls for a clock, but they were all bare aside from the shelves. It did seem like I had been down here forever, but I knew that focus wasn't my strong point. There were times in class that one hour had felt twice that, just because my eyes had taken to strain and my head to strife.

I laid a hand on an unopened book that sat on the table, pushing my finger along the spine. I could keep reading. Researching. I indolently flipped the front cover open, pulling my finger along the binding. When the words swam like tadpoles, I slammed it shut. Not a chance.

I crossed to the hallway and casually angled my back to the wall, fighting the unease that tickled the back of my throat.

After all that had happened, I was still afraid of having my back to monsters in dark rooms. Who was I kidding? I was the fucking monster in the dark.

Bitterly amused at the absurdity of it all, I peered into the yawning hall.

Without the smudging light of day, the old furniture and elegant wallpaper felt stale and haunted- a bitter collection the dead left behind.

"Eli," I called out.

No answer. Of course. That man was smoke when it suited him.

The wooden floors grumbled beneath my weight as I crossed into the kitchen. I'd all but ignored the understated room when I'd passed through, but now, in the soft dim light, it was remarkable in its simplicity. A smooth countertop was linked to the walls in an 'L' shape, broken up only by the old gas stove and chrome sink. The window above it was cracked open and let in a cool, crisp breeze that lifted the hairs on my arms towards the ceiling. The sight of it had me drawing a comparison to Harris' kitchen- hers with the peeling paint, crumbling plastic, and the holes in the table that she could never seem to fix or get clean no matter how hard she tried.

A transport wagon went rattling by outside, the home-made muffler shouting along with the men and screamed its way across the property line. I cringed and flinched away, the quiet moment tarnished by the dirty fingers of the outside. Idiots, breaking curfew. It was easy, too damn easy, to be disruptive and noticeable when you're the only moron outside in the span of four acres.

Idiots, I thought one more time, as I left the kitchen as I had entered it. They were just asking for trouble.

The rest of the main floor was deathly still and sealed tight against the outside world from Eli's frenzied grab to block out the windows. His cigarettes and lighter were left where they had fallen, a soft indent on the thin carpet. Impulsively, I tucked them in my pocket. Just in case.

Only the faintest humming of noise continued from outside, and I assumed the late-night riders had either ran out of momentum or realized their foolishness. Suddenly wildly envious of their careless youthfulness, I too felt the taunting call of the envelope of night. You could be anyone, do anything if you were a shadow. I bit the inside of my cheek. You could be nothing.

Remembering Eli's words, I slithered along the wall to the back door, not quite breaching the threshold but meeting the eyes of the dark and unbending night. I must have been in the basement longer than I thought.

I shifted my weight foot to foot, tossing around Eli's cryptic statement. Why wouldn't I go outside? What kind of demented security level control restricted me to one cramped house?

Ah, fuck it, I thought. I wasn't about to wait around for a chaperone.

But you promised, a quiet voice nagged from the back of my mind.

Snorting derisively at myself, I grabbed my cloak off the mid-table and tied the knot tightly around my neck, flipping the hood up. It was familiar, reassuring: the weight against the back of my neck, the feel of the coarse fabric brushing against my ears. Indulging myself, I turned my face into the fabric, breathing in.

Harris had brought me to the Service Shop herself. I sighed, wading through the tinted nostalgia. It had been a long way from the floppy hooded sweatshirt tossed on me in the empty sewer. Smelled a lot better too. It was the first and last time Harris had brought me there.

The door rasped as I pushed the screen panel open and slapped against the doorframe's loose hinges.

My breath caught, and I left my hand limply on the handle of the door.

Tiny bright lights twinkled brilliantly from a small circle in the vast blanket of darkness, glimmering like crystals swimming beneath the dark ocean floor.

Slack-jawed in reverence and confusion, I stepped off the porch, craning my neck to get a better view. What was that? Looked too high and far away to be light from the Centre. Could it be a cluster of BirdsEye drones?

No. I shook my head. That would be stupid. They wouldn't be grouped together like that. They couldn't possibly be stars. Not possible. Not like this.

I hugged my arms close to my body to fight the chill of the night and turned my attention back to our level plane. Small winking lights wavered in the near distance, and I briefly compared them to those in the sky. Satisfied that they were different hues, I drifted into the shadow of the porch, pulling the cloak around me. Those lights I was familiar with- flashlights.

For a moment, there was only the sound of my shallow breathing. Then I heard voices vibrate from behind the blinks.

There were few laws on the Plate the Council actively enforced. For the most part, it was anarchy. You could get away with murder if you wanted. I would know.

But you could not openly break curfew.

In the seventy-third year, when Hartwell drew up the original treaty to allow settlers to make homes, the first condition on the page was not to disturb the upper class. Silence by dusk. The men and women in the Pod could not and would not know we were out here.

I squinted at the men whooping from inside their motorized wagon. They didn't seem too concerned by that rule, as they slowly rolled to a stop beside a stack of hay bales facing the road. The closer they got, the more aware I was of their adolescence. Made up of gangly limbs and soft jawlines, they stumbled in bodies not yet wholly theirs. Bottles clinked against each other melodically as they shifted them out of rucksacks.

I twirled the cigarette I had stolen from Eli's coat pocket between my fingers while I watch them. I hadn't decided if I was going to light it or not. If I did, it would be the last one I ever had. I had to promise myself that.

Their frumpy, unmarked clothes were those of the sustenance handlers, dusted from a day's work. I knew the token they earned today would be laying heavy in their pocket right about now. As if on cue, the boy nearest to the haybale rubbed a palm against the flap on the side of his cargo pants.

Making sure it's still there. I scoffed quietly, slipping the cigarette between my lips. So naive and predictable. You don't keep that shit on you. Ever.

I cupped the end of the smoke and flicked on the old gas lighter, hovering it above the tip until it lights.

The first drag was horribly bitter and rubbed salt in my lungs, but I held my cough in. I wasn't a weakling. The second wasn't much better, but I eventually found a degree of inhalation that worked. God, it was putrid. The taste was borderline acidic. How I used to do this on the regular was a mystery.

I'd taken my eyes off the boys for only a second, but when I look back, they had roamed into the broad, empty plain and were tossing around a ball. I was just beginning to wonder if the rules in the North were different when Eli's neighbour's door opened. Thinking he was merely drawn to discover the source of the late-night noise, I pulled myself further into the shadows and puff, puff, puffed tiny grey clouds of smoke that disappeared into the deep night.

Without a hitch in his step, the man straightened his hat and sauntered across the road, leaving his fingers tucked lightly in his belt loops. The hushed notes of an old tune were eerily whistled as he neared the boys.

"Hey boys," He drawled out. His voice was lower than I expected. It rumbled like rushing water. Peculiar, but there were a lot of peculiar things around here.

I took another drag as the boys gather around each other in a haphazard crescent.

"What's it to you, old man?"

I rolled my eyes. Always so combative. Human beings were such inherently disorderly creatures.

"Go back inside," The taller one sneered, squaring his shoulders in a failed attempt at bravery. "Ain't nothing out here that concerns you."

The neighbour removed his round spectacles from his face and brought them to his shirtfront, where he gripped the hem and began to polish the glass.

"You're being awfully loud, son, and I do believe that concerns me."

"You can't just shut your damn window like everyone else' round here?" The tow-headed one gestures widely at Eli's unlit home.

"You're breaking the law." There was something I didn't like about the way he was talking, though why I couldn't be sure. The tone was an alive thing, something slick and limbless, slithering and winding, slow only until it decided not to be.

"Oh, come on," the front boy stepped towards him, fists clenched at his sides. "No one cares about the law around here. Look around you. There ain't no one out here for miles that gives a damn about Jebediah's stupid rules."

The neighbour chuckled, returning his glasses to his face and swiping the brim of his hat. "That's where you're wrong." Unperturbed by the boys' angry vibrato, he stepped closer, so close their noses almost touch. "I care."

Catching the whim of the upcoming drama, I tossed the cig to the ground and crushed it with my foot.

"No one gives a damn what you think."

"Yeah, get the fuck outta' here," the young one echoed.

Not wanting to be a voyeur of what was bound to be a fight, I slipped back inside. I was dusting off my shoes when Eli appeared in the kitchen entrance.

"You were outside," he said, his voice low and heavy.

"Yeah." I shrugged out of my cloak and draped it on the back of a chair, guiltily tucking my hands in my pockets. "Just wanted some air."

Eli watched me silently, his eyes nearly as dark as the sky outside.

"It wasn't a big deal," I continued, still leaving one ear cocked for the altercation outside. Rule two of the street. Know the danger.

"It is," he said forcefully, drifting to my side. "Who's out there?"

"I don't know, man. Just some kids."

The lights from their flashlights bobbled through the windowpane. Eli pushed me aside, squinting outside. "Who else?"

"Nobody, they're just being stupid."

"Who else?" He asked, this time his voice a deep rumble.

"The guy who lives next to you. He was giving them shit for violating curfew or something. Looked like the kids were looking for a fight."

I heard the first shot just before the last consonant left my lips. I was about to turn back to the door when Eli grabbed me, dragging me down into a crouch behind the counters. Kairo's blood-stained tunic flashed so violently into my brain that I was blinded by it.

"What are you doing?" I peeled my top lip back, sneering at his iron grip. "Let me go. I'll even the playing field." I pulled again. He did not release. "Eli, they don't stand a chance alone. They're just idiot kids. I don't know who the fuck that guy was, but he wasn't one of us."

"That's enough, Valencia."

When the second shot sounded, I shoved at Eli in a bid to free myself. They were stupid, idiot kids, but they didn't deserve to die without a fair shot. They didn't. Kairo swam back into my mind, pale and dusted against the ground. Too weak to protect himself, too small for a world so hungry.

I pushed against Eli's chest, twisting my arm from him, and made a line for the door. I was able to see another van pulling up before Eli wrapped an arm around my waist and pulled me back.

"So much for caring about the kids, huh, Eli?" I spat out, digging my fingers into his forearm until I knew it was hurting him. I hated being held like this. I hated it. There was a memory biting at me, something I didn't want to think about. It was bile in my throat, fire in my gut, acid on my skin. My heart was pumping words into my brain. *Free, free, free, free.* "Guess you're not the fucking saviour you think you are."

"We can't help them now, for God's sakes, shut up."

I watched the neighbour crank open the back doors through the window above the sink, calling twice for help until someone exited the front seat. The two men grabbed the limp bodies and threw them in the back, the image numbing and humbling me.

I was still seething as the van pulled out and whistled away down the street, leaving only tire tracks and no hint of the chaos and destruction it had just brought in its midst.

Eli loosened his grip now, letting me sprint out onto the porch. I stared into the dark street, willing the van to return. Willing for it to come back and be a channel for the anger that was now itching for a fight. When it didn't, I whirled on my heel and stomped back into the kitchen, fury a fire in my chest.

"Why did you do that?" I asked, spitting venom. "How could you do that?"

Kairo, Kairo, Kairo. Weak and stupid and too damn delicate for this world. I suddenly and violently wanted to cry. It was humiliating.

Eli had collapsed in one of the chairs, resting his head on one of his hands. "There was nothing that could've been done."

"Are you kidding me?" I slammed my hand on the table near his head. "I thought you were supposed to be the good guy."

He rubbed the bridge of his nose. "Valencia. It would've been much too big of a risk. Those kids would have died or disappeared either way. The only difference would be that you would be in the back of that van too."

I snorted without humour. "I can't-."

"Die," Eli finished, nodding his head. "But I can guarantee you would have been taken all the same. Men like him never work alone. It's not just one enemy you're up against. The enemy isn't always just the guy in the field. It's the hundreds rallying behind him."

"You make excuses just so you don't have to think about what that choice makes you," I whispered, not trusting myself at full volume. "Those kids deserved someone on their side."

"Valencia," he said, exasperated, but I had heard enough. The anger was greater than the both of us now, and it wrapped around my body, squeezing until my eyes felt like they might've popped from the pressure.

"You're no better than they are," I snapped out, whipping my cloak from the table and heading to the column of stairs.

He hadn't shown me the upstairs. The fact halted me on the bottom steps, my foot hovering in the air. Did he not want me up there? I brushed it off, forcing the chip off my shoulder and stampeding up the stairs. I couldn't be near him right now. I didn't care whose house it was. I needed to be as far away as possible without breaching curfew conduct. We saw what happened when people didn't follow shit. Tossed in the back of a van like sacks of meat.

Kairo's gap-toothed smile pushed back in my mind, and I gritted my teeth against the tears. I knew the difference. I wasn't confusing it. I wasn't.

I used the flat of my hand to bash open the upper hallway's first door and found myself faced with a room full of boxes and scraps. Making a sound of frustration, I left the door swinging open and stomped to the next.

When I found a room with a lumpy mattress and a lopsided dresser, I dropped onto the bed and stared at the ceiling while tears burned unshed in my throat.

No, it wasn't right.

None of it was right.

16

The Neighborhood of Death and Misdeed

The next day started slow- painfully so. I woke up on the same broad, bumpy bed I'd finally surrendered myself to sleep on, mourning strangers that I'd never know, in the same clothes I'd worn the day before. I wiggled my toes in my shoes. Great.

Yesterday's events started coming into focus, pushing my hazy sleep fog out of the way with extended arms. I had acted foolishly. I knew that. I had confused my past with the present, which only made me feel more stupid.

Too restless to stay in one spot for long, I left my perch to wander back to the washing room and use the shower, which I found in an even worse state than the last I had used. It released only the most pitiful of trickles of freezing, grey water that did little to wake me up from my crusty-eyed, creaky-bodied state.

The glimpse I took in the mirror did not bring mental repose, as most of the bruises from my alley scuffle had only become worse with time, rearing their ugly heads as they fought their way to fruition.

Cranky and quickly moving to irritated, I slipped back upstairs. I had failed to bring a change of clothes, so the musky shirt and pants were clinging desperately to my skin like plastic wrap.

Garbage day. Garbage, garbage day.

Feeling foul, I toed my newly minted bedroom door open, surprised to find a platter carefully sat at the end of the bed. The neatly plated sustenance was fried to golden, speckled with black marks of seasoning and a shimmering powder on top.

Too hungry to be cautious, I dropped onto the windowsill and ate it from there, sipping at the tepid tea in the chipped mug and staring out the window. Eli had left no note, but I was sure the gesture was a sort of peace offering.

It was nice, really, but unnecessary.

I stared at the black smudge on the opposite side of the road where the van's tires had burned the tarmac.

What would I have done? I leaned my head against the pane of glass and let my chest swell to capacity with each breath.

Chase the van down, rip the heads off those grunt workers and make them choke on their pistols? What good would it do?

Eli was right. Those boys were dead whether I'd chased after that car or not.

Fuck. I opened my eyes. I was wrong. I hated being wrong.

Deciding I owed him an apology, albeit a stiff one, I carted my dishes downstairs- deliberately avoiding the weakened steps that would creak beneath my weight.

When I didn't find him in the kitchen, I checked the backyard and the front porch.

"Eli," I called out, spooked by the way my voice echoed in the house. It was deceptively hollow, even with all the furniture and historical knickknacks taking up space.

I checked every other room in the house- all still and untouched, like a museum of a dead man- before wandering into the drafty study. This time, I'd entered the frigid box prepared, a patterned quilt around my shoulders like a shield against the brisk air.

I plunged back into the texts with more reverence than the night before, pouring over the neatly scrawled notes and meticulously recorded anecdotes.

Child after child, neighbourhood after neighbourhood. Dead ends. All of them. Kids we'd seen at the Institute, kids we knew like the back of our hands- yet not a single person could claim knowledge of them being taken in the first place. And none of them ever returned.

It was, inexplicably, fascinating.

Of course, we all knew about it- Claiming Night started as the third Thursday of every month and had been the same for decades. It was a promise hung over every family's head, just waiting for the desperate to get desperate enough. Force their kid to stick out for all the wrong reasons. They really didn't need to try so hard. I knew that now, after being on the inside.

You work hard; you get snatched. You're disobedient; you get snatched. The only safe way from the Council's claws was to be nothing at all. A lifeless, figureless smudge, drifting until you accepted your designated placement and began your training on the eve of your tenth birthday.

It was common knowledge that over half the youths were claimed. Everyone talked about it. Everybody knew about these damn kids.

But when it came down to it, not a single person could name or recognize one of them.

Not one.

~~~~~~~~~~

I was buried in an old, dusty book when Eli popped his head through the doorway.

"Just letting you know, I'm going to grab dinner soon."

"What?" I sat up in the chair, letting forgotten papers fall and scatter from my lap. "What time is it?" I foolishly scanned the walls for the clock I knew wasn't there.
~~~~~~~~~~

Eli glanced at his watch. "Just hit four."

"Oh," I dropped back, tucking unruly wisps of hair behind my ears. "Still early."

Eli crossed his arms over his chest, blocking off most of the strange t-shirt graphic from my view. "Sure, but I've got to make a run into town and swap out some tokens." He shot a hand into his pocket and jingled the loose change. "It's been a while since I've been home, so there's not a lot of food around."

"Well, I..." I paused, cleared my throat. I could be polite, damn it. Didn't Harris spend plenty a night trying to teach me that very thing? "I appreciate you gifting me with some this morning, even more, knowing that."

He shrugged. "It was nothing. Anyway, I just wanted to let you know I was leaving so you wouldn't think I'd abandoned you here."

Like you already did this morning, I thought but didn't say.

"Okay, thanks." The silence ebbed on.

"I wanted to apologize."

Eli lifted an eyebrow in his strange and sharp way, keeping his eyes steady and direct on me. Since he said nothing, not even a prompt, I bumbled on.

"I was upset, and I acted irrationally. I didn't expect to be affected the way that I am by all this, and I guess it brought up some stuff from when I was kicking it on the streets," I said, but my chest felt tight. "You were right. It would have been a much bigger risk than reward."

A whisper of a smile played across his lips. "I certainly wasn't expecting that from you."

I sucked in a sharp breath. "I can be mature."

"And wrong," he commented, his eyes infuriatingly beginning to twinkle as they did when he baited me.

"Yes, Eli. I already said you were right. Mostly. Mostly right. There was nothing we could do." I heaved a sigh and began to organize the papers that had fallen off me onto the floor. I hated having to humble myself. It was a new pill I'd have to learn to swallow if I was to work with others again.

"So..." Eli drew out the 'o' in a goofy drawl, "You want to come downtown with me?"

I blinked slowly, "To the square?"

I tried to mentally calculate the distance to the downtown off the top of my head but didn't have enough geographical awareness to situate where Eli's neighbourhood was on the plate.

"No. We've got a swapper out by the town."

I gripped my stack of papers tightly against my lap.

"Registered?"

Registered Swappers mandated by the Council had access to the full extent of City Centre amenities. They were glorified price gougers. It cost nearly triple what it did to get anything at the square to have it close to your house.

Yet another thing to force us closer and closer to the Centre. *The belly of the beast.*

"Unregistered."

I made a noncommittal sound in my throat and raised from my perch. "That's some risky business. If you got caught..."

I didn't need to finish that statement. We knew what happened. We all knew what would happen. Disobeying the system was one thing. Frauding it was another.

"We won't be. He knows what he's doing. Hank's an expert," Eli said conversationally. "People've been doing this business down here for as long as City Centre's been running."

The statement made me uneasy, though I couldn't put my finger on why. "No one's caught on to the guy with a hundred tokens in his pocket every day?"

"Nah," Eli shook his head to accompany his verbal dismissal. "There's too many of 'em. It's hard to prove, in any case."

I hesitated for another second before moving towards the yawning door.

"Alright. I'll come. I think if I spend another minute in here, my eyes are going to fall out of my head."

Eli raised himself off the frame, bringing his body to partner mine. "Do you not do a lot of reading normally, Valencia?"

I scowled, gently shoving past him to start to walk through. "Why do I feel like you use my name to mock me?" I asked, annoyed. "And I read, plenty, thanks."

"I can't tell you why you feel what you feel." His voice carried down the hallway in a low echo. "Maybe you care too much about what I might think of you?"

At the top of the hallway, I resisted the urge to shut the door in his face to prove I didn't. "I don't care what you think of me. You don't have to like me to get the job done." I said once in the main sitting area.

"Oh," Eli rocked back on his heels and shot me a quick grin. "But I do."

"What?" I knitted my brows together and warped my face into an expression of distaste.

"Like you," he said, beginning to rummage in the side desk, apparently searching for something. "More than I thought I would," he muttered before uttering out an 'aha!' and whirling around with a set of keys on a thick chain.

"We're taking the car?"

"Oh, no." We crossed to the front door, where he unbolted the locks. "Can't make you spoiled, can we? We're doing it the old-fashioned way."

I sent him a dry look, crossing the threshold into the evening air. "With our legs."

"Yep." The door slammed shut with a solid thud. I didn't bother turning around to watch him as he turned all the locks. "With our legs."

~~~~~~~~~~

The walk wasn't as bad as I thought it would be. Eli's area was a lot quieter than those near the Centre, and nearly everyone seemed to mind their own business. We were stopped
~~~~~~~~~~

only once by a beggar, and even they scurried off after a gentle shake of the head. When I asked Eli about it, he shrugged the lack of buskers as just a note of the neighbourhood, stating that barely anyone had enough for themselves, let alone enough to share. You'd have to go closer to the Centre to find inhabitants with heavy pockets and a willingness to part with their coin. I'd remembered sharing the same viewpoint but reversed.

I had commented that they were hard to come by anywhere and earned an evasive grunt from Eli, putting a temporary hold on my stream of questions.

It wasn't until we reached the bridge that I asked another.

"Where do you get all your tokens?" I asked as our feet sloshed into a sludgy muck at the edge of the boardwalk. I could only assume- hope- that the consistent water stream was a leak from the Spillout.

"Where does anyone?"

A question for a question. Damn near every time.

"From what I've seen, you don't seem to take much seriously, which leaves less than a few employable options."

Eli waited for me to reach the top of the incline. "Oh, you mean like an assassin?"

I scowled and turned away from his offered hand and clambered the rest of the way myself, only slipping slightly when my foot careened against a slick, flat rock. "I hate that term."

"No reason to put a bow on ugly just to lie to yourself," he pointed out.

The familiar trickle of annoyance shot up my spine, but I worked to keep the flames at bay. I was beginning to realize that Eli pushed me the most when he needed a distraction.

God, I was both the rattle and the baby.

"I know what role I play. Do you?"

Eli's eyes were on the stretch of road in front of him, darting from one side to the other. "Of course, I do,"

I waited for a beat, then pressed a little harder. "So, why-."

"Fuck's sakes, Valencia. Please, shut up for a second."

I was about to snarl back when I caught movement in the shadows of the buildings. The bodies moved like cosmic energy, pushing and pulling off each other in a dark magnetism. I could make out only one man with any success, and the lip of his cap hung low, shading strange and ghoulish features. He was too thin, too crooked, and he clung to the crumbling side of the building like a spore.

After him, I began to pick up on the others milling about in the dwellings of the haunted town.

There must have been at least twenty in the first ten feet. The open street, however, remained quiet and empty save for Eli and me.

Two black iron trash cans had been pushed together to block off the doorway to what used to be 'Pincadilly's Eats' but the sign was faded and worn, losing the last letter to time's hungry, wanting mouth.

It would seem the only things left in the open were boxes for the dead.

I was caught up in the patterns the blackened factory soot had made on the windows and narrowly missed Eli slinking away into one of the alleys. Because I had no explicit invitation, I merely halted my exploration and focused the study on the buildings closest to me.

I was no stranger to the concept of the loss of small, independent businesses. I had missed most of it because once they started going, they went fast. Once the Council seized everything from twine to shiny plastic, selling anything was out of the question. The service storefronts stayed open only moderately longer, as there were always things others couldn't- or wouldn't- bring themselves to do.

I crouched in the dirt and pried a flat tin sign out of the ground. It took only a few brushes to clear the writing from the dry dust. Killarna's Seams.

Clothing. Of course. I glanced at my plain black pants, now spattered with flecks of mud. The Council seized control of that, too, once they realized patterns and graphics meant originality and freedom. I traced the raised lettering and checked the backside for a date but found nothing. I wondered what happened to Killarna, and if she had lost her life when she lost everything, or if she had become a factory worker, too. Slaving away to the old crank machine.

"Alright."

I straightened at the sound of Eli's voice, dropping the sign guiltily into the sand, not unlike a child caught pawing through their mother's precious jewelry coffer.

"Done?" I asked incredulously, instinctively seeking a glimpse of the trader. "Already?"

"Yeah," Eli said casually, impervious, or merely apathetic to my current anxious state. He raised the bottom-heavy bag to eye level, swaying the contents. "It's good stuff, too. Hank says some of it's flavoured."

Even his displaced sense of coolness was weak against the childlike excitement that wiggled its way to the surface.

"No way," I said, but the tone was more reverent than dismissive. Sustenance usually tasted like one thing, and that one thing was often the absence of taste- a little bit like the way the back of your tongue tastes when you first wake up.

It cost next to nothing for the Council to add a flavour- Caleb had known a guy who had worked in the slop-house (earning its name due to the bubbling broilers of the slimy, gloppy mess)- and the addition of flavours took merely one slight adjustment to the chemical compound. The token markup, however, was a different story. Flavoured sustenance could go for sometimes two, three times more than regular, and in much smaller packaging.

I peered at the parcel Eli was holding and felt my saliva pool at the 'smoky, salty, savoury' label on one of the cubes.

"That's wild." I poked at the rest of the bag. "You've got enough food for a whole week in there. Two, maybe, if you stretch it."

"That's the idea." He grinned childishly. "I have to treat my guest right."

He playfully bumped my hip with his. Dutifully, I tried to remain stoic and uninvolved, but the smile was creasing my face like a fold in paper.

God, it felt good. It was all I could think as we talked and laughed our way back over the sloshing boardwalk and the empty streets. It was an impenetrable moment. The darkening sky and the whispers of the night had no sway- it was just Eli and me, and a heavy bag and excited hearts.

I felt foolhardy, gloriously so, and the feeling bubbled and danced in my throat. Just two people, a knobby-kneed assassin with a black eye and too many scrapes and a dark, compelling man with hair that tumbled like black water, giggling like children who didn't know what the world was.

It was the closest to normal I'd felt since I died. Hell, since before I was even admitted to the Institute. The last time...

Caleb's face swam into my memory like a photo developing- blurry, cloudy, then sharp in the second it took me to suck in a breath. The pain was swift and fierce, striking a lit match beneath my breastbone.

"Hey, are you okay?" Eli asked, concern whispering beneath the surface of his voice.

"I'm fine," I replied tightly.

"You just stopped talking," He glanced at me warily, our childish joy dissipating like sand in water.

Truth be told, I couldn't remember the last thing Eli had said to me: the nonsensical banter was already slipping away from me, leaving me with traces of, 'Oh man, and those fake silver plates that'd leave flakes in our food' and 'After the Institute, any food seems like a delicacy'.

"No, I just..." I trailed off for a moment, taking a deep breath. "I just remembered something." *Someone.*

"Something you want to forget?" Eli probed. His eyes were direct, searching. I wondered why he asked when he looked like he could see right through me.

And forget Caleb? I swallowed thickly, watching the little explosions of dry dirt puff out from where I stepped.

Hundreds of memories raced through my brain; dark nights, sunny days, running through the flooded tunnels, our feet slapping the water, chasing our giggles as they bounced back to us. How many of those tunnels had collapsed now? How many of those were lost to the unstable environment beneath the plate? Just like Caleb and I, they could no longer exist in the way they once did, not ever.

If I didn't remember them- if I didn't remember him- the way he was in those moments, then that Caleb would cease to exist. And I wouldn't allow that.

Couldn't.

"No, just something painful to remember." I sent him a weak smile. "Didn't mean to bring the mood down."

"It's okay." He gestured towards the street in front of us, where his house waited at the end of the lane. "Good time to ruin a trip is at the end of it."

"Wow," I was taken aback. It was unnerving just how fast time went when one forgot to pay attention to its passing. "The walk there seemed so much longer."

Eli matched his pace to mine, brushing the spattering of light debris off my shoulder.

"One way always does."

I stayed quiet until the front porch, where words snuck up on me as Eli was unlocking his door.

"Do you have any remember-hurts?" I asked, my voice sounding soft and strange in my ears. I don't know why I asked. Maybe it was the softening light, and the way the streaks of the sun became delicate paint strokes, hovering on something for just a moment before they moved on. I tried to blink the blurry spots from my vision, but more danced in.

Jeez, I thought. Where was my head at?

"Don't we all?" Eli's smile was easy, but it did little to distract from his haunted eyes. He looked for a moment the way he had looked when the storm had nearly taken in the front room: entirely absent.

"Yes," I said simply, "But I wish that we didn't."

17

The Disease of Truth-Telling

I was still dizzy by the time dinner rolled around, but I was sure as I watched Eli slice the smoked cubes into a frying pan and drool pooled in my mouth that food would fix it.

I shifted in my spot on the long wooden bench and cringed as my lousy shoulder hit the wall. It annoyed me that it was there in the first place, but more so that the pain was yet to subside. That was supposed to be the good part about being dead - the fucked-up nerve endings.

"Hey, space cadet." Eli tossed a dishtowel at me, and I scarcely caught it before it was able to slap me across the face.

"I asked you three times how you wanted your sus'."

It had been so long since I'd have flavoured sustenance, I didn't even know.

"However you do yours normally is fine," I said casually, skirting around the truth.

"I would have thought kill-for-hires would naturally have a pretty sophisticated palate; with all the dough they must rake in." Eli whistled through his teeth as he stirred the bubbling food. "How much you make off a hit, anyway? Ever kill anyone important?"

The question made my stomach roll, but it wasn't anything I hadn't heard before. Once, at the Harris house, her new errand boy had barged in while I had my tea. It took him all of a minute to take in the dark cloak, the blood under my nails, and my unfriendly disposition and realize that I was the weapon. I hadn't felt much like answering any of his questions, so I left him stuttering and glopping like a fish on land. I could hardly do the same with Eli.

However, there were other ways to make him squirm.

"I'll tell you what you want to know." I smiled slowly, each tooth scrape carnivorously against my lip in the gesture. "If you tell me what I want."

Eli sent me a quizzical look from where he was scraping steaming sus' onto plates. "What?"

"I asked you earlier, in the yard. What you do for your money. You hedged."

He chuckled, dropping the plate in front of me. The faded blue placemat crumpled beneath it.

"I didn't hedge." He slid into the seat across from me, folding a napkin over his lap in a gesture so foreign to me it was absurd. "There are just things you don't do around Swappers. Talking about yourself is one of them. Those guys will do anything for a buck. They swap supplies, sure, but they're just as likely to swap information for the right price."

"Eli," I said, with more patient than I felt.

"What?" He asked, food dribbling down his chin.

"You're hedging again."

He laughed then, rich and warm.

"You're right, sorry. It's been a while since I've actually spent time with someone and been genuine about it."

That makes two of us, I thought, as he sipped from his tin cup.

"I'm actually a pretty decent Finder. That is where I get my money."

I raised my eyebrows in authentic surprise. Finders were rare. So rare, in fact, I couldn't remember a time I'd actually met one. But that was the point, wasn't it?

Finders were incredibly private, wisping people that spent every waking second cataloging you, your things, and your every move- they could find anything, from a dropped pen to a dead aunt.

They could find a needle in a haystack with their eyes closed.

Fuck, the right kind of Finder could find your specific needle in a stack of needles.

They were tireless. Conniving.

"Did somebody pay you to..." I trailed off, poking at the rapidly cooling mush on my plate. "You know, find those kids?"

'Find me?' was the question unasked on my lips.

"Not this time," he said, chewing carefully.

"So, why are you looking?"

"Nope," he waved a fork at me. "My turn."

Indignant, I took a bite of my food, and the burst of flavour immediately started taking chunks out of my sour mood. "Fine."

"Have you ever killed someone directly employed with the Council?"

I thought of the first guard when I had woken up, the one who had chased me into the alley. "Yes."

"Was it more physically difficult than killing a citizen? Did he put up a fight?"

"Mmm," I took another bite, then swished my water around in my mouth. "It wasn't anything, really. I don't have the same pain receptors that I used to. Kick me in the face, and it just pisses me off."

"That's incredible." Eli's eyes sharpened, and I could tell he was about to shoot off another inquiry, so I held up a hand.

"My turn. Are you working any other jobs while on your personal interest one?"

"No." He thought for a moment, then amended. "Well, sort of. There's a man on the street desperately looking for a lost brooch. It was his late wife's. She was murdered by a bunch of thugs, and they pillaged her body. He seems to think having the brooch will make up for the fact she's dead, but it won't. A lot of the jobs are like that. People thinking that having an item from the time will bring back that time and that person, but it never does." He shrugged, but it seemed as false and forced as his sentence had been. "Pays the bills."

"Do you ever feel bad taking money from people who barely have anything when you know it won't solve any of their problems?"

"Do you ever feel bad taking someone's life?" He tossed back. When I didn't respond, he said, "That was my question."

Did I feel bad?

I certainly had before. But there were equal times that I didn't. Sometimes I felt like the human part of me was getting smaller every day.

"Nothing is that simple."

"It can be." Pause. He was watching me so carefully. Studying me. I felt the urge to squirm, like this was no longer a friendly conversation but rather, an interrogation. "Answer the question."

I cleared my throat, unable to look at him. "I feel bad, often. Or I used to. Maybe when I first started. But I was angry.

Maybe I'm still angry, and I've just gotten so used to it that it just seems normal now." I exhaled laboriously, frustrated with the unclear explanation. "It used to feel like I was cursed, and that it wasn't my fault that people died because I carried around this curse. Now, it just feels like I'm more curse than I am human. And with that, nothing."

My monologue hung in the air like an omen, dark, and shifty. I laughed then, breathless and nervous. "Sorry if that didn't answer your question."

Eli ate slowly, focusing his gaze on the small bites. "I don't know if it did, but it might've helped me understand your perspective a little more."

He swung his eyes to mine, the amber blazing in the warm orange light, and my throat closed. I turned away, flattening the sustenance with my fork. "The answer's sufficient then," I said shakily in forced good humour.

"Yes."

"So, it's my turn."

Eli smiled, wiping the corners of his mouth with the napkin. "If you want it to be."

"Has there ever been something you just couldn't find? Something just… too far gone?" I asked but wasn't expecting the reaction. He dropped his napkin to the table and pushed the almost empty plate away. The energy in the room shifted, bubbling, and swirling around his tension.

"No," he said flatly.

Curious, and unable to help myself, I leaned forward on my elbows when he leaned back. I should have taken the apparent cues- his sharp tongue, the abrupt body language- but I pushed forward.

"Are there not things that are just too beyond for any mortal being to assess? What about when things merely waste and burn away?"

"I would never leave a job. If it burns, then I bring back the ashes." Eli stood, gathering his dishes into one stack, squashing the leftover food with his glass. He brought it to the counter but did not return to the table. I was staring at his back, dumbfounded, until I found the strength to speak.

"Sorry, did I say something wrong?"

Eli stopped his restless movements and braced a hand on the open cupboard above him, leaning his forehead on the raised forearm.

"No. I'm sorry." He chuckled softly, rolling his head to rest on his cheek and stare at me. "It's just one of those things."

I watched him from the bench, my hands gripping the edge of the table. "One of what things?"

"You know," he said, strained. "Remember-hurts."

He dropped his face back into the crook of his elbow. The stove continued to buzz, a low steady drone that remained untouched by the swell of human energy.

I moved before fully realizing I was going to, leaving the warmed bench and glided towards Eli.

What was I doing? I was never any good at any of at comforting. Still, my hands reached for him- crooked, ugly things that took more life than they ever gave. I grazed them along the tight muscles of his back, hesitating when he jerked at my touch.

He lifted his head, only slightly, but the new angle was enough to send his breath fluttering into his fallen hair and moving it like wind-chimes swaying above a doorway.

Neither of us moved, my fingertips laying on his shoulders, his head hung low and frozen in time.

Finally, I drifted my hands to his waist and wrapped my arms around his torso, ignoring the instant magnetic jolt that raced through my body as I pressed it flat against his. Cautiously, I laid my cheek against the curve of his spine, listening to the breath 'whooshing' in and out of his lungs.

I'm sorry, I thought, closing my eyes. I could feel his anguish as true as I might've felt my own. *I'm sorry*, I thought again. How strange it was to say I'm sorry and not have it be a private admission of guilt.

After another minute, I stepped back, twisting to lean on the counter next to him.

"Are you okay?"

Eli cleared his throat, pushing a hand through his hair, and darted a darkened glance at me.

"Yeah. Just... I need some air. Maybe you could, I don't know, grab that book you were reading earlier? Sorry."

And he was gone. Strange, how I'd already forgotten he could move like that. Here one second, gone the next. Struggling not to feel the sting of humiliation, I half-took his advice and stole another book from the living room.

I wasn't going to cry. I wasn't. Not for some random stranger living in a private museum. I didn't feel anything. I furiously fought the lump in my throat all the way to my self-proclaimed bedroom, and it wasn't until I shut the door behind me that a single tear spilled out.

Why was I doing this?

Torturing myself, when I knew what I was capable of. What I was meant for. These stupid hands brought no good to anyone.

I'd accepted that. I had. So why was I pushing it now? Trying to reclaim some bullshit sense of humanity when that didn't even mean anything to anyone around here anyways.

Fuck. I painstakingly wrenched the book from my clenched fist, prying the fingers off the already wrinkled spine, and tossed it to the bed.

God. Stupid, stupid, stupid. I crossed the room with aggressive paces, eating up the minimal square footage with jerky, halting movements.

How could I face him now, after humiliating myself like that? We were colleagues. Not friends. Not anything.

The moment got to me, was all. That's all. Diving too fast, too hard, into a friendship that was- and should be- no more than business.

I stopped my restless pacing and quickly dashed away the few rogue tears, twisting my hair to one side and taking a deep breath. Some soft lights, warm food, intimate conversation. It would get to anybody. He couldn't blame me for that. It had been so long since I had connected with anyone. The nostalgia of a life left was unlike any...

I pried my shoes off and kicked them into the corner, feeling a swift knock in my chest at the sight of my belongings strewn around the room. Even at the Harris house, I'd kept most of my things carefully organized by the door. Maybe some part of me had known that was all temporary.

Maybe some part of me was hoping this wasn't.

I pulled my shirt over my head, stripping down to the clinging tank. Gingerly, I pressed the sore spot on my shoulder. I hadn't bothered to redress it after my shower this morning, thinking that the fresh air would do it some good, but the damn thing looked even worse than before.

More frustrated than concerned, I moved to the mirror atop the end vanity. At its awkward angle, I was forced to raise myself onto my tiptoes to see anything. Once I did, I was able to get a good view of the stripes of blackened veins that snaked their way along the ball of my shoulder.

Impulsively, I dug my finger into the ragged hole, ignoring the queasy feeling that rushed through me as the torn flesh squelched like a muddy puddle.

I pushed in all the way to my first knuckle and tried not to gag as a smell of burning rubber floated out of the wound like a pungent cloud. While digging, I scraped something sharp and hard, and for a second, I thought it might be bone, but I could feel curved irregular edges.

Shit. I was so stupid. The bullet was still in my damn arm. Of course it was.

'Where's your head at, Val? Where's it at? The damn girl has always got her fucking head in the clouds,' Auntie bit out, Cal at her hip, tiny hands bunched in the sides of her faded apron. Watching me. Judging me.

Mentally, I tried to rebuild the cobwebs around the voice and pulled the top drawer of the vanity open. It had no place here. I wouldn't let it follow me. Pushing away crumpled paper, plastic beads, and twisty elastics, I settled only once I'd found a pair of pliers with a sharp point.

When they, too, were too thick to shove in the wound, I impatiently wiped my bloodied hands on the sides of my jeans, breathing heavily. I had to get it out, that wasn't a question. The damn thing had been eating me from the inside, and I hadn't even noticed because I could barely feel anything. Fuck. I slapped a hand on the vanity and threw down the pliers, fighting the anger that exploded like a crack of thunder. What if there was a tracker attached to that thing?

Shit. I pushed my hair back from my face, using my sweat to slick it into a shiny mane. Idiot. I tried to bring the shooter's face to my memory, but it was slippery and intangible. Could it have been a Councilman? His group definitely wasn't.

But that farmer had seemed like a plate-dweller before he'd taken out those boys.

They could be anywhere.

I had to get this thing out.

I moved to my bag that I had left hanging on the bed and flipped it upside down, dumping the contents onto the covers. Besides the one change of shirt, there wasn't much else. A dry stick of moisturizing clay, that guy's wallet from the train station (now empty), and the knife Cal had given to me for my tenth birthday when he'd thought I needed to start looking out for myself. I had been such an insolent little fuck. The memory made me smile. He'd made it almost ceremonious, in the basement bunker of what used to be an old pharmacy. The place had been ransacked virtually immediately, most people looking for a way to numb the pain, no matter how expired those old powders were. I'd been so angry with him for the suggestion that I needed something bright and shiny to tempt me to be strong. I'd whipped the knife at full speed into the back of a storage cart, where it sat, straight and unmoving. If the crate had been a man, he'd have been dead.

Caleb left in a huff. I'd stayed down there two more nights without him before I went to find him. The knife had been forgotten. Once I was back on my feet with Harris, I'd hit a mark in the same neighbourhood. Out of curiosity, or some sort of sense of nostalgia, I'd found myself wandering into the decrepit building. Other people had bunked there, until a group of people had either committed mass suicide or been slaughtered. Their blood was old and dry, coating the walls with flaking brown. It had smelt impossibly foul.

I found my knife where I left it, downstairs in the side of the old upturned wine crate. No one had taken it, so I did. It was one of my last connections to who I had been. Insolent, mouthy, cowardly. Grimly, I glanced at myself in the mirror.

Well, look at me now. Running into danger instead of away from it. Going to save your ass too, Cal. Wherever you've ended up. *Promise.*

I flicked open the blade. Though I hadn't opened it in months, the point was still as sharp as it had been the day he gave it to me, and the light caught the tip in a glimmering beam. If this didn't do it, I didn't know what would.

Moving away from the blanket- even if I was mad at Eli, I didn't need to wreck his artifacts- I braced myself back against the dresser, trying to achieve the angle where I could see the edges of the wound.

I was slicing open the bottom edge when the knock came.

"Hey, Valencia? You in there?"

I held the breath I was exhaling as if it was a secret, slipping the knife into the baggy pocket of my pants.

"I thought you were going out."

There was a soft chuckle from the other side of the wood. "Can't go far after dark."

The blood was rushing from the slice in my arm, dripping down the length of it and pooling onto the carpet. "Oh, well, I'm glad you're feeling better."

There was no reply for a moment, and I thought that he'd headed back downstairs before he said, "Can I come in? I want to talk to you."

I had my shirt pressed against the waterfall of blood, silently willing it not to go everywhere- after all, I was a guest- when I started to feel dizzy. Fuck.

"It's not a good time," I said, but my voice was thin and shaky. If he would just fuck off, I'd be able to dig this sucker out. I was sure of it.

"Are you okay?" The door was already being shoved open before I could respond, and Eli's rangy body barreling through. I watched him take in the messy room, and the blood splatter before landing on me and the crumpled t-shirt against my arm. "What the fuck is going on in here?"

Using my free hand, I rubbed my face and started to laugh, the hysteria playing into the chaos and creating a cocktail of emotion. "I promise it's not as weird as it looks."

The expression on Eli's face was bafflement and something that might've been concern, but I wanted it so badly I rejected the interpretation. "Well, it looks pretty fucking weird. What have you done to yourself?"

"I didn't do it to myself." I scowled, moving the t-shirt to show the oozing wound. The frantic blood flow had, thankfully, halted into more of a trickle. "I was shot."

"When were you shot? What?" Eli moved towards me and grabbed my arm, yanking it upwards for the light. "In here?"

"No." I pulled back but was weak against his grip. "In the alley."

"That was ages ago. You've been bleeding this whole time? How are you not dead?"

I laughed for real this time. "I am dead."

"Shut up, Val. You know what I mean. Have you been hiding this from me?"

"No, no, god. Let me explain." He was still trying to poke the wound. "Can you back off for a second and let me explain?" I couldn't think with his hands all over me.

Reluctant but obedient, Eli offered me a foot of space and let his hands swing to his sides. They were already stained red.

"I got shot in the alley by one of the men. I didn't think anything of it, but it was taking longer to heal than it typically does. My wounds would usually begin to close a few hours after they happen. I checked it out when we first got here and cleaned and redressed it. I thought it was just taking longer."

"Okay," Eli responded, but his eyes were still on my shoulder. A muscle in his jaw was jumping.

"Then I noticed these little black lines. You see them?" I pointed at the dark streaks.

"See them? How could I miss them? It looks like you've got oil under your skin."

"Thanks," I said sarcastically, scowling that I had to explain any of this, "I started poking around-."

"With your hands, I take it," he gestured at my one hand covered in small, black chunks. "That's sanitary."

"I started poking around," I began again, louder and more defiant, "And I felt something in there. So, I wanted to get it out."

Eli rocked back on his heels, pressing his tongue against the soft part of his cheek. "Using your finger, an old knife and a rusty pair of pliers?"

"It's not like any of that would kill me."

"Well, maybe, but you're giving it a damn good attempt."

Annoyed all over again, I turned my attention back to the mirror. "If that's all, I'd like actually to finish what I've started here."

Eli moved smoothly behind me and gathered my hair into the palm of his hand, pulling it to the side. He gently coaxed my hand from my arm and took it from me. "Valencia. Let me help you. Please."

The soft, humble request dried my annoyance and scraped it clean like an empty mine. I hesitated only a moment longer. "Fine," I said, but only because I could feel the feathering of his breath on my neck, and I wanted it over with.

He was gone for less than five minutes, ordering me to lean against the desk while he gathered supplies, stating that it would only make a bigger mess if I fell.

Eli clunked back in with an armful of towels, a folding chair, and an unmarked, snap-shut case with a few scuff marks on the bottom side.

"You look ridiculous," I said, smothering a snort as he stumbled through the door like a drunken horse.

"Happy to know you're amused instead of annoyed by me right now." He proudly popped the chair open next to the bed, dropping the towels onto the padded seat. "Does that mean we're friends again?"

"We'll see how this goes." I eyed the set up suspiciously. "What are the towels for?"

He draped two on the bed and gestured for me to come over. "For you to sit on."

"I thought that's what the chair was for."

"Chair's for me. Sickly gets the bed. Everyone knows that."

"Oh, excuse me," I said, rolling my eyes, "I didn't know you were experienced with medical care."

"Gotta do what you gotta do." Eli waited for a beat, but when I didn't move from my perch, let out a sigh. "Can you just come here and sit down?"

"I don't know what you've got in that case there." The dull metal thing was nearly as ominous as my wound. "You're not going to do anything weird to me, right?"

"How many times do I have to tell you to trust me?" Then a head shake. "I feel like I'm starting to sound like a broken record. Just... please. I'm trying to do right by you."

Still feeling the stubborn edges of resistance, I crawled onto the bed, awkwardly trying to keep the dripping arm at a point of leverage. "Sorry about the mess."

"Not the first time a house on the plate's seen blood and won't be the last," he said, cheerfully. "You ready?"

"God, Eli." I leaned back on the headboard and closed my eyes. "Don't sound so excited. It makes you seem like a psychopath."

He laughed lightly, and the sound brought a tingle to my gut. Val, I warned myself, don't do this. It's just projection. First person you've touched in years. Don't make it into anything.

His hands were warm and quick as the dabbed the wound with a damp cloth. I reopened my eyes, too cautious to sleep through the ordeal though I was tired, deep in my bones.

"What's that?"

"I'm cleaning it," Eli said patiently, his brow creased in concentration.

"I already cleaned it."

"With water, I assume. Which isn't that clean to begin with." He picked up a glass bottle from the nightstand and passed it to me. "It's alcohol rub."

"Jesus." I flipped it in my hands as he dabbed. "This costs nearly eleven tokens at the Centre."

"Fifteen from a Swapper," he replied idly.

"Do you just like... not eat usually?" I questioned. Sustenance was two tokens for one meal. Most people's wages went directly to food, and even that was barely enough. Malnutrition killed nearly a quarter of the population yearly.

"Just lucky. Stop moving."

I stilled my fumbling, too stubborn to admit that I was nervous. "It's not that big of a deal."

Eli shot me a look and pulled a cylinder from the case. I was casually speculating on what it could be as he unwound the packaging but shot straight up when he brandished a needle. I was back on a metal slab, back with my hands tied above my head. Back with hands on my body. *'Keep still,' the nurse whispered. 'Keep still.'*

"Hey, what the fuck. No way."

"Valencia," he said. "What you have is bad, okay?"

"I said not to worry about it. I'm dead anyway."

"You know, you keep saying that. But from what I can see from the blood all over my damn floor and your rapid heart rate is that your body's still going. But you let this thing sit long enough, and it won't be. Jesus, this thing's like acid. It's chewing through bone. You think because it doesn't hurt, it won't kill you. But it might."

"I've recovered from a seventy-foot fall and a broken neck."

"Okay," Eli replied slowly, but the look in his eyes didn't change. "So, you're durable. But whatever this is, it might be impervious to your fucked-up system. It's discharging poison faster than your body is spitting it back out."

No. I wouldn't have a needle.

More than stubborn, the internal voice was desperate. I couldn't let it bring those memories back. I couldn't remember the long hall at the Institute; the amalgamation of pills, the nurses with the covered faces, the slabs. The way it happened every day until you thought you'd go insane from it. Until you weren't sure you hadn't.

"Let me do this, Val." Eli looked up at me, his eyes wide and alert, framed by thick, spidery lashes. He was calm- centred. I wanted to trust him. I did.

I closed my eyes. I wanted a friend. "Okay," I finally said.

A small sting of the needle followed Eli's sigh of relief, and I tried to force my body to relax. "What is it?"

"It's a chemical that's going to fight the spread of the poison. Draws it out."

"Like a magnet?"

"Sort of. Yeah."

I could feel it moving under my skin, but it wasn't altogether unpleasant.

"It feels weird."

"Oh, so now you can feel stuff."

I lightly smacked him, but I felt groggy and tired. "Sometimes. It's just pain that doesn't come through. It's like a bad signal. I'll get flickers, but it gets rerouted."

"Does this hurt?" He poked a pair of tweezers into the skin's initial barrier, separating the thin tendrils of flesh that stretched across the mouth of the wound. It was a dull pang, but nothing else.

"Not really. I'm aware of it. But it doesn't make me feel like I need to pull away. It's hard to explain." I leaned my head back and allowed myself a weak smile. "Everything about me is hard to explain."

"It would seem that way."

My eyelids began to droop, and my saliva felt sticky and hot in my mouth. "What's happening to me?"

"It's okay. Relax. It's just a side effect."

"Side effect?" I slurred out. "You didn't say side effect."

"Well, there's bound to be with any drug."

"You didn't tell me about this one." My tongue clunked awkwardly around the words.

"You wouldn't have taken it."

He was right. I wouldn't have. I hated the feeling of the darkness closing in, unyielding and hungry. Like a vignette, it crept across the outskirts of my brain and pulled the doors shut, yanking against the neurological insistence to keep myself awake. "I don't want..."

And then I slipped away, slipping into the murky waters like it was a maternal embrace.

~~~~~~~~~~

"You're an asshole." The statement was husky from sleep.

"You're an idiot," Eli chirped back. His teeth were gritted together, making his words sound tight and muffled.
~~~~~~~~~~

"Stop touching me." I tried to shove at his hands, but my limbs were still heavy, and weak like gravity had suddenly become especially besotted with me.

"Yeah, I would, but if I did that, you'd keep bleeding all over my stuff," he spat out, wiping his brow with the back of his bloodied hand. "So, stop squirming and let me finish sewing you up."

"Don't know why you bother," I mumbled, but drop my head back onto the pillow. "I said what I said about death and meant it."

"And I meant what I said."

I winced as the needle burrowed its head into my flesh and tugged the thick sutures behind it.

"Why can I feel it?" Then softer, "Why does it hurt?"

"Must've been made vulnerable by the stuff swimming in your veins."

"You mean the stuff you put there."

Eli sent me a dry look. "Yeah, maybe. But more likely it's the two combined."

"Anthoxyaprophin," I murmured,

His fingers deftly tied a tight knot in the elastic string. "What?"

"Anthoxyaprophin." I sighed. "I just remembered. It's what they started putting in the Council's bullets."

"And how would you know something like that?"

I lifted my hands to my face.

"Caleb."

"Okay." He said, but his expression was unclear. If I wasn't so groggy, I might've thought it disgust. "Take a breath."

I opened my mouth to make a snarky retort about how I was already breathing but lost it when he stabs the thin point back into my flesh. "Jesus Christ."

He laughed breathlessly, an airy sound similar to his constant state of anti-solidity. "That's a name I haven't heard in a while. Do you still believe in something beyond Valencia?"

It was painfully apparent he was trying to distract me from his ever-busying hands, but I was grateful for such. The dragging of foreign metal inside of my skin was making me nauseous.

"I'm not of anything but myself."

He paused thoughtfully, stilling his hands for a moment. "That's an odd thing to say."

"Is it? I only think it's not worth believing in anything anymore. If someone was going to save us, I think the time might've passed."

"You never prayed while you were at the Institute? Maybe to make it through to the second round? Most kids I knew were so desperate to be chosen."

I raised my chin defiantly. "I was never like that. I never begged or prayed for anything in my life. I didn't lose that."

Eli looked up at me, curiously from beneath his mop of curly, dark hair. "But things were lost."

My bottom lip slipped out and caressed the top with a gentle kiss. "Are you going to depress me while you've got your hands buried in my flesh?"

"You're right, I'm sorry." He smiled slowly, white teeth glinting in the low light of the bedside lamp. "It's such lovely flesh, too."

"Yeah, right." I found myself wanting to brush the stray hairs from his forehead, so I fisted my hands at my side. "I'm fine, you know."

That wasn't the entire truth- I had the mother of all headaches, and the persistent ringing in my ears didn't seem to have a yen for stopping- but I couldn't have him hovering over me like this. It was doing weird things to my brain.

"You're fine because I've got that damn thing out of you." He tossed a bloodied rag onto the table next to the bed; the only other occupant a geometric ashtray filled with metal pellets that preened beneath the light. "You're fine, but it's not by any accident."

He must've caught me eyeing them because he picked one up between his forefinger and thumb and rolled it carefully.

"Is it just me who thought it'd be bigger?" He asked, but I didn't feel like he was addressing me. "All this trouble wrapped up in a microscopic ball bearing."

"A microscopic ball bearing on performance enhancers."

We shared a smile before he dropped the piece back into the glass bowl.

"Why is it that..." He trailed off, shaking his head. "Forget it." Eli tossed the surgical instruments he'd been using on a mangy towel, and he began to swaddle them in one bundle.

"Why is what?" I'd propped myself on the points of my elbows, and it put me at direct level with his gaze. "I couldn't think of a better time to ask something. My judgment's impaired." I'd meant it lightly, like a joke, but he didn't smile this time.

"Why is it that you don't take your life or your body seriously in the slightest?"

I raised my eyebrows and felt the distinct chill race along my spine. "Pardon?"

"You just brush off this shit like it means nothing. What if one day you don't come back from it? And that's just it."

"It doesn't mean anything, Eli. It doesn't. I'm already fucking dead."

"That's a pretty brash thing to say. If you have a heartbeat- if you bleed- does that not classify you as the living? If you can laugh, cry, exclaim, care- does that not mean you're alive?"

I made a small, contemplative noise and focused on the vibration of my tongue against the roof of my mouth.

"Is that all it takes to make a human being, Eli?"

"Is it not?"

The room is suddenly deafening with its silence, a patient, and a baritone wail that hummed along with the soundwaves like the tide.

"I know I am dead because I was there for my death." The words felt unbearably awkward in my mouth. "I felt every bone in my body crack and split, and then I woke.

Everything was the same, except it wasn't. The world no longer felt like mine. Some days it was as if my feet weren't really touching the ground, the air wasn't really going into my lungs." I closed my eyes. "My skin felt like an ill-fitting suit jacket that I couldn't take off. Venomous insects crawled beneath my skin. I came back, but it was all wrong. I was all wrong. I died and then brought death back with me in my hands, a curse in my skin.

It would feel an awful lot like a sin to say that I am one of the living." I opened my eyes just enough to look at him and was shaken by the steady, unreadable gaze. "I don't expect you to understand. It's just a feeling."

"You say you're dead because you feel like that's the only way to justify why you're still here."

"That's not what I said."

"I think that the fear of finding the real reason that a body- a human body- could be capable of such horrible, awful things- might be more terrifying than just writing your life off as a crude, horrible mistake. And that maybe all of this," he gestured broadly at me on the bed, "Was by intention, not accident. And you were somehow created to be this way. What would that mean to you? To know it wasn't an accident?"

Eli grabbed his case and turned to leave the room, giving me a last lingering stare. "What would it do to you to know that you didn't stumble upon death? That this reign over death was given to you? Not by misfortune, but by duty of someone else's wielded hand?" He flicked the light by the door, gliding out like smoke. "Good night, Valencia. Get some sleep."

18

There Are Too Many Ghosts Here

We didn't speak of that night again. I wanted to bring it up, but the time never quite seemed right, and Eli seemed more than happy to leave it behind us. I didn't ask him any more questions about what he'd lost, and he did the same for me.

For me, at least, the lack of intimate conversation felt like a form of intimacy. With both of us clearly on either side of the room, I felt more comfortable sharing his space with him. It was a waltz of respect and tapping of feet that never seemed to stop.

It was on the eve of our fourth night together that Eli bridged the emotional gap. We'd finished dinner over a quarter-hour earlier than we had the nights before and gone back down the hallway to review our recent material. There was a lot of that. Studied learning. I had gotten used to the ebb and flow of education for the most part, and I did find myself more often than not enjoying the intellectual stimulation. Still, there were just times that after dinner, I wished Eli and I could go for a walk before the sun slipped away or laughed and told stories over the fire. I worried that I had done a horrible thing by pressing my dirty little fingers into his wounds, fuelled by curiosity and tactlessness. I had lost a friend before I'd even made one. It was a shame that I was so good at bringing things to ruin.

"Valencia," Eli began, a floppy white map blanketing a considerable amount of his face from view.

I had been staring at the City Centre's blueprint for god knows how long, too long, without absorbing any of the material. The letters swam and kissed like fish in a pond and left speckled dots on my vision.

"Yes," I responded, but I didn't want to hear any crap about my lack of focus. I'd studied more in the last few days than I ever had.

"Do you feel like I've been working you too hard?" He asked casually, folding the map down the middle and angling his unreadable eyes towards mine.

"That's what I'm here for, isn't it?" I jerked my shoulder in a shrug that felt sharp and awkward. "To work for you."

"Not for me." Eli reached for my blueprint, but I slid it away. He sighed. "I don't want to be a tyrant."

"You're not." And it was true. He wasn't that bad. I was only a little antsy, but that was more than likely a result of being in the house for so many days in a row.

Eli leaned back in his chair and raised his arms out in a stretch, flexing the taut muscles in his shoulders and cracking his spine. "I am. It's a character flaw. A fatal one, at that. I get consumed by all this crap."

"It's not wrong to care about things."

"No, I suppose not." He rose from the chair and began to refile some of the loose papers into the worn binder. "But if I'm realistic, a day's time isn't going to make a difference. We don't have to work to the bone." He smiled at me. "What do you say? Want to take a break?"

"Is that a trick question?"

Eli laughed, tossing his head back. "Why would I be trying to trick you?"

Sheepish, I crossed my ankles in an anxious gesture. "That's what people do." When he chuckled again, I kicked him beneath the table. "Don't laugh at me."

"I'm not. I'm just delirious." He sobered, stilling his face. "Bordering on hysterical."

"I thought this was your whole life." I felt the tension slipping from my shoulders along with the easy conversation. This, right here, was Eli. Though we had been together for days, I felt as though I had missed him.

"Ah, well. I'm usually out in the world gathering stuff. I'd just reached a point that there wasn't anything new to gather." He stood and crossed to the bookshelf, pulling out a thickly bound book. "I don't know if you've looked through this one yet, but this is my recollection of all the kids I knew in the Institute. It's a lot of dead ends, honestly. It's not even worth looking at at this point."

I followed his movements and joined him at the shelf, peering at the worn cover. "I hadn't seen this one."

"As I said, it's not worth looking through the thing. I thought that if I started cataloging the kids, it would be easier to find their families or at least people who knew them. God knows how long I spent trying to find anyone who knew Richie."

The blood in my veins ran cold at the name, though I'd never forgotten about him. Richie was always there, hovering just behind my ears, and I'd never stopped running from it.

"He was the reason I ran," I blurted out. Saying it out loud for the first time felt a bit like spewing acid. The back of my teeth felt the heat.

"What?"

"I started running because of what happened. I was there when they wheeled him out." I rubbed the spine of the book as if I could drag the kids out from beneath the script and pump the life back into their veins myself. "And then everyone started talking. About how it was so stupid for him to do what he did and that we were lucky and all this shit."

"That changed things for you?" Eli was leaning casually against the shelf, but his eyes stayed intense despite the apparent nonchalance. I couldn't put my finger on it- couldn't quite decipher the shift, but it was as if his entire corporeal form changed, rippling like scales.

"I don't know. I guess at some level, it did. I couldn't let it go. Couldn't stop thinking about it."

"Yeah," Eli replied, taking the book from my grasp easily and smoothly re-shelving it. "I know the feeling. It hit me in the same way."

"You were his roommate, right?" I approached the topic hesitantly, tiptoeing on the eggshells that surrounded the memories of the Institute like landmines.

"Not for long. I had a single hall for most of my stay." His tone was distracted, but not cold.

"How did that happen, anyway? You must've been the only one without at least two people on the floor."

"Lots of kids hit Solitary."

"Only when they've done something really wrong."

Eli shook his head and drifted back to the table, gathering the finished books into a pile.

Stubborn, I traipsed after him. "I've been wondering this since before I left. It was like you had special treatment. Why?"

"I don't know if it was special."

"Different, then." I stayed on his heels as he tucked in the chairs around the table.

"I guess."

"What made you different?"

"I don't know, Valencia." He sighed, stopping in his tracks. I had been following too close and had to brace my hands on his back to prevent myself from stumbling atop him. "What makes you different?"

"You mean to say all of it was random?"

Eli swiveled around to face me. There were times I forgot how tall he was, but when I was up against him like this, I had to crook my neck back to glimpse at his face.

"Do we have to talk about the Institute right now?" Eli asked softly.

"Why? Does it upset you?"

"I don't know." He bumped my hand with his. "It just makes things feel wrong."

My breath was catching in my throat as he twisted his index finger around mine. "Things?"

"Everything." Deliberately, he lifted my hand and turned it palm-up. Insecure, I tried to curl my fingers to hide the unsightly maroon blotches, but he forced them open. "Stop. You don't have to be ashamed of these."

"You know what they mean to me," I murmured. "To everyone."

He raised my palm to his cheek and held it there. "Not to me."

The heat rose to my cheeks, flushing the skin and making me uncomfortably warm even in the damp room. I gently tugged my hand away, slipping it safely into my pocket. "You shouldn't do that."

"What?"

"Tempt fate."

The smirk glided across his face, smooth and easy. "What are you saying about us?"

I lightly smacked the front of his half-open flannel. "I meant death."

"How many times have I told you that you don't have that effect on me?" He offered me a sly wink, and I couldn't help but back away, giving myself a cagey, cautious distance between us.

"You have no way of knowing that. It could change at any minute."

The grin stayed on his face, near-feral. "Why would it? You have no evidence that it even could."

"And you have no evidence that it couldn't! Just..." I held my hands up in a barrier gesture. "Don't touch."

"Are you an art piece, Valencia?" He purred, clearly finding enjoyment in the torment. "Something classic... timeless?"

"You shut up. I know you're trying to rile me up."

"And I know it's working."

We stayed in a comically timed balance, our bodies angled towards each other like they were suspended on a wire.

"Is this what you had in mind when you said we should stop working? Because if it is, I'd rather go back to the books." I said it casually, but my pulse was throbbing in my throat. He was watching me like a hungry cat.

"You're a joy." He chuckled, and I realized in that minute that it was a sound I hadn't heard since he left my room nights before. "An absolute joy."

"That's a rare take on things," I muttered, feeling mildly shrewd at being the butt of some joke I didn't quite understand.

"It's not a bad thing. You... delight me." His eyes flashed. "Interest me."

"Because you have a toy," I challenged, raising my eyebrows.

"More so that you don't buy into my playing with you." Eli strode to the stairwell, leaving his hand on the light switch but not yet flicking it off. "I had other things in mind, Valencia. Away from the study."

"Outside?" The small strip of glass along the top wall didn't allow for much light to seep through, but even I could tell the sun was dwindling low in the sky. "That's risky."

"No. Just up."

"Like to my bedroom?"

"Your bedroom?" He asked, clearly amused.

"I didn't see any names on it."

"I sometimes sleep in it if I'm around."

Once I was beside him in the doorway, he turned the light off with a low electrical hiss. Without the artificial illumination, the shadows deepened and made everything seem harsh and exaggerated.

"Did I take it from you?"

"You might've, but it's fine. There's another bed on the main floor that I've been sleeping in. You want to head out?"

I remained where I stood, lingering at the threshold and gazed at the angles and planes in his face in the dull light. I'd think that if this was a different time, someone might've painted him - the sullen boy with the sharp face and magic eyes.

"Why don't you go first?" There were many reasons I never slid into leadership roles, and being followed close behind ranked high on that list. It meant there were people you'd never see, always nipping at your heels, leaving you vulnerable.

It wasn't enough to be a part of the shadows - you had to be the shadow and make people forget you were ever there.

"Gone back to not trusting me at your back, huh?" Eli asked, his tone lilting. Despite the almost not quite agitated comment, he slipped effortlessly in front of me and drifted down the hall, leaving me to follow or be left behind.

Such a strange little dynamic I'd stumbled into. Shaking my head, I trudged after him, flinching at the creaks and groans of the boards as I walked.

"This house makes it impossible to be inconspicuous," I commented, gritting my teeth as the landing grumbled in response.

"It's a good thing there's not a lot of sneaking around to be had in here," Eli replied, going back to the drawer as he had this morning to retrieve the key ring.

"Wouldn't it be easier to just keep those on you?" I asked, spinning in between suspicion and excitement.

"I guess." But that was his only reply.

I hovered in the basement doorway and waited for the next move, assuming we'd be leaving the kitchen and heading up the main staircase.

To my surprise, he walked only further into the room and kicked a swaying cabinet door shut. It stubbornly swung back open.

"Damn thing."

"What are you showing me?" I asked dryly, attempting to take in the kitchen set up more objectively. All I saw were stained counters, cracked tiles, and the few dishes from dinner in the sink.

When Eli picked up a broom that had been leaning on the wall, I backed up and shook my head. "No way. I'm not cleaning your kitchen."

Incredulous, Eli looked at the cleaning tool in his hand and then back at me. "I'm incredibly hurt by that, Valencia. You're a guest in my home."

"So, what are we doing then?" I asked, putting emphasis in the middle.

Eli slapped the wall, a boyishly charming expression on his face. "I told you. We're going up."

I squinted at him dubiously. "Eli... that's a wall."

He shook his head vigorously, kicking a bucket aside. "It's not! It's just disguised as one. It's been here since the house was first built." When I didn't move to join him, he huffed impatiently. "Get over here and look."

"So bossy," I retorted but slid to where he was standing. It was easier to make out the slight edges where the door has been wallpapered over and pried open from up close. "Okay, so there is a door," I amended.

Eli took down a soft-edged knife from the counter and dragged it along the seam, separating the clinging wallpaper from its desperate embrace.

"When was the last time you even went up there?" I asked, wincing at the sound of the tearing paper as Eli pried and wrestled the door out.

"It's been a while," Eli said, stopping to stare at the yawning entrance.

"How come?" I had yet to formulate an opinion on the looming secret passage, but I wasn't getting reassuring vibes from Eli's disposition.

"Well, I..." he paused in his speech, starting up the short staircase. "My... father used to always warn me about spending too much time up here."

"Why?" I trekked up after him, leaving my hand limply hanging on the skinny, rotting banister. The flakes of paint stabbed into my palm, but I refused to let go. It was too dark to travel without an aide. Eli waited to answer until he popped open the door at the top, leaning into it with his shoulder.

"There are things in history that draw you in so deep they can swallow you whole," he said softly, disappearing into the room. "It comes down to knowing your limits before that happens."

The lamp crackled on in a puff of flame, casting an orange glow on Eli's face. The illumination reached only as far as our partnered stance in the middle of the room, leaving the walls and corners still caught in velvet shadows.

"I'll admit it," I said with more confidence than I felt, squinting into the dark, "I am intrigued."

"Good," Eli replied and smiled brilliantly at me. I could've sworn that grin was brighter than the lamp, damn it. My skin crawled.

"I should warn you, I'm not exactly patient. I don't like to wait for things," I said in a tone that was crisper than necessary, but this dark moment felt far too intimate. Eli raised both his eyebrows.

"I'll go get the other lantern." He waited for me to take the lit one from his hand before drifting away. The room couldn't have been any more substantial than the one I'd been sleeping in upstairs, but when Eli crossed to the other side, it seemed like miles between us.

The second lantern puffed on in the same manner as the first, and with the addition, granted the room with enough light for me to start to understand where I was.

It was a room much like the basement in its casual academic disarray, with stacks of books and papers leaned sloppily against each other on crooked stools.

"Your family must've liked reading," I said, picking up a paper from the table. I didn't recognize the scrawlings on the page, as they were marked up with lines and angles, and small numbers along each side. When I failed to understand the markings, I dropped it back into its place. "I don't get it. What's so special about all this?"

"Oh, you mean besides the fact that all this stuff survived the Council's eradication of 'alternate theory'? That's not interesting enough for you?" Eli shook his head, disparagingly. "Really, I thought better of you."

"I don't know," I mumbled, lifting my shoulders in a shrug at his chastising. "I mean, it's cool." I didn't want to admit that I didn't understand most of what was surrounding me.

"It's okay if you can't pick it up. I can't read most of it either. I'm not an engineer," his tone lifted and fell in a moment that was almost too quick to pick up on.

"Is that what this is?" I looked back at the paper and tried to see the shape in all the diagrams.

"Well, yeah. It's science. But unlimited science. Not just our life here, on the plate, but beyond."

"Beyond," I repeated, and tried to formulate an idea of what it might look like past the wall. What would be left? Would it just be endless, empty nothingness?

"Yeah. Beyond. Which is what I wanted to show you."

I hadn't been watching him- which I should've known to be doing, but somehow always seemed to forget- and he had pulled something out of a cramped closet that scuffed the floor as he dragged it to rest between his knees.

I drifted over to his perch, peeping into the creased cardboard box. The frayed edges of photographs pushed against each other in a swollen, passionate battle for space, married with old toys and broken puzzle pieces that scattered deep into the bin.

"What's this?" I questioned with genuine intrigue.

"This was my great-grandfather's, from when he was a boy," Eli explained, gingerly removing the first stack of yellowed photos from the top.

"It's such an incredible thing," I commented in reverence, reaching for the first photo. "Knowing your lineage. I never even knew my ma', let alone her entire family tree."

Eli graciously let me slip the photo from his hands, and I stared blindly at an out of focus image of a tire on a rope, dangling in the foreground of a body of water. "What was their place called?" I pressed, but Eli didn't have an answer.

"I don't know that much. I'm sorry." He took the photo back, carefully wiping it on the front of his shirt before placing it at the bottom of the stack and resting the bunch on the desk next to him. "By the time this stuff reached us, the knowledge was thready. All we have now are pieces." Eli's eye twitched in annoyance. "He didn't even want to keep it. Said it was all bullshit, anyway." He hesitated, giving a small smile. "My dad was a conservative man. Through and through. Loved the plate." The laugh was short and husky, hinting of a deep, burning wound. "Wouldn't even give a thought to a life without it."

It had only taken the better part of the week, but I felt as if I was beginning to understand the complexities of Eli through his strange and weaving commentary and was well on my way to building an image of the life he had before the Institute took it away.

I couldn't have been more wrong, of course, but that's how these things go.

That's how we must learn.

"That must have been hard," I'd remarked, then winced at the seeming falsity of the statement.

"It was what it was," Eli replied, and the brief window slapped shut. He held out the stuffed bear- an innocent, dirty little thing with a missing eye and a cracked nose- and waited for me to take it. When I did, Eli clasped his hands together and dangled them between his knees. "He was just a kid when they made the journey. His entire life changed in the blink of an eye." He shook his head. "Just like that."

I turned the bear over in my clumsy hands, feeling the harsh line of the seams against my palms. Time had faded the colour and unwound the fabric, but the love beat in the shabby toy like a heart of its own. "Did they have to travel far?"

"All the way over the seas," he replied.

I knew about the sea. It had been so much greater than the Spillout, carrying on for miles and miles of deep blue and rusty grey. People got lost in its tide. I remembered hitting the water of the Spillout and closed my eyes against the offending memory.

Bigger.

"They swam?" I asked, and my arms felt heavy like they had the day I fought the small waves.

"No, of course not," Eli chuckled. "They would have never made it. They took boats."

"Wasn't that dangerous?"

"Everything was dangerous." He slipped another photo from the pile and passed it to me. This one was of a crooked house on uneven land that oozed dark goop. Confused, I looked back at him.

"That was their home." He tapped his finger on the sinking building. "When the Reckoning started, the land was the first thing to go. The earth just started swallowing itself." He made a twirling gesture with his finger. "Sucking stuff down below ground and crushing it beneath the weight of the land."

"So, either way, they were in danger."

"Yes. Leaving by boat, at the time, was the safest option."

"But why come here? If it was so far away? Was there no salvation in their homeland?"

"That's where certain things got complicated, Valencia." Eli took the photo from me and began unfolding a thin, crinkling sheet of paper that he had at the ready. The markings were dull and confusing, but I could see a pattern in some of the shapes. "It's a map."

"A map? But it's all broken up." I'd seen maps, back in the Institute in the study room. There were distinct landmasses all around, not tiny speckles.

"After the Reckoning started, there were no countries anymore. Only islands. The earth was splitting at every weak and low point, flooding with water and burying entire villages.

They heard of this base from an army man that had come to steal from them. He had taken orders from above to get hold of a motorized boat and visit the lasting islands to find things to start a new civilization on his big vessel."

"Only to find items? Not survivors?"

"No, not survivors. The Pod was at capacity, he said, so the legend goes. There are theories. I find it more believable that they were selfish, greedy cowards without a benevolent bone in their bodies. They didn't want commoners taking up precious space and breaking the weight capacity. It wouldn't last if it were too full."

"But it didn't do anything," I said pointedly, knowing full well the plan had been for much greater than a sedentary building in the middle of a field. "Because Hartwell's men couldn't make it do anything."

"Well, they might've eventually."

"But they didn't."

Eli chuckled, shaking his head. "No, they didn't."

"So they stayed holed up in that big egg feeling very self-important. I know this part of the story."

"Ah, yes. I forgot how studious you were."

"You forgot, hmm?" From where I was sitting in front of his chair, I rested my chin on the crests of my knees. "Doesn't that imply that you once knew?"

Eli met my eyes. "You doubt that I did? I paid attention, Valencia. You spent a lot of time in the history section at the Institute. That's why I thought you'd appreciate this." He tapped the tip of my nose with his pinky finger. "You are like me. You like to not only look but know."

I ignored the fluttering in my chest at his light touch and sat back. "I never seemed to find any real answers in that library—just more aversions and redirection.

One time, I wanted to look for information on the tunnel system, but there wasn't any record of it existing. Every book said it was just us, the Pod, and a big-ass plate on the ground. Except I knew that there was a tunnel system because Caleb and I used it, all the time."

"So, where did you find your answer?"

I raised my shoulders. "Logic, I guess. Which now that I think of it is hardly more than a guess."

"And what did you conclude?"

"Well," I sat up straighter, crossing my legs. "It's more of a theory than anything. It's sometimes hard to figure things out when they're so much bigger than you are."

"I'd like to hear it."

"Okay," I stalled, biting my lip. Knowing that it was half-baked, but I'd opened it now. "I started formulating the first time I visited the wall."

"The wall?"

"Yes."

"What was so interesting about it?"

"When everyone talked about it, I thought it would be a shabby old thing. All spotty and slapped together with leaky holes and poor patchwork—a rush job. Like a last-minute addition to protect the Pod. I assumed because the settlers were able to get around it, it was a tiny thing. Easy to scale."

"I imagine the truth came as a surprise."

"It did. I stayed at that wall for hours."

"It's huge, right?" Eli laughed, his eyes sparkling in the warm glow of the lantern. "Just fucking huge."

"I couldn't believe it. I could barely see the top. And when I touched it, it was cold. Freezing cold."

"What did you deduce?"

"It's made out of the same stuff as the plate. It's practically seamless." I made a gesture with my hands, outlining a curved crescent shape. "Like a flat-bottomed bowl."

"And how did this help you understand what the tunnels are for?"

"Don't you understand?" I asked, delighted to be on my way to understanding something Eli didn't. "The tunnels must have something to do with water release."

Eli tilted his head and squinted at me dubiously. "That's what the Spillout is for."

"No," I said, running over the end of his statement. "The Spillout is backup public water usage, for when our rain collection isn't enough." Most residences were outfitted with a rain-collector, which was little more than a large barrel with a winding of pumps that climbed the sides of the houses, but for larger families and residences, they had to turn to the Spillout to collect pails of water and bring them back to their homes. "The tunnels are for letting out the excess runoff."

"Then why are they people-sized? Why were they made so perfectly for settlers to breach the Plate?"

"Well, I-." I stopped myself, sinking teeth into my bottom lip. "I don't know."

"I didn't mean to invalidate your theory." Eli dropped a hand on my shoulder, warm and heavy. "You know, without answers, there are only theories. I would hate to make you feel bad for building them."

"I don't, not exactly," I gingerly removed his hand. "I'm just..." I fluttered helplessly. "It's frustrating. It's like you said. We have pieces of understanding, but no real knowledge of how any of it works. Like, why would Jebediah build the plate and wall around a town that was already here? Why not destroy the town and wipe it clean?"

"Wonderful question," Eli twisted in his seat. "And why not seal the tunnels when they did the access points from the Outside?" He said the outside like that- like a title.

"So when the plate was put in the ground, they expanded the wall at the same time."

"But they left that town accessible." Eli finished. "Why?"

"Do you think that they knew people would come for salvation? That they'd find a way in, past the wall?"

Eli was quiet for a minute, watching me, until- in a nearly imperceptible moment, he shifted his knee so that it bumped my shoulder. "And if they were supposed to find a way in? Maybe they were always part of the plan."

"Like a trap," I said, feeling sick. "Like he set a trap for us. But why?"

"That," Eli said, his voice soft and haunted, "... is finally the right question."

I collapsed into breathless silence, trying to make sense of everything he was saying.

"Do you really think he would do that?" I asked softly. "Lie to everyone?"

Eli snorted, but it was a bitter sound, void of joy. "I think that he was a man who thought he was a God. And I think that he thought of people as nothing but building blocks for his gain."

"Hold on," I squeezed my eyes shut. "This isn't making any sense."

"Hey, speak for yourself. I'm just out here expressing truths."

I sent him a glare, tucking my hair behind my ears. "We agree that the plate was built beneath the town, and the wall somewhere after?"

"Yes."

"And that the buildings must have been before the Reckoning, but somehow after the plate? Why would Hartwell leave an entire town on the plate? What good would that do him?"

"It's possible that..." Eli trailed off and furrowed his brow, narrowing his eyes.

"What?"

"He wanted to preserve the town, exactly how it was. Habitable. Reminiscent."

I drummed my fingers on the floor, considering. It had already gone further than the speculation I did on my own. But was it plausible? "Why?"

"For the people that would inevitably come, and think they were doing something awfully clever. It's easier to trap an animal if they think it's their idea."

"But how would he even do that? Spread a plate like that underground?" I scrunched my face in thought.

"People would just think the rumbling was an earthquake," Eli said dryly, and I realized the error of my thinking.

In an era of plate separation and constant natural phenomena, one rumbling earthquake from a distant hill, theoretically, would go unnoticed. "It doesn't explain the wall. It wouldn't be easy to build something like that without raising questions."

"No," Eli agreed. "It wouldn't."

I lapsed into silence, picking at a ball of fuzz attached to the leg of my pants. It was hard to even imagine where all of it came from in the first place. There were the facts of Hartwell's legacy, his material invention, but creating something like that... I shook my head at the thought. I couldn't even fathom.

And that was why I wasn't sitting in some cozy apartment downtown being paid three tokens an hour to do the science for the Council.

Just didn't have the brain for it.

"I wish there were a record somewhere of unbiased facts," I commented, propping my chin upon my hand. "I feel like everyone else is fine to just take the word of the Council and call it truth, even without any proof."

Eli took a slim cigarette from his pocket but left it unlit, toying with it between his fingers. "It's a lot easier than figuring it out yourself."

"So you think they're just lazy?" Distracted by the slender stick twirling in the air, my tone was light and airy, my eyes trained on the dance.

"It is certainly less daunting to let yourself believe a semi-inconvenient truth than realize you're trapped in a system that benefits from your sufferings."

"But isn't that a scary realization? To wake up and realize that the people put in power to protect you may actually be causing you more harm than if you were to be without?" When he didn't reply, and merely watched the cigarette go around and around, I added, "Though, the world outside isn't known to be merciful."

"Neither is the Council," he commented, inspiring a breathy laugh from my chest.

"No, that's true."

A curl from Eli's hair sprung free from the hand-pushed hair, breaching the smooth skin of his forehead and bounced across his face. I remembered him as a child then, a quiet boy with lousy posture, clinging to the back of Senator Griggs' shirttails. "And yet they always seemed to have mercy for you," I murmured again, so quiet it was almost devoured by the stuffy room.

Eli replied with a laugh of his own, but it was tight and sharp. "This again?" He shook his head. "If what they'd showed me was fucking mercy, I would've preferred being left to the wolves. I don't think anyone of them even knows what that word means."

He shifted his body and tucked the cigarette back into its case, untouched.

"Change your mind?" I questioned, gesturing at his pocket.

"I don't smoke up here."

"Why?"

"I don't want to ruin any of this." He gently nudged the box with his foot. "It's all I have left, and it's barely holding together."

My brows knitted together. All he has left? He had the house, the job, the network- why would a ratty bear and a blurry picture be all he has?

The wind rattled the small window above Eli's head, sending flecks of dust drifting between us. Though the sun had just disappeared beyond the horizon moments before, the skylight already was displaying a charcoal sky that allowed only a small section of the near-transparent lines crisscrossing above distinguishable to the naked eye. His foot bumped mine. I tried not to let my eyes glaze over at the casual contact. Clearing my throat, I twisted away. "Does the weather make you nervous?" I asked if only to put some distance between us in the intimate silence.

"In what sense?"

"You know," I stretched my legs out as far as the confined space would allow. "If it were to take the house down, and you'd lose everything in it."

"I suppose it does, but I'm hoping to have at least the photos transferred to a computer before any of that happens."

"A computer? How are you going to get one of those?"

"I already have one."

This piqued my interest and straightened my spine, pushing me forward until I was nearly sitting on top of his feet. "It's against the law for civilians to have any kind of communicable technology."

"Lots of things are against the law," he pointed out.

"Is it in the study? Why haven't you shown me?"

"It's for me," Eli said, then cut himself off. "I thought you didn't want to talk about the job."

"I didn't say that." I found myself souring again and fought to keep myself composed. "You offered for us to take a break. It's not like I bailed."

"Why does that make you defensive?" Eli inquired.

"Defensive? I'm not defensive."

"You are. That part wasn't the question. You know it's not a bad thing to need a break, right?" His eyes twinkled in silent laughter.

"Maybe not for you," I replied, "But every time I've stopped running, the clock started ticking down."

There was a long pause, one that almost always seemed to follow my brash statements, and it was just long enough to make me question if I should have said anything at all when Eli spoke again.

"It must be a difficult thing to not have somewhere safe."

I made a noise somewhere between one of derision and amusement, brushing off the comment as effortlessly as I'd brushed off the falling dust from my shoulders. "I had the Harris house, once I was out. She kept that place like a damn fortress." The memory made me smile- though I had never had a conventional relationship with her, she was an absolutely fascinating, wickedly smart brick of a woman.

"Physical safety isn't the only kind of security one needs," Eli added thoughtfully.

"It's all that I need," I said quickly. The last thing I needed was Eli thinking I was a soft-handed, soft-hearted fool that wanted to be coddled. "Besides, you're holed up in here all by yourself, too. You're the last person I'd expect to preach the importance of keeping human company."

"I brought you here, didn't I?" A smile graced his sharp face, easing the lines back into soft slopes.

"For business, not pleasure," I said directly, pointedly moving out of reach.

"I'd consider being with you a pleasure, Valencia." The simple statement was spoken clearly and without guile or ulterior motive, but it still made me wary.

"Why do you always have to say things like that?"

"Like what?"

"I don't know what you're trying to achieve."

Eli shook his head at that, rising to his feet, suddenly distracted. "I'm not trying to achieve anything. It's just genuine."

I felt helpless and small from where I was on the floor, but I didn't have enough room to get up with him standing in front of me. "Where are you going?" I asked.

"I want to get out of here." He massaged his brow. "It's stuffy."

It had yet to bother me, but his sudden discomfort eked into me.

"Oh, okay."

Preferring to get up myself, I waited until he had stepped over my bent leg and into the middle of the room before awkwardly bouncing upright. Standing, I was able to feel what Eli was talking about. My head swam with dizziness and nausea, pressure building in my temples. "Ugh," I muttered, gently kicking a path between the antiquities.

"You okay?"

"Yeah, just a head rush. What about this room makes that happen?"

Eli clicked his tongue, waiting with the first lantern. "No ventilation. That skylight doesn't open, and there's no carry through from the rest of the house. The pressure up here is ridiculous."

I hadn't even noticed him turn off the other light until I looked over my shoulder, and the room was awash with shadow. Startlingly, I found myself yearning to return to the corner and the box of the Beyond, breathing in the little boy's toys.

Silly, Valencia.

The last light puffed out, and I heard the door creak from behind me.

Don't you know it's already gone?

19

The Fire Hatred Started

It took me close to an hour to get comfortable in bed that night, and even once I'd begun to drift off, my body remained restless and uneasy. The ghoulish wraiths I kept locked inside my head pushed against the front of my skull and urged me to shed the comforts of this old creaking home, chase the winking stars in the sky and disappear into the oblivion.

My dreams had been full of agitated turmoil and the faces of my past, with Caleb's driving to the foreground and whispering words that no longer sounded like language. I was hot and prickly, though I had long since kicked the sheet off my body.

I lied awake in bed, staring at the ceiling and wondered what time it could've been. There were no clocks in this room- a small fact I had overlooked during my stay- and so I was left wondering, the ever-present silence of the night my only hint.

A cough that started small quickly escalated into a short but harsh bout that left my throat dry and my chest heaving for air.

"Fuck," I said, frustrated by the difficulty of the night. Why was it so hard to get a decent sleep all of a sudden? The one period of time I would have a secure residence to safely slumber in, and my body stopped cooperating halfway through. It was bullshit.

After another minute of obnoxious throat clearing, I admitted defeat and elected a trip to the kitchen for water would be the only thing that would soothe it. I was about to climb off the bed when Eli burst through the door, the light from the hallway streaming against his back and silhouetting him.

"Get up, Valencia. We've got to go." Eli frantically tore the drawers of the vanity open and began to throw things in a rucksack.

Groggy from my fuzzy half-sleep, I scrambled to my feet and quickly began to pull my discarded jeans over my bare legs. Too confused to feel ashamed of my unclothed state, I briskly did up the button and grabbed my belongings off the nightstand. "What's happening?"

"It's a raid."

Bewildered, I moved to the window. The darkness still smudged the horizon with massive strokes, but in the distance, I could see the faintest flicker of a red glow. "A raid? Why?"

I swung my cloak over my shoulders, following Eli's suit and grabbing the last of my belongings from the room.

"They're in the denser blocks. It's a breach."

"A breach?" He was moving out of the room, rapidly charging the staircase and forcing me to barrel after him. "What happened?"

"It's got to be the Swappers. Somehow the Council must've caught wind of it."

From outside, someone let out an agonized, blood-curdling scream. My skin itched at the sound. I knew what that meant.

The blaze wasn't just taking down buildings.

"They're going to destroy the whole quadrant with firepower like that." I was fascinated, hideously so, by the spread of the flames across from the front window. "It's gaining speed."

Eli was busy rummaging through a closet on the main floor, his face hidden from me by the arms of sweaters. "They're just looking for a fucking excuse. Been looking for one for a while. They don't make any money down here from us."

"What about the factories?"

He let out a harsh laugh that sounded like smoke seared in his lungs. "Factories. Right."

He tossed me a briefcase with a broken silver clasp. "I need you to go to the study and fill this with as much as you can. Blueprints, maps, and any information about the personnel, okay?" I was still fumbling with the bulky case when he rose and grabbed me by my arms. "Do you understand? Nothing about the kids."

"Nothing about the kids?" I asked, astounded. "But don't we need it to-."

"No! If this all works, we will have everything we need about every fucking kid that has ever been in that godforsaken place. But we need the maps. Go! Now!"

Dutifully, I raced into the room we'd spent the last week in, feeling a pinch around my heart. I clutched the ripped handles with sweaty hands and tried to slap on the lights. They didn't even buzz.

"I can't see anything!" I called, catching my breath while waiting for a response.

"They cut the power!" Eli yelled back, and I heard the rough strain in his voice. "They're forcing us out to the street!"

"Fuck, fuck, fuck." Sweat was pilling from my forehead and dripping into my eyebrows. Why was it so fucking hot?

Remembering the last thing we'd been working on, I squinted into the darkness for a pile on the table. When I spotted the wink of the white folded paper, I cracked open the case and started to stuff the documents inside.

On a whim, I moved to the bookshelf, trying to remember the shape and feel of the first binder Eli had shown me on the night I'd arrived. It was chipping on the spine. I remembered that much.

"We've got to go, Val! Now!"

Ignoring his desperate and aggressive call, I continued combing the third shelf until I felt an irregular texture. Trusting that the book's lumpiness meant the metal specimen was inside, I forced that into the case as well and desperately snapped the locks shut. The broken one hung loose. Deeming it good enough, I took the hallway in strides twice my usual length and met Eli in the front room, where he waited, resignedly, by the front door.

"What took you so long?" He barked out but restrained his aggression as he gingerly took the case from me.

"I had to find something off the shelf."

Indubitably disinterested with my reasoning, Eli wrenched the door open but halted when it was halfway open.

"What's wrong?" I asked, not seeing anything on the quiet street even after I'd muscled my way beside him. "I don't see anything."

"Yeah, that's the problem." Eli leered forward, his chin brushing the top of my head. "People should be evacuating."

"Maybe they don't know?" I suggested.

"No. There's an alert system rigged in almost every house past the Beamline. One guy pulls the wire, and every house gets the vibration. That's how it works."

"And you got yours? Did it wake you up?"

"No, I wasn't sleeping." Agitated, Eli pushed the door open another fraction of a foot. "It buzzed so many times I thought the thing would rip out of the wall."

"Maybe they've left."

"Maybe," Eli said, but I could tell he didn't buy it. "Stay low and stay behind me. We have to make it to the next street over before they get down here."

The Council's sirens sounded a deep and bassy moan that shook the ground. It was the first I'd heard, but it couldn't have been a good sign.

They were getting closer.

"Okay, now." Eli slipped onto the porch, carefully leaving the door slightly ajar. I recognized it as an old raid trick I'd picked up from Auntie- I hadn't seen a raid before, not in my time- but they used to be a lot more common, back when residents were less susceptible to control. Propping the door open gave the appearance it was abandoned, and they were less likely to rip it down.

Eli and I dropped to ground level, skirting around the buildings' edge, and kept our backs flat to the siding.

The raids were a vicious, violent scare tactic, meant to destroy any inkling of life beyond obeying the system. In the downtown, we never saw any because nearly everyone just clicked along the edges of the law. We were, at the core of it, more subtle about breaking it.

When we ran out of the length of the house, we dropped into a half-bent hurdle, ducking our heads as we struggled to maneuver our way to the next. Tires squealed closer and closer, the sound like a barrage against my eardrums.

"They're getting closer," I yell-whispered, tucking my flopping bag beneath the flaps of my cape.

"We're almost there," Eli hissed back.

I remained confused until I realized we were making a beeline towards the canopy we'd parked his car under just days before. "We can't take a fucking car out of here, are you crazy?" I asked incredulously, forgetting to whisper in between the wheezing bouts of breath.

"We're not driving it," he replied tightly, smoothly ducking beneath the drooping shingles.

Following suit, I joined him in the damp concave. "Then what are we doing?"

Eli popped the trunk and began to rifle through, pulling out something boxy and slim. "We need the computer."

"Well, shit," I paused, catching my breath. "How are we going to get all of this out of here? If you get caught with any of that, you're either getting killed or detained."

"If we want any of this to work, we need it."

He tossed me a small plastic baggy of various plug-ins. "Keep that somewhere dry."

I wrinkled my nose, trying to see through the fogged plastic. "What is it?"

"They're for data transfers." He efficiently shoved the briefcase and the laptop into one larger, less conspicuous bag. It was a typical resident carry-on with the thick lining and dull colours.

A smattering of shots was fired from somewhere near us, raucously popping like miniature explosions and punctuated with calls of terror.

"It sounds like they're nearly on top of us," I murmured, moving to the front of the canopy to see if I could see the contention from where we were.

Cautiously, I poked my head around the siding, keeping my hood low over my face.

At the end of the short alley, flashlight beams busied themselves bobbling and bumping against each other. A man's voice yelled, "Clear!" but I couldn't see the origin.

Dismayed, I pulled my head back under the canopy.

"It's crawling with them," I commented, warring against the smoke that was thickening and filling my head with clouds.

"Shit," Eli said, tying a band around the top half of his untamed curls. "They moved fast this time."

"This has happened before?"

"A couple of times." Eli gently parted the dangling shingle and gazed out into the street as I had. "The men almost always stayed closer to the main channel."

Something crackled, then popped, loud enough to make me cover my one ear with a gloved hand. "Well, they aren't holding back this time."

The backpack on Eli's back fell askew, with one side sliding down his muscular shoulder as he tried to scope out our surroundings. I reached for the strap to tighten it, lightly resting my free hand on the back of his arm. I left it there amid a horrible feeling that it would be one of the last times I would get to feel his skin, warm beneath mine. "You got a plan?" I asked, but my voice was hoarse.

"Working on it," Eli twisted his neck to look at me, his eyes drifting lazily over my face. "What are you doing?"

"Tightening your straps," I replied simply, dropping my hand from his arm as if his words had seared my palm. "You know, if we can find an entrance, I can take us through the tunnels past the Beamline."

"I wouldn't even know what to look for." Frustrated, Eli puffed out a breath. The thickening smoke rippled in front of him.

"We've got to move soon." The smoggy cloud was starting to tickle my throat. "The fire's getting closer. The tunnels are going to be our best bet."

"You got any ideas of how to figure that out? I'm not about to run out in the line of fire like some idiot who doesn't know left from right. I need to know what to look for, and we need a direction."

Frustrated, I pinched the bridge of my nose and inhaled deeply, my chest rattling and wheezing in the bowels of smoke. "How well do you know your neighbourhood?" I asked.

"I'd say pretty well," Eli replied confidently. "I've got a straight grasp on nearly everything in the entire city. I've been pretty successful in my ability to find and organize information." Male bravado saturated his voice.

"Pop quiz, then." I rubbed my hands against each other, attempting to offset the tingling burn of the marks against the harsh air. "How many streets do you have in this quadrant? Once you have that number, split it; how many clicks between here to the Beamline?"

Eli scrunched his face in concentration, his lips silently parting and mouthing along to the thoughtful crusade.

"I'd say nearly seventeen parallel, maybe, if you're counting the smaller roads. From where we are, four, maybe five. We're nearly at the turnaround here."

"If we're taking the side roads-"

An explosion shook the ground beneath me, sending my joints smacking against each other. My teeth gnashed against the tender pink flesh of my inner cheek, slicing it open with the blunt force. I swore then, unable to keep my composure against the assault.

My anger boiled in its membrane, bubbling and foaming up the length of my esophagus and swelling the woundedness of my mouth. If they thought they could just... I fisted my hand at my side, pressing my knuckles against my thigh in an almost forgotten habit.

"We've got to go, Valencia!" Eli pushed his hand around my rod-straight arm, yanking fast and hard. "You'll have to guide on the way!"

He was yelling, but I could still barely make out his voice amidst the gunfire and screaming. Seething at the screeching in my left ear, I cupped a hand over it and loped into a quick jog, pushing in front of Eli and shaking his grasp.

The streets were already set ablaze, the edges of the crimson wave tinted with gaseous auras that shimmered in the light. I didn't see any Councilmen, but it did little to soothe my wariness.

"Eli!" I called out, not bothering to spare him a glance. I trusted him to be behind me.

Trusted.

The realization made me stumble and stub my toe against the raised curb, forcing me to flay my arms forward.

"You alright?" He asked, panting to a stop beside me.

"I'm fine," I snarled out, though I hated the physical interruption. "I need to know if it's left or right to the Beamline from here."

"Ah," he started, but paused, squinting into the intersection. "We've got to take a right."

"City layout says the lowest point of the city is almost always two and a half roads from the Beamline."

I picked up into a run again, lightly batting a low hanging pipe out of my way as I jogged around the corner.

"And that's where tunnel entry points are?"

Careful not to let my guard down, I kept my eyes peeled for any movement in the reaches of the sparse buildings. The flames had yet to touch this sector, leaving the dilapidated establishments to continue to lay victim to their personal story of ruin.

The lack of chaos could only mean one of two things- one: the guards had come and gone, writing off the small street from their tirade and deeming it as an unnecessary risk, or two: we had stepped onto their next track and into the line of fire. I thought of the crackling flames and quietly remarked, literally.

"No, it's just an old trick to remember an easy entrance," I waited for him to join me before making the dart across the empty street. "They're all over the city."

"How many entrances?" Eli shot out, and I realized he was ceaselessly cataloging and storing the new information as I regurgitated it to him.

We were close now- I could feel it. The ground was getting thinner, marked by how the dirt spread over the plate was patchy and inconsistent.

"Maybe twenty accessible, but probably more counting where the ground is a bit thicker."

The distance would've been, at worst, an arm's throw from where we were- I could see the small turn-off I wanted to go down- but there was a rather large and unforeseen problem roaring into our path.

A raid wagon.

Eli spotted it mere seconds after I had, leading both of us to a near-identical tucking of our heads close to our chest and ducking behind a protruding staircase.

"Shit." He said, struggling to keep balance against the weight of his pack. "They caught up to us."

I shrugged. "Or us to them." A sticky line of sweat was blooming along the small of my back.

"You think if we wait, they'll keep moving out?"

It was unlikely, but it wasn't impossible. I rose on my haunches just enough to peep over the chipped concrete steps.

The raid wagon had four rows of seats and a capacity of twenty. The men were already hopping down, but you didn't have to be a math whiz to realize there were more than that. A lot more.

"They're packing off, Eli," I whispered, keeping my eyes trained on the broad chest that stayed secured to the centre of the wagon.

"You get that fella you were after?" One of the men called to the other, his voice dull and muffled by the masks the Council required they wore. The head-pieces hung low over their nose and mouth and matched the silver goggles that blocked their eyes from the fumes.

"Bastard got away," the other one spat back. "Fire'll get him now."

Then they laughed, bucking and heads whipping like they'd been grabbed hold of by something demonic. The words echoed in my head.

Fire'll get him now.

Fire'll get him now.

"Not the smartest bunch," Eli commented idly.

"Definitely not." I peeled back the top half of my gloves and buttoned them down, setting my fingers free from the confinement. I saw Eli's eyes dart to them, but he said nothing. "Raiders are the lowest of the Guard." I spat out gooey saliva to emphasize my point. "Bottom feeders."

"What are you about to do?" he asked, hushed.

"We're going to get to that tunnel entry." I secured the button of my cloak at my neck. "But you need to trust me, and we need to be fast. Can you do that?"

The flicker of surprise and suspicion in his eyes was quickly subdued, and I silently thanked him for it. It wasn't the time to think.

It was time to move.

There were close to eleven men on our side of the street. Each had a handheld spout with a twisted coil cord attached to a pack on their backs, but only two were at the ready. There were at least three other explosives strapped to their vests, but the pull triggers on each would take five to ten seconds to detonate after aim.

I wasn't going to give them that chance.

"Follow me and don't say a word," I said.

I plunged into the heart of the action, the tails of my cape flying in the wind. I didn't check but merely hoped Eli had followed behind me.

"Hey! Hey!" One of the raid-men blustered, glancing around to see if the other men had seen the same as him. "Stop where you are!"

We had acquired most of the men's attention now, and their casual dawdling had quickly snapped into hungry violence. Their feet slapped the ground with the weight of lead, fumbling to get a steady hold on their weapons.

Making sure Eli was close on my heels, I shot him a quick glance then slipped into the alley. As I suspected, the short path was blocked off by the next building over.

"I don't see it," Eli sharply hissed. Someone fired a shot, but it was widely mistargeted and hit the crumbling wall beside us. "Val, there's nothing here."

It had to be here. I clenched my teeth and pulled a wooden palette down to obstruct the pathway, but it wouldn't hold off a small army of men. The only other things in the alley were a pile of garbage, buzzing with flies, and a dirty old mattress half-folded against the wall.

"Look at the morons," sneered a lanky raidman that successfully blocked off the mouth of the alley. "You kids have gone and cornered yourself." When another guard flanked him, he was waved off. "No, man, they're mine."

The comment made me smile. It wasn't hard to make any of them think they were smarter than us. I pulled on the frayed edge of the mattress, but, when it was too heavy, gestured with my head for Eli to take the other side. Together, we flipped it upright just as the raidman released the valve and spewed the first streams of fire into the alleyway. The puffy mattress took most of the hit, but it ignited quickly, the flame consuming and inhaling the available cotton. We were able to snatch our hands back, but I saw Eli's quick wince. If he got burned, that was his problem.

Sixteen seconds. That was about all we had before the flame went down enough to get a clear shot. I dropped to my knees and began to rub my hands over the dirt, pushing the loose mounds aside. Relief flooded my body when I felt the raised edge of the utility hole cover.

"Eli, over here!"

Eli left his watch to join me, shoving at the dirt. With both of us clearing, I was able to find the tab.

Seven seconds.

Groaning with effort, I shot my fingers into the small opening, acknowledging the wave of discomfort that meant an abrasion or breaking bone and pulled at the cover. After a creak of its own, it came loose.

One second. A bullet whistled by my ear.

"Get in, Eli."

He stared dubiously at the dark hole. There was no way to see what lay ahead. There wouldn't be, no matter how long you stared. "Now."

Obediently, he braced his arms and lowered his body halfway into the hole before giving me a slight head shake and letting himself drop. I heard the splash that meant the tunnels had a waterbed.

The fire licked at my back, the reaches of the inferno stretching into the alley. Whatever chemical they'd sprayed as ammunition was doing its job.

I turned my head for one last look and grinned as the men's dark silhouettes remained trapped behind the blaze. Thanks, comrade, I thought and offered a small salute before dropping into the tunnel.

Game on.

20

The Hungry Tunnels

Eli was quiet the entire time that I strained to close the lid from below- an ordeal that never seemed to get easier, no matter how many times I'd done it- but spoke once the darkness enveloped us.

"This is where you tell me we have nothing to worry about, right?"

Submerged in the shimmering black of the tunnels, I couldn't see but a foot in front of me. "Oh, well, Eli. There are always things that breed worry." I undid the flap of my pouch and struck a match, the weak flame doing very little against the hungry dark. "It's just an active choice not to participate."

I was still grinning, the sides of my cheeks puckering into deep dimples that marked my oval face.

"Well, I'm glad you're feeling chipper."

The excitement was well and healthy, brimming at my core. "Just in my element."

"Your element is stinky, slimy caverns?" Eli asked dryly, lifting his palm to the light and showing me the smudge on his hand. "What is this, anyway?"

I hesitated, investigating the blemish as if I didn't know what it was.

"I'm going to be honest with you, Eli. You don't want me to answer that."

"What the fuck?" He wiped his palm on the leg of his jeans. "Then why are we standing in it?"

"Because," I drawled, "We'd have turned to crisp otherwise."

My match puffed out in a small burst of smoke.

"What's stopping them from following us down here?" Eli asked as I groped blindly to light another.

"Oh, no, nobody would risk coming down here. Really, Eli. I'd thought you'd known." Eli reached out when I continued to struggle to light the flimsy match and blocked my fidgeting hand with his.

"I've got something better."

Moments later, a tiny spark puffed alit. The cigarette lighter.

I studied the sides of the tunnel, seeking anything I could use for a larger light conduit. "You wouldn't happen to have anything in your pack that I could safely light on fire, would you?"

Eli blinked slowly at me. "You can't just do some funky voodoo shit?"

Incredulous, I pushed an exhale out of my nostrils. "Nothing I do has anything to do with the supernatural." Spotting his small smile, I lightly shoved his shoulder. "Oh, a joke. Funny guy."

"I don't have much in here, but you're welcome to look." He turned to face the wall and hovered his pack in front of my face in an offering.

Later in the day, it wouldn't matter quite as much whether we had a light source or not, but for now, we'd be lucky to make it five feet without falling over ourselves.

Jerkily, I pulled the zipper open and forced myself not to wrench my guilty hand back when I saw the shimmering laptop just below the cover. 'It's okay,' I reminded myself. It's just a computer. Just a stupid computer.

Expelling another heavy breath, I pushed it aside and rummaged through the rest of the contents. A thick sweater, a crinkled book, a bent comb, half a short bottle of clear liquid.

At the bottom of the bag, the fleshy pad of my hand gripped the flat steel of what I could only assume to be a small sword, engraved with shallow grooves and twisting curls.

"Dude," I said, the word slipping from my mouth though it hadn't belonged to me in years. The juvenile was already smoking back into oblivion as I pulled the blade out. "Do I want to know what you were planning on doing with this?"

"You're the one who wanted to go through my stuff. Can't complain about what you find."

Grumbling, I tossed the slender weapon back into the sack and slapped the top flap shut, giving his shoulder a small tap to signify I had finished. He swiveled to face me, the lit lighter still flickering shadow creatures on his face. "Don't know how to make a lantern out of a dagger, Valencia?"

I was cranking my mouth open to respond when an engine rumbled to life above us, the splash of the tires making the soft ceiling dip with the weight.

Without so much as a second thought, I grabbed his arm. "They're going to start blasting," I hissed out, taking full, rapid strides.

"I thought you said we didn't have to worry," Eli puffed out, but I didn't need to drag him anymore. His feet slapped in the puddles alongside mine, and the sound comforted me, long after the lighter hissed out, and I was no longer able to verify he was with me visually.

"Follow my voice, okay? Stay with me." Stay with me. Caleb laughed from somewhere in front of me, ample and dark. Stay with me. My heart thudded dimly.

"I can see the tail of your cloak at some corners," Eli responded, and I realized he was right. The tunnels were brightening- only by a fraction, but it was happening. "How much further?" He pressed, and the detriment of having a travel companion was starting to irk me.

"Not much," I responded hastily, cutting myself off when the arm of my cloak snagged on a low hanging iron bar. The familiar feel of tearing flesh registered but blipped away. "We just needed to put some distance between them and us."

"Would they actually toss a bomb down here?" His statement was broken up with laboured breathing and sloppy footfalls.

"Some might," I replied in what I hoped was the verbal manifestation of a shrug. "Others are too afraid of what it might do to the plate."

Comfortable now that we'd weaved several turns between us and the entryway, I jogged lightly to a stop and braced an arm to block Eli from trampling me.

"We're stopping?" He asked breathlessly.

"If they were going to send something down, they would've already."

"So they're just letting us go." Eli snorted, lightly dusting his palms against the front of his jeans. "If I'd known it'd be that easy, I might have considered checking out the tunnel system earlier."

I sneered, though I knew the darkness would keep the expression between it and me.

"They aren't letting us go," I mumbled, biting my tongue at the insult that threatened. "They're assuming the tunnels will kill us, so they don't have to."

Eli's arm grazed mine as he shifted beside me, and I could almost picture the look of quiet speculation as he struggled to make out the things that went bump in the dark.

"It doesn't seem nearly as bad as everyone makes it out to be. Sure, a little dark, a little wet. But not overly threatening or dangerous," he commented, and from somewhere north of us, a stream of water began to pour into the tunnel.

"It's not what you can anticipate," I said softly, wrapping my arms around myself in a tight hug. "It's what you can't."

"What?" Eli's voice was incredulous. "What does that even mean?"

"When you're down here, you're out. Out of the bubble. Out of protection. Out of safety." I fidgeted. "Closer to the real world than people have been for a long time."

"Yeah, but you're not all the way out. If we're down here, we're still encased in Hartwell's special metal."

"You'd think that makes it better," I said, remembering the days those stubborn statements pushed their way from my chest, not his. "But sometimes the walls become your coffin."

The tail end of my sentence stumbled into softness, almost being drowned out by the lame trickle of water that continued beyond us.

When people spoke of the tunnels, they spoke of monsters and demons and things beyond our control- hunters and predators that would crush our bones with hungry fists and slanted eyes. A threat from a world outside of ours.

There were no monsters down here aside from the ones we brought down here ourselves. Without sentience, the tunnels could not be or do evil, but that was what made them so dangerous.

They would never spare mercy, no matter how you cried for it.

It was minutes before we moved again, this time accepting the absence of light.

"Have you seen their dangers firsthand, then?" Eli asked, and I could tell he was tiptoeing around my unreadable mood.

"In a way." Screaming. Running. Scrambling.

Stay with me.

"And what does that look like?" Eli asked, and his fumbling hand found my elbow in the dark. "So that I know when to be afraid."

Disregarding the slimy film on the wall, I laid a hand against the cold metal. "The sides will get hot. Warm, at first. But then it grows. Like a disease. You take off your first layer, but it doesn't matter. Every effort you make to cool yourself down, the tunnels will match it with another degree hotter." My tongue darted out and moistened my lips. "The shakes start after. Sometimes it's hard to tell if it's just you. But then the entire thing starts to hum. Like a car rumbling to life.

Before you know it, the floor starts to feel like it's just slipping away. You try to get your feet planted, but it's like the swamp water begins to bubble and pull at you. What seemed like a half-foot of goop-" I raised my shoe off the floor, accentuating my statement with the squelching release of my foot. "-suddenly seems like tar, and you're caught. Next thing you know, it's in your mouth, your lungs- behind your teeth like sour candy. If you're lucky, it ends there. If you're not..." My mouth felt sickly and dry from the explanation.

"If you're not what?"

"If you're not lucky... well, it gets hot enough- the metal starts to warp. Men get their legs twisted in the bowels of this tunnel system." I cleared my throat.

"Does that mean we..." Eli had stopped walking, but his hand remained wrapped like a vise around my soft-fleshed elbow.

"What?"

"What are we walking in, Valencia? Fallen men?"

I cracked the krick in my neck and freed my arm. "Something like that."

"Man," he said in a strange, barely-there voice. "That's fucked up."

"Isn't it all," I replied.

~~~~~~~~~~~

It was impossible to know what time it was when the noise from outside had roused us from our sleepless nights, but it must've already been close to morning. It was apparent in the short hour after our journey began when the sun started to rise and pour dribbling light into the underpass.

Our trip through the tunnels had been monotonous, but that was the magic of the risk. More often than not, you could get away with it.

You only needed to worry about the one time you didn't.

We'd stopped again only once, taking a swig of the single water flask Eli had had the forethought to pack. Our conversations stayed light and sparse as if we both knew the other needed the time to think.

There was a question hanging over both our heads that neither of us wanted to ask, though I was sure it needed to see the day. We had been heading for the Centre since we'd escaped from the South, but now that we were nearing it, I felt my stomach sinking.

"Eli," I started, but he was already nodding along.

"I know."

"What are we going to do?"

"Plan stays the same," he said firmly, his jaw set.

"How can it stay the same?" I pushed. My feet swelled with pressure and itched from the moisture seeping through the
~~~~~~~~~~~

sole. "Seriously, Eli. We're wet, cold, tired, filthy. Not to mention we reek. How will we make it past the City Centre's threshold like this, let alone the fourth floor? They'll stop us within seconds under suspicious activity."

"I'm not quitting. Not when we're this close," Eli spat out. "We have everything we need; we just need to get in."

"And I'm not saying we don't do it." In a rare move, I slid in front of him and braced a hand on his chest, forcing him to a stop. His erratic heart pounded beneath my palm. The move to soothe and comfort flashed so quickly into my brain, heat shot to my cheeks in a blooming stain. "But if we want to do it right- if we want actually to make a difference for those kids- then we need to make sure we're successful. And stumbling into a hive of our enemies like a couple of bumbling fools, we're not going to get far."

Muscles still tensed, but not denying what I was speaking was the truth, Eli exhaled, his warm breath fluttering the strands of hair around my jaw. "What's your plan, then? We're way too far to try to go back to my place, and the people downtown are a bunch of rats. No offense," he added quickly, "But we can't trust any of them."

"Rats," I replied, unable to fight back the smile. It was true. "What if we didn't need to see anybody?"

"What you got in mind?"

Feeling a spark glimmer to life beneath my breastbone, I pulled my hair back into a loose ponytail and slipped it into the neck of my shirt. "There's an exit point that connects directly to the Harris house. We could stop there, do some recon, find a change of clothes."

"You think that's safe?" He was dubious.

"They've already conducted their search and tear," I commented, referring to the aggressive and careless way of stripping down a house. "They'd be long gone."

"That's a pretty big risk, Val."

Agitated, I shook my head and pulled at the cord of my handbag. "Even if it is dangerous, we need the practice. If we can't take a few grunts on the ground, we're never going to make it to the fourth floor of the Centre."

Eli deliberated, scrunching his brow into a crinkled fold. After another quiet moment, he nodded unambiguously.

Suddenly filled with a brimming cocktail of excitement and nerves, I danced back to movement, shifting my weight from one soggy foot to another.

"How does one find a specific entry point in this godforsaken place?" Eli lifted a paper draping off the tunnel wall with pinched fingers as we walked. "It all looks the same."

"To someone inexperienced, maybe," I tossed back, though I knew after enough time in here the repetitive views could cost you your sanity.

There was only one way to figure out which was which, and to do so, you needed at least a preliminary knowledge of the codes and synopses the original Settlers had developed. Most exits had a yellow number, though most had been faded down or covered by the tunnel barnacles that grew and ate at the hardest bits of the cave. If you couldn't see the numbers' curves, they were similarly identifiable by the amount of dots that followed in succession. The Harris house was one of the only exits that were utterly wiped out by the churning throat of time, a door with an absence of a marker.

Though, now that I thought of it, I was sure Harris had something to do with the obscurity. She had always been a cautious woman. A smile warmed my numb lips. A fascinating, rumbling, overbearing woman.

"Hey, Val. Is this one?"

I turned to find the source of the sound- Eli, awkwardly shifting while he adjusted the bulky pack, was pointing at a ladder leaning against the wall that stretched up to the ceiling.

The tunnels' muddy waters were thicker here, forcing me to wade through the molasses with haste. I aimed to bundle up the legs of my pants to keep the dampness from expanding, but it was futile. There was hardly any hope of saving what I was wearing right now. I felt a small pang at the thought of my cloak being irreparable but brushed it off and redirected my focus to the task at hand.

The wall across from me showed no immediately visible markings of an access point, but upon closer inspection, I was able to identify the edges of a sign. I hopped up onto the raised sill and grabbed hold of it.

"Come closer, would you?"

Begrudgingly, Eli slid over to me, his eyes slanted and trained on the attenuated edge of the tin sign I had curled a finger over. "What?"

I jutted my chin at the shirt he had stripped off and tied casually around his waist. "Give me that."

"You can't be serious."

"Do you want to get out of here or not?" I asked pointedly, then stretched out my free hand. "Hand it over."

Reluctantly, Eli untied the slipshod knot and passed it with a faltering movement, a grimace gracing his face. The fabric, warm and damp from his body, landed in my hand with a 'thwop.'

Up until now, so consumed by the movements of the cavernous tunnels, I had paid Eli little mind. Now, as the insides were in the midst of a flood of soft beams of light, I could make out the slopes of his muscles and the sheen of sweat that glimmered over his buttery skin. The pack must've been burdensome, as the straps were leaving deep red marks on his shoulders. Should I have offered to carry it?

"You just going to stand there or what?" Eli asked, annoyed.

"No," I jeered back, uncomfortably warm from the heat spreading to my cheeks. Who was I kidding? Had I offered, he'd have merely tossed it back in my face anyways.

Channeling the fuels of embarrassment after being caught in what could've been construed as a longing gaze, I rubbed furiously at the grime burned atop the sign. The goop fell off in gobs, splashing dirty water up around my ankles.

"See anything yet?"

I was midway through the third character, which was all I was going to need to determine what side of the Beamline we'd be popping out. My knuckles rubbed raw on the metal, snagging in the wrinkle of my second finger. Softly letting out a single curse, I finished polishing the surface. The bold, block title read: 45D.

"What does that mean?" Eli poked, unable to quiet his inquiring nature.

"Anything in D block is around the suburban area of middle city."

"So, we're close."

"Close-ish. There's a fork coming up that will take us out towards Harris."

I hopped down and offered his shirt back with an outstretched hand. When he didn't take it, I shook it impatiently. "You don't want it?"

"Honestly?" Eli pinched it between two fingers and twisted it in front of him, staring with glazed eyes at the dark smear on the front of the shirt. "I don't think I could feel clean wearing this bad boy ever again."

I laughed and reached out, unclenching his fingers with mine and let the shirt fall to the ground. "Just leave it, then. These floors have seen many things left behind."

"You say stuff like that with such ease," Eli said as we started moving again. "As if it doesn't bother you to think of the people who lost their lives here."

I shrugged, keeping my eyes peeled for the split path. "The risk is a reality of using this system. Everyone knows that going in."

"So that makes their deaths less sad?" Eli hiked the straps of the pack higher on his shoulders, redistributing the weight. "That makes them less worthy of grief?"

"There are too many things worth of grief to distribute it properly," I replied, "People die up there, on our land, every day. If we were to stop and give a moment of silence for every life lost, we'd never speak again."

"That doesn't mean you shouldn't feel a little empathy for them," Eli contended, but I was too distracted to feel even a dim spark of argumentativeness.

Empathy was something I might've known once- something I might've dabbled in, rubbing it into the soft skin of my wrist like a subtly scented perfume- but that wasn't me anymore. There was no time to grieve the dead when I, too, wielded a hand that brought people there. I had no right to feel such emotion. I peeked at Eli's face and his tight jaw, the aristocratic nose, the delicately slanted eyes. I had no right to any emotion at all.

"Toxic," Eli suddenly said.

"What?"

His eyes swung to mine, tinged with mania. "The shit we're splashing in. Is it toxic?"

Casually, and because I didn't know for sure, I raised a foot out of the puddles and studied the blackened smudges. "Nah."

"If its bodies, it is," he accusingly retorted, a drop of pride in his voice as if he was catching me in a slip-up.

"I said it was something like bodies."

"What exactly does that mean?" He pressed.

Dusting off my shoulder, I was impervious to his anxiety. "They've been baked to a crisp, Eli. The moisture is just leaking down from the plate. Oils, fuel." I gestured at a leak that was drip-dropping from a hose. "Rainwater."

"Yum," he said sarcastically, but my answer seemed to soothe him.

"Tell me, Eli," I started, but cut myself off when I spotted the opening. "That's it!" I exclaimed, scrambling towards the intersection.

The entire clearing was only a few feet wider than the tunnels and split off into two more exit points.

Lightly jogging, Eli joined up with me in the circumvent. "Which one do we take?"

It was a good question. Fuck. It looked the same. It all looked the same. How did I figure this out before? What was it?

Breathe, Valencia. I closed my eyes. I forced myself to go back to the week before. Leaving the sanctuary of Harris' home. Noises against the door. Running into the tunnels.

Splashing. Cool walls. Cooler water. Turn. Run. Turn again. There.

The circle. Into the circle. Straight across from me- suburban.

I opened my eyes and stared into the deep black of the opening in front of me.

"That one."

~~~~~~~~~~

The corridor was long and dark- one of the only sections of the tunnel that weren't broken up by the streams of light coming through the open holes in the ceiling. There were no stops between the intersection and the Harris house, and if there had been before, they were long blocked off by structures and buildings alike.

It was a journey I had taken many times, just me and the darkness, a slip of paper tucked in my breast pocket. There was a newfound comfort in traveling with Eli- the soft whooshing of his breath reminded me I had started a new story; one that was void of those slips of paper and what they meant.

The ground beneath my feet was softening and becoming malleable, my weight pushing down into the boggy floor.

"We're close," I said, the moisture rapidly dwindling in my mouth.

"How can you tell?" Then, crash. Something clattered from his side, accented with a softly spoken curse. "It's dark as hell."
~~~~~~~~~~

"The ground's been mulched." I reached out a hand to try to feel the wall. "Harris put it in to absorb moisture so it wouldn't flood."

I lurched forward as my shin came in contact with what could only be the first step in the shabby stairs that lead up to her cellar. Carefully, I pressed my hand into the air in front of me, rubbing it along the ridges.

"Hey, Eli. Over here."

There was a smattering of rustling as he breached the distance and landed his hand on the small of my back. Deciding not to comment, just for this once, I started up the ladder.

I poked my head through the hole, catching sight of the small strip of light from beneath the door, and the shape of the bookshelf still shadowing along the line. I pulled myself through with Eli following close behind.

"You got any juice left in your lighter?" I asked, fumbling at the crooked lock.

When I'd made my way through here in scrambling haste, I'd done a bit on the lock, desperate to keep even the flimsiest wall between the Council's men and me. It had seemed like a good idea then- maybe not so much now.

"Maybe, but probably not a lot. What about your matches?"

I lightly laid a hand against the purse that rested on my leg. Moisture had made its way into the fibres of the hanging bag, leaving a damp spot on my upper thigh. "Wet."

With a final triumphant flick, the lighter puffed on, emanating a meager glow that illuminated the knotted coil I'd tied around the padlock.

"Do you have the key?"

"Do I have the key," I muttered mockingly, pushing into my bag and rummaged through the hidden compartment sewn into the side. "Of course I have the key."

With wet, blundering hands, I groped at the padlock, the slimy metal fighting me the whole way. It was amazing how things would grow down here. How fast an object could get swallowed by the dark ooze that coated the tunnels.

The padlock gave way, though unwillingly, and bounced down between the cracks of the stairs, quietly disappearing into a yearning black.

"Wow, hope you weren't hoping to save that," Eli commented, laughter dancing on his tongue.

Ignoring his inane pestering, I busied myself with the unraveling of the light cord, getting stuck on a tight knot in the middle. I swore under my breath as my nail was caught and tugged backward in the process. "You've got to be kidding," I murmured, too engrossed in the activity to register Eli's lighter had, once again, fluffed out.

"Do you hear that?" He asked, confusion laden in his tone.

"What?" I grunted in frustration at the knot, straining my tired, numb fingers to crook a hook into the tangle. "I don't hear anything."

"Stop," Eli said, resting his broad hand on my busy ones. "Listen."

For a moment, there was only silence but then- a distant creak. "Somebody's in there."

I shrugged his hand off and finished loosening the knot. "Maybe."

"You don't care."

The vinyl cord slipped off in a slither and dangled limply in my hand. "I just want to be out of here, Eli. And I'm confident in our abilities to tackle whatever lies on the other side of that door. Okay?"

An intelligible mumble from Eli's side gave me all the encouragement I needed to twist the knob. I leaned my weight against it, but the door only groaned back.

"Hey, big guy," I commented, the edges of taunting in my voice. We both knew he was more lean and rangy than formidable. "I could use some muscle on this."

"Oh, now you want my help," he teased back, but I felt the landing shift as he joined me near the door. "Want to count to three?"

"Just push," I said firmly.

With the two of us applying pressure, we were able to crack the door open a few more inches.

"Jesus," I said, blinking furiously at the sudden blinding nature of the sunlight. "I almost forgot what the sun was like."

"A giant ball of fire?"

The door jolted forward, pushing the shelf out of the way and sending the two of us tumbling into the day. I barely saved myself from wiping out, catching my falling frame on the edge of the desk- an item once tucked beneath the front window, but now lived in the middle of the room toppled on its side. "Shit," I breathed, caught in an exhale as my brain registered the room.

The floor that Harris had been so meticulous about keeping clear- 'A cluttered room is an obstacle course we can't afford,' she'd always say- was shrouded in loose papers and torn fluff gouged from the slashed couch across from me. The desk I had used as my safety harness was missing its drawers with one long, ugly scratch across the tabletop.

"They really went to town on this place," Eli said, lifting his foot to peel an empty envelope from his boot. "What were they looking for?"

"Information." My throat scratched in a surprising physical response to the trashed room. "Harris had tons of it. On nearly every member of the Council."

"Even down to the Chairman?"

"She always said she did. I never believed her," I said, picking my way through the debris. A broken vase- one of Harris' little tasteful decorations she had littered through the house- smashed to smithereens at the doorway, the sand rifled through with the thin lines of a comb. "But this is making me think maybe she did."

"It's pretty rare that they wouldn't just torch the place," Eli shifted the pack off his back and dropped it onto the couch, sighing in relief at the shifted weight. "She must've been some special kind of lady."

I snorted, peering into the hallway. "A lady she was not. Special, yes. Sometimes..." I trailed off, pausing to scan the long hallway for movement or sound. "Sometimes I feel weird calling her a woman at all. It was like she transcended all gender and labels. Harris was merely Harris."

"Huh," Eli replied noncommittally.

"You shouldn't leave the bag down here," I said when he joined me at the doorway. "The house isn't secure. We don't know if we're alone yet. Keep it on you."

Huffing in frustration, Eli rounded back to the couch and grabbed the bag, wincing as the weight pulled at his sore shoulders. "You're right, again."

"Here," I said, reaching out and pulling at the strap. "I've got it, okay? Let me do it."

Eli stared down at me, an expression of puzzlement delicately glazing his face. "Okay, thanks."

"Okay," I said, avoiding eye contact as I slipped the bag onto my back. My cloak bunched around my arms, awkwardly folding into the slope of my armpits. I'd need to take it off at some point but preferred doing so in the comfort of my room-whatever it looked like now. At least it was smaller, and easier to verify a safe perimeter.

"Watch our backs," I tossed over to Eli as I lead us toward the staircase.

"Does that give me permission to check you out from behind?"

The smile that graced my face was small and involuntary- nothing more than a mere turn of the lip, but Eli caught it. "Is that a yes?"

"Can you save your jokes until we've secured our position?" I deliberately stepped on the edges of the stairs, carefully avoiding the sagging middle that was bound to creak. Eli, of course, moved soundlessly regardless.

I was in the middle of speculating on those impossible movements again when something creaked from the top floor. "Okay, I heard that one," I whispered.

Noiselessly, we reached the top of the steps. The upper floor was in slightly better shape than the lower- some of Harris' frames were still dangling skewed on the wall, and her patterned rug lay unwrinkled in the middle of the floor. I turned to Eli and crooked a finger in a slight angle, gesturing towards the open door of my living space. If I knew anything, I knew this house- and I knew each creak, whine, and whimper of the old plaster.

Holding my breath back in a restricted inhale, I nudged the crooked door open with my toes, pausing when I heard rustling from inside. Whoever it was, their training was feeble and uninformed. They should've been aware of us the second we stepped into the living room. I shook my head in casual judgment but still decided to leave the gloves sedentary in my purse.

No matter experience, you always needed to treat your adversary as a worthy one.

I pushed the door open with the crest of my knee, knocking it wide open and revealing the room that was once my home.

You couldn't take a single thing for granted here. Not a single, goddamn thing.

21

Tell Me You Know How To Save The World

The man on the other side of the room hunched his crooked back over the table Harris had once carefully set below a triangular window, his dirty fingers knuckle deep in the drawer.

"Who are you?" I asked, but my voice was muted and non-confrontational. Eli was no longer behind me, but I knew better than to worry. He would, no doubt, appear once again when he was needed.

In a clumsy and awkward movement, the man turned away from the desk, guiltily slamming the drawer shut and fumbling to the side of the long table.

"I was- it was- they said-." He stuttered out, his eyes darting from one side of the room to the other.

I was visible, intentionally so, but kept my back to the wall and my face in the shadows. "Who are you," I repeated, firmer.

"Me? I'm nobody. I'm just dirt. Garbage, really," the man blathered on, taking breaks to nibble at his dirty fingernails. "They said it was empty. They said it was up for grabs. They said we could just come right on in. Take what we want." He giggled then, a decidedly unpleasant sound coming from his mouth of broken, rotted teeth and a fishy tongue. "What we want."

"Who said?" I pressed. The man seemed less and less like a threat every minute, but I wasn't finding myself wanting him around any more despite that. The guy was drugged out- on what I couldn't be sure.

"Tall guys. Tall guys with short hair. White, white, silver, white."

Senators. I pressed my tongue against the back of my teeth and considered. What were they playing at? Why would they be sending bottom feeders to clean the place out? A new use for the previously labeled useless members of society? I couldn't be sure.

"You need to leave," I said, already fatigued by the interaction. There was no use warring for information with people who were as far gone as he was.

"That's not fair. Not fair. They said. I want what I came for. It's mine."

Caught in the tense and unyielding limbo of a man's sheer will and my inherent stubbornness, I relented, leaning a hip on the corner of the sagging mattress to support the added weight of the bag. "What was it you came for, then?"

The man scratched at the skin behind his ear- a habit he must've been fond of since the flesh there was ragged and raw, puckered with sores that had been picked at until they turned to canyons. "I was looking for somma' that stuff they use. They use to make us better." He mimicked puncturing his thigh and pushing down the syringe. "It makes me alright." He lifted his head to meet my eyes, the soft amber of them wet with sadness. It was there that I saw a glimpse of the man he might've been, the boy he once was. "I need to be alright again."

"What are they making better?" I pushed gently. "What are they fixing?"

"Me," he said forcefully, then, quieter, "Me, me, me, me, me."

"What's so wrong with you?" Damn it, Eli. I glanced at the doorway but saw no movement. Where are you?

"I don't know, girl. Girl. Girls." He twitched, whacking his head with the side of his palm. "They just kept saying they needed to fix me, fix my code, re-code, re-code. So I need the-

"He paused and mimicked the stabbing gesture again, this time in his neck.

"You know," Eli's conversational voice came from the other side of the room, near a narrow closet. "I think I saw some downstairs."

The man whipped around, rapping his shin off the leg of the table. "Y-you. Who. You. Nowhere. Him. Like before. Magic man. Magic man. Magic man." He scrambled backward, nearly overshooting the doorway. "Magic man knows. He knows."

I waited until he'd left the room- gauging the distance by his continued mumbling- then turned back to Eli.

"Did you hear that?"

"Which part?" Eli busied himself with removing his shoes, pulling at each lace, and letting it unwind before kicking the sodden pair to the floor.

"All of it. To start- the Council giving him something off the street," I slipped the backpack off my shoulders and left it on the cushion, knocking the door closed to secure our perimeters. "He's not some runaway kid or an eligible transfer, not to mention, he doesn't seem as if he could afford it himself. That man was worn down," I said, watching Eli as he paced restlessly around the room.

"You know that people can make money in a lot of different ways, Val. Maybe he's a hustler. Or a swapper."

"You can't buy injections from any site I know. Needles are impossible to source down here. Any medication comes in liquid gels. The Council is treating him for something under the table," I replied confidently, "The question is what, and why. If he's sick, why do they care? They've never bothered before."

"And if they're even administering something he needs," Eli pointed out, always more ready to indulge in a conspiracy than I. "Maybe they're looking for those kinds of people on purpose. The people who seem too far gone."

I mused at that, letting out a grumbling exhale. "Taking the next step in their plight of scientific correction, I guess."

"Another day, another issue." Eli unbuttoned the snap of his jeans, letting the waistband hang open.

"Getting naked again, Eli?" I averted my gaze, staring furiously at the space on the wall beside his head.

"I need a shower, man," he dragged a hand raggedly through his greasy hair. "You might be used to that skanky tunnel, but I can feel that shit on me like a coating."

"Not sure if the water's still on," I said as it occurred to me. "If the Council's out there encouraging people to come in and take what they want, they probably took out the amenities already for safekeeping."

"Guess it's good I'm going first then," Eli drawled, lackadaisically strolling to the open door on the opposite side of the room.

"Check the tub for murderers," I said it playfully but stood guard at the door to the hallway.

"Why would I have to check?" Eli asked with a quirk at the corners of his mouth, pulling his shirt off in one effortless motion. He paused to deliver a lingering glance. "You're out here."

I was still shaking my head moments later, long after he'd shut the door. Funny guy, I thought to myself, glancing around the room. Real funny.

Fuck, it felt weird to be back. Following Eli's lead, I slipped my feet from my shoes and let my feet sink into the threadbare carpet, as I had so many times before. It was my room, still with the modest touches that showed I lived here- engravings in the surface of the desk, the worn mattress, the small writing on the wall- but it no longer felt like it belonged to me.

So awful how fast that happened. So awful... the ache pressed into my chest with a lead foot. How quickly we adapt, evolve. Change. Exhausted, I rested my face in my hands and closed my eyes. Was that a blessing or a curse, to be so ready to part with the things we once claimed to love?

I heard the shower sputter on from the bathroom and, at least, found relief in the knowledge I too would soon be bathing the stink off of me.

That was where Eli found me- curled like a question mark on the bed, my fingers pulling at the edges of my face like tape too tight, my shoes discarded on the carpet.

"You okay?" He asked, his low voice rumbling at an octave that made my stomach feel warm even though the rest of me was trembling from the cold. I looked up at him- took in the low-tied towel on his hips and the way he rubbed another, smaller hand towel over the spiraling curls atop his head- and then dropped my face back into my hands, barely suppressing a groan and rubbing at my temples.

"Just a headache or something," I bluffed, knowing very well the strange and nauseating feeling wasn't coming from any physical pain. "Water worked, I take it?"

"Yeah. It's cold, though. Like bloody ice pellets." Eli grinned then, a cheeky, childish grin that exploded across his face in quicksilver glory. "No heat whatsoever."

"Ack," I sounded, raising from my claimed stoop to meet him at the entryway to the bathroom. "The hot water was always bullshit even when the bills were getting paid. Shit's nonsense."

"So, you're still gonna do it?"

Despite the melancholy hovering over my head like a storm cloud, I paused at him and cocked an eyebrow. "I'm sure as hell not staying dirty and stinky while you smell and look like a damn feast to a starving man."

Eli feigned shock, pressing a veined hand against the muscles of his chest and left his mouth gaping comically open. "Valencia... are you flirting with me?"

Exasperated, I glided past him and proceeded to slam the door smartly in his face.

"A door won't stop this," he called out casually from the other side, and since I knew he wouldn't be able to discern my reaction through the door, I allowed the smile.

Harmless fun was a luxury I'd all but forgotten- especially such that involved flirtatious taunting. Intense, brooding types tended not to be caught up in the frivolity of romance, joking or not. Eli seemed to fall on the other side of the plate in that sense, lapping up the jokes as if he needed it to survive. I was beginning to think that maybe he did.

Methodically, I began to shed my clothing layers, dropping them into one heaping pile in the corner of the small bathroom. I wondered if Eli had even started to feel the acute anxiety about what we were about to do. If he had, he was awfully good at pretending he wasn't.

I bent into the tub at an awkward angle and cranked at the thin rubber hose.

The water flooded out in choppy waves, splashing droplets up the sides of the greying tub. When some splattered on my arm, I sucked in a sharp breath and pulled myself out of the splash zone.

Eli wasn't kidding. The water was fucking cold.

Gritting my teeth, I stepped into the needling spray, standing tense as the water slid off my naked form in sheets.

It didn't feel possible that I was back here, in this bathroom- where I'd washed the blood of many off my skin, where I've sobbed, stricken by guilt and grief, where I'd stared at myself in the mirror until I looked like a mere guess of what a person might be.

How was this real?

We were just in Eli's study, looking at notes, studying for a day that seemed light-years away. How could we already be on that day? Thrust upon us like some fucking push of destiny.

The tub's bottom was filling with black gunk, the water no match for the thick mixture that slowly slithered towards the gurgling drain. I used the last of a nearly finished bar of soap to wash off what was left of the tunnel's discharge from my skin.

The flicker of doubts began again, buzzing behind my eye sockets. Two rejects, taking on an entire army of sociopathic missionaries hell-bent on keeping us lower than them? I slammed the shower faucet off and stood shivering in the tub, goosebumps bubbling up on my flesh.

I reached for the last scraggly towel Eli had left hanging on the tarnished rack. We were charging towards a disaster that had the potential to be our end of times, with our eyes closed and our heads down. It was an awful idea. A horrible one. I'd just have to tell Eli it wasn't the right time.

There it was, softly- in the back of my head, that damned voice again- *coward.*

Leaving the sloppy pile of clothes on the tile, I wrenched the door open.

"Eli, I have to," I began, but my words fell away like rain when I saw him at the end of the bed, dressed in a charcoal grey t-shirt and dark jeans.

Caleb's grey-shirt. Caleb's jeans.

"I hope you don't mind." He gestured at the wardrobe choice. "I found this in a bag in the closet. Figured they were too big to be yours."

They had been too big for me, too big for Caleb too, even when he got them. Swaying, I pressed the pad of my hand to my skull. He had been what, fifteen or so when admitted, and I hadn't seen him wear those clothes more than once- his interview clothes that he'd left in the Pharmacy basement. When I'd returned, five odd years later, they were still there, wrapped in plastic beneath the rock and smelling just a bit like him.

God, they were different- so different- Caleb dark and ever-shifting, tall and broad, Eli, all tones of warm amber and terra-cotta, wiry and slim- but perched at the end of that damn bed, they might've been twins.

"Um," I cleared my throat, averting my gaze to hide the sudden dampening of my eyes. "It's cool."

"You alright?" Eli rose to meet me, giving me a few feet of space.

"Yeah, just..." I paused, tightening the knot of the towel that was my modesty. "Just worried," I fibbed.

"About the mission," he soberly stated.

Restless, I shoved by him to the dresser and pulled out one of the drawers. When it was empty, I scoffed with exasperation. Of course, my clothing had been looted. Why wouldn't it have been?

"Mission implies someone's assigned us to do it," I said, my voice prickly and tough.

"Maybe something did."

I let out a short, barking laugh, rubbing my hand over my face. "Don't you start that now."

"I'm sorry, I thought we were on the same page here," Eli replied, crossing his arms over his chest. "Are you having doubts about going?"

"Is that so weird?" I pivoted to face him, the fresh shirt I'd finally discovered draped over my forearm. "It's a hell of a lot weirder to not be worried. Yet here you are, like some fucking sage, acting like we're not running a suicide mission here that I don't even fully understand."

"I didn't know you were unclear," he said, infuriatingly patient as his gaze stayed steady.

Feeling suddenly silly standing across from him soaking wet and barely clothed, I self-consciously crossed my arms over my front. "I get it. Get in, get to their control room, download the information. And then what? All we have is more information. All this fucking information."

"Valencia," Eli said softly, crossing to me. Gently, he cupped my chin in his hand and tilted my eyes to meet his. "Information is power. Thus," he stepped back, allowing me space but kept his eyes smouldering on mine, "The more we inform ourselves, the more powerful we become. Only a fool would discredit the irreplaceable value of knowledge.

We are going to free those kids, Val." He turned around to face the wall, giving me privacy to change. "Then we're going to free the whole fucking town."

22

Here, Now (For You)

The exchange with Eli did little to soothe my anxious mind. I wasn't sure how one man came to have so much faith in us, and I sure as hell wasn't envious of it. That blind faith was dangerous, and it felt as if the siren screams of *'danger, danger, danger'* were swallowing all conscious thought.

I was trying to stay confident- to remain clear, grounded- but my mind kept trying to formulate measly excuses for why we shouldn't do it.

Coward.

Eli, on the other hand, was as steady as the drip of the leaky faucet, maneuvering around my prickly mood with a deft hand and expertise. He had stayed in the room while I changed, delicately enforcing that someone needed to guard the door- though I had locked and secured it- and then, when finished, had made the seamless transition to unloading the backpack of any non-essentials.

The entire transition was wrapped up in less than ten minutes, leaving my long, twisting curls still wet from the shower.

"We're really doing this, huh?" I asked, hugging my elbows to my chest in an infrequent exhibition of vulnerability as Eli fiddled with the laptop on the old desk.

"Yeah," he replied, but he gave me a warm smile. "I know you're scared, Valencia, but you have to trust me." He slipped the USB drive into the port, downloading something into the pill-shaped device. "I know what I'm doing. I've been planning this for a very long time."

"Run it by me again," I nervously demanded when he passed me the drive. It felt heavy and hot in my hand. "All at once."

Eli rotated the chair to face me and leaned back, stretching his legs out in front of him. It made me think of the night he showed up at the motel, strange and cryptic. Had it only been a week ago?

"We head down to the Centre. When we arrive, we get into the respective lines of Sustenance Distribution A and House

Repair Inquiry. Midway through the line, we should be perfectly lined up to Stairwell C and D. You following so far?" I was, but that wasn't surprising. I'd heard each piece spelled out a hundred times. "Using the magnetic strip I'll be wrapping on your finger-" he held up the roll, "-you'll be able to freeze the scanning system momentarily and slip into the stairwell. You'll likely run into at least one guard on that landing, as they usually have someone making patrol rounds." I'd already decided I wouldn't be killing him- I couldn't be wasting my energy. "You'll take the stairs to the fourth floor, whereas I'll be dismounting on the third on my side. I'll be hooking up my computer in Janitorial Sector Four. You clear the passage on the fourth floor, make your way into the Security hub, kill the watchmen, and plug in the device. I'll sync my computer through the signal and download their screen access." Eli smiled, though it was more like a baring of his teeth. "Easy as pie."

"You say that," I mumbled, but tucked the device safely in my breast pocket. "But you're not the one in any danger."

Eli sighed and dropped his head to look at me sternly from beneath a furrowed brow. "You've said so yourself; you can't die. You won't be in any real danger."

There are some fates worse than death, my brain whispered, but instead of speaking it aloud, I offered up a grim smile. "All while you will be safe and snug in a little linen closet."

He scoffed, rising to his feet and slamming the laptop shut. "We'll both be exactly where we are meant to be. Trust in that, if nothing else."

Unconvinced, I ignored him while he began to pack, turning my attention to my own preparation. It was just another mark, Val. Relax. I rotated my stiff shoulder and rolled my neck, trying to shake off my woes.

How many of these had you been on? I slid my knife into the pocket of my pants, burying it next to the strip of magnetic tape Eli had tossed to me earlier. How many guards have you killed before? This wouldn't be any different. In and out. It was just an information recon- the real work hadn't even really started yet. It would just be like a regular day down to the Centre.

The pep talk was working, much to my satisfaction. Eli didn't need to know the person he chose to tackle this with was just a cowardly mutt.

Fuck, I wouldn't let it be the Jockeys all over again. I wasn't a watchdog. I could do this. I pulled my shoelace tight around my hand. For god's sake, Val, how hard was it for you to do something that actually meant anything?

"I think we're all set," Eli said conversationally, his tone carrying the casual cadence of a man packing for a day trip. "You got everything?"

I patted the lumps in my pockets for peace of mind, then, resolving I had my small collection of trinkets, granted him a thumbs up.

"And the drive?" He inquired.

Unwilling to even do a check with the knowledge it was secure, I pursed my lips in disapproval. "Come on, Eli. I know I've been a little on edge about all of this, but that doesn't deem me completely incompetent."

Engaging in a small battle of wills, Eli balanced on his heels and squinted at me, laptop in hand. Then, finally, "Alright. We should get going."

He absentmindedly turned from me, scanning for the bag of which the laptop frequently resided.

"Looking for this?" I grabbed the backpack strap from its place on the floor, swinging it in an outstretched hand.

Apparent in his gratitude, Eli took the canvas bag from me in a graceful dismount. "Are you good?" I asked, able to see his cloudy and distracted state now that my anxious one had cleared.

"No, yeah, I'm okay. I do wish we had more time- that I agree with," Eli replied, but his tone seemed more melancholy than distressed.

"We could always put this off, wait around here for the night," I said slowly, attempting to sound impartial, all whilst wiping my damp hands on my thighs.

"No," he replied, shaking his head firmly. "It's not a secure base. We have no idea what they've got planned for this place, or who they've got coming in. It's way too big of a risk. We've got to go now, while the Centre is open to the public, and we're on our game."

“Fine,” I said, slipping my gloves on, “Then we go.”

~~~~~~~~~~~

No other looters were roaming the downstairs when we passed through, and for which I was grateful. The still-fresh memory of the hunched man was seared in my brain like an ugly branding- an evident and atrocious outlier that didn’t fit with his surroundings. A fluke. A mistake. I swallowed thickly as the acid in my stomach curdled.

We wandered out into the street, where residents of the neighbouring homes were just beginning their day. Most avoided my gaze, casting their eyes downward and shuffling forward as if Eli and I weren’t crossing their paths. A few looked upon me with a familiar reverent horror, a look of ‘is that Harris’ girl?’ pasted all over their faces as they murmured amongst themselves.

“What’s up with that?” Eli muttered to me as someone crossed the road to avoid us.

“People around the neighbourhood have their stories,” I whispered back, linking my arm with his as we took the turn into the downtown, “And many of them have heard of the kind of business Harris runs.”

Gallantly, Eli took my arm in hand. “And I am sure many of them made use of that business when it was beneficial to them.”
~~~~~~~~~~~

"Yeah," I murmured, "It seems hypocrisy runs as rampant as corruption."

"Hypocrisy is corruption," Eli replied through a smile as he gave a passerby a friendly nod.

We were gliding through the town amongst the hustle and bustle under the guise of a happy, although simple, couple. Dressed modestly, we blended in with the rest of the working folk- my bare face and Eli's unruly hair sold the idea that we were of the lowest class- and people paid us little mind. Too wrapped up in their tribulations, even an accidental bump from one of us wouldn't shake them from their troubled state.

It didn't change the fact that the closer we got to the Centre, the more eyes I felt following us like slimy snakes in the night.

"Are you sure no one is looking at us?" I asked Eli, sweat bubbling on the back of my neck. It was still early in the morning, the yawning sun just lumbering to its peak above us, but somehow it seemed hot, too hot, as we made our way through the marketplace.

"No one's looking anymore, Valencia," Eli whispered back, his breath hot on my ear. "No one knows who we are."

God, I was itchy. Was there something on the shirt? Maybe it was the tag. I unwound my arm from Eli's and wriggled in the fabric, pulling at the sleeve.

"Can you relax?" Eli hissed over. "You're going to cause a scene."

The Centre loomed in front of us like a starving demon, the ample doors propped open and ready to chew on the early risers and desperate people that clambered in. I made a small noise in my throat and tugged at my collar, desperately fighting my flight instinct as Eli dragged me forward by my elbow.

"Maybe it's not a good time," I stuttered out, blinking the panic spots from my vision, "There's probably not enough people for us to slip in unnoticed; we're coming in way too early."

We climbed the stairs together, me, reluctantly, and Eli with confidence, and ranged over the threshold, submerging ourselves into the buzzing chaos of the Centre. People swarmed from every angle, all but jumping over each other for a better spot in one of the many lines. Two people engaged in a shoving match stumbled into our backs, sending us tumbling forward. Laughing, Eli steadied me with both hands on my forearms.

"What was it you were saying?" He asked sarcastically, maneuvering himself to circle me. "This place gets busy from dawn there on out. No one wants to wait in line for hours just to be kicked out by closing. You know that."

I shook his hands off of me, indignant. "You never know."

"Yes, you do." He shook his head at my contrarian ways. "Are you going to be able to do this?" He asked after, his voice sickeningly low and kind.

Insulted by the suggestion I couldn't, even though I myself had been doubting it just moments before, I straightened and met his eyes with a stubborn stare. “I can do this, Eli.” I jolted past him, muscling my way into the swarm of people. “I’ll find you when it’s done.”

“Hold on,” Eli landed his hand on my shoulder, waiting for me to turn to him. His face was close to mine now, less than an inch away, and there was something urgent in his eyes that I couldn’t place. “We’re in this together. Don’t forget that. Don’t ever forget that.” His grip tightened. “This is our game. This time we win.”

Perplexed by the insistence in his tone, I rubbed my gloved hand on his bare one. He looked surprised by it, an expression so vulnerable that it was quickly extinguished. “I know,” I said, tongue thick on the words. “I get it.”

After a moment of pause, Eli smiled, released his grip. “Okay.” His eyes searched mine. Seeking. “You’ll come find me afterward.” It was a demand.

In lieu of responding, since anxiety was a hand around my throat, I sent him a joking salute, then plunged into the crowd and weaved my way to the furthest line that twisted around the high walls.

Sustenance Distribution.

It had been lightyears since I’d waited in one of these lines. Before Harris was bringing me home neat little packages with a week’s worth of cubed sus’, even before the Institute, I’d played the tune of the underground market like a damn orchestra player. Thievery, I mused as I stepped into the end of the line, was a hell of a lot more efficient than baking in the heat of human bodies for the bottom of a barrel the Council would dish out.

"Hey! No cutting in line, princess!" Someone barked out from behind me, just moments before a fat glob of spit landed on my shoe.

Disgusted and seething, I whirled to face the miscreant, anger flushing my skin.

"You've got to wait like everybody else," said a woman with crooked teeth and a fat, twitching mole on the bridge of her nose.

It had been a simple mistake- nothing more than misgauging where one line ended and another began- but the crowd was quickly becoming shifty and agitated, a growing rumble from their conglomeration of murmurs shaking the buzz of the room.

"Okay, fuck," I muttered, stepping out of the line, where the patrons behind me all rushed forward to fill the gap. "Give me a break."

I hiked all the way to the end of the line, where it had petered off into a small point. I was able to see the access route to the stairwell from where I stood, but it was minute and far away.

Did Eli really expect me to stand in this line for hours just to get to the starting line? I squeezed my eyes shut and rubbed at a headache that was brewing just below my skull. Someone coughed, then sneezed. There was a shifting of bodies as we gave the person a wide berth; none of us able to afford an illness.

It took nearly twenty minutes to move our first five feet. The air was sticky, hot, and smelly. A man a few people up had stripped down to his bare chest, proudly displaying a patch of scraggly hairs and scabbing lesions.

The mania pushed at the edges of my brain. *What are you waiting for, Valencia? This isn't you. All this waiting. Just waiting, waiting, waiting. What are you waiting for?*

Someone behind me nudged me forward, as I had been a second too late to make a move with the flood of people.

What are you waiting for? The voice hissed again. Then again, and again, until it was all I could think- all I could hear, and feel- that awful, pushing voice, leaving a trail of slime in its wake.

What are you waiting- I slid forward, flattening myself against the wall. No more waiting. No more.

I kept low, tucking my chin close to my chest as I burrowed forward.

Shadows don't deserve to walk in the light.

I pulled the strip Eli had gifted me with from my pocket, winding it around my finger until it was so tight that my fingertip bloomed purple. The short, white fabric was fitted with spikes that poked out from the bed, their heads a darker, near impossible, shade of black that absorbed all glimmers of light.

"Hey," someone said as I bumped their elbow, but I didn't stop. Couldn't. I was so close now. I just needed to get it done. I just needed...

I pressed my finger onto the waiting panel, gnawing on my lip as the machine whirred and beeped back at me.

"Get back in line," someone shouted.

Come on, I quietly willed. Almost there.

The door shot open, seamlessly gliding into its slot in the wall. People around me noticed the suddenly open door, their confused minds all scrambling to gain a closer look at me. I could all but hear their speculations- could I be working for the Council? Why would I have an access pass? Did I know something they didn't?

I bolted in, my weight shifting from the loading panel and sending the signal for the door to snap shut.

Then, nothing.

Alone in the quiet stairwell, the brimming chaos from just beyond the wall was blocked off, deleting those people and their pleas from existence as easy as the act of pressing a button.

It made me think of the protests that had once been lead against the Centre- the campouts of people shouting and chanting for change, for justice- and how they'd been yelling at people who hadn't even given them the grace to listen. All the changes they'd thought they'd achieved with their loud mouths and their hearts brimming with passion had all been a calculated move from the Council, deciding what to offer and what to withhold.

Fuck. I tucked my shirttail back into my pants from where it had shaken loose and smoothed my ruffled hair. I wondered if Eli knew about the soundproofing, or if it would be just another sliver of information awaiting its addition to the collection. I started on the steps, feeling naked and vulnerable without my cloak, and kept my ear perked for any movement above.

There was no reason to be afraid, I said to myself. You've done worse. Hell, you've seen worse. It's just a recon mission. In and out.

The stairs themselves were kept clean but dimly lit and stood nearly half a foot taller than a standard set. My shoes squeaked softly on the mats, echoing into the dark hall. It was almost serene, the ebbing silence, the lack of company. As much as I'd enjoyed Eli's camaraderie, it was nice to be alone. I stopped walking suddenly on the second landing. Alone.

Where was the patrolling guard?

Surely, he would've been through by now. At the very least, my entry into the stairwell would've pinged on the mainframe. Yet no one had been by to check it out?

Unease crawled up my shoulders with pin-pricking legs and a wet tongue, lapping at my ears. It was a near sure thing they knew I was here, in some form, so what were they waiting for? I gulped down the anxiety, feeling it travel in a lump through my throat. How much did they know?

Nervous, I felt for the drive tucked safely in the folds of fabric, soothing myself when the edges met my fingers. In and out.

In and out.

I continued to climb, using the railing like a crutch until my hand protested the pressure with a quick spasm up my arm. I wondered how far Eli had made it into his stairwell, and if he'd had a run-in with a guard.

He could take care of himself, that much I knew, but what if something had gone awry? How would I know?

Third floor.

I hesitated, staring at the irregular shape of the doorknob that graced the narrow entry door. Could he be in there already? Setting up the computer, waiting for my go ahead?

How would I know?

The last flight of stairs felt the tallest. Each one felt like its own mountain, the crest sending spikes into my shins as I pulled my weight over the peak. I was breathing heavily now, my lungs struggling to suck in wheezing breaths as I lumbered onto the final landing.

There was nowhere left to go, no stairs left to climb, no floor above me. I had reached it, and now, there was just me, and this door and whatever might lay behind it. There was no running now, no cowering behind empty barrels or quaking in swampy shadows.

I was afraid, I dropped my hand onto the handle, but I wasn't running. I was here- wholly, fully, every wisp of the ghost I'd become- I was here.

I was *here*.

I closed my eyes and thought of Eli and Caleb and Missus Harris, thought of the empty fields beyond the Beamline and the sweet sugars of the Morris' old bakery. I thought of Kairo and his cherry-bright blood on the front of his sweater, and the hardening of his brother's eyes.

I was here now. I pushed on the handle. And I wasn't running.

23

Gone, Tomorrow

The day I died, there was a light- a brilliant light- so unlike anything I'd ever seen before. It had filled both the air around me and inside of me, warm as a water bath on the twentieth day of summer.

It was the last time I had ever felt whole, submerged in that light.

Maybe I'd been chasing it all this time, ever since that day, peeling back skin as if people were hiding it from me. Just waiting for the day I cracked a ribcage and found it nesting there, just so I could call out a triumphant 'I told you so' and disappear with what was so rightfully mine.

I never found much of anything inside anyone besides blood, and guts, and wretched old secrets. If there had been light there once, it had long since burned out.

It was that same light I was thinking of when I pushed open the fourth-floor door and nearly blinded myself with the fiery white glow of the fluorescent fixtures. The shouting began almost immediately.

There wasn't any time to think, or even breathe. Isn't that the way it went? I clambered onto the back of the nearest guard, flicking open my blade and dragging it across his neck, using his body as a shield for the spray of bullets that began to assault the room. When his dead frame became too heavy for me to carry, I let his body thud to the ground and wrenched his firearm from his holster. There was never any time.

The first bullet to hit me tore through my shoulder, just inches above the one I'd gotten last week in the alley. The pain was a mere flash, a small message notice to my brain I'd been hit but faded off into the deep oblivion. It was all bullshit. Didn't they understand that? Didn't they get that?

I fought with the gun clip, unfamiliar with the pistol's slope and the length of the firing arm. My first shot barrelled into the carpeted floor, splintering plastic and sending shards into the air. I was more successful with my next few, managing to nail the nearer two guards and disarm the further.

My hands began their familiar tingle- something that was near a burn- as if they could smell the death that drenched the hallways and spread like fire. They called to me in a siren call only I could hear, begging to be freed.

An alarm started, a blaring scream that came from all around me. More guards flooded in from an open elevator, roaring through their heavy masks.

Now.

I stripped the gloves from my hands, flinging them towards the bodies that now littered the hallway. The last man I had shot lay bleeding in his injuries, his body desperately clinging to life as it fought the tremors of pain and shock.

"Poor boy," I cooed, dropping to a squat and crawling around him. "Poor, poor boy." I dragged my hand across his face and watched his eyes roll back. "Mercy for the poor boy," I whispered, then closed his eyelids for him.

"Put your hands up!" Someone shouted at me.

I whipped my head up, snarling. They dare direct me? They dare think...

I rose to my feet, moving so fluidly that I barely touched the ground. Who did they think they were?

All they did was take and take and take.

I leaped, scratching one man's arm. He fell like a crumbling building, collapsing in on himself. I must've screamed then, because I heard it, like an unfamiliar friend. A song you once knew, but the melody had been stripped from your brain.

Stolen.

"What is it?" A horrified guard called, caught in a trembling stare with me. "What is she?"

"What are you?" I crowed, wrapping both hands around his meaty neck, feeling his life being sucked out from his skin like an empty pack. "What are you?" I yelled, this time louder as a bullet struck my spine. I threw my head back, yowling at the swaying chandelier light.

My body vibrated like a power surge, shuddering as it flooded through me. There was nothing but this.

I clambered on all fours, building momentum to charge into the quivering knees of the bewildered men. One man freed himself from my form, getting a high enough angle to plunge his blade towards my forehead. I swerved, avoiding the initial impact but feeling it clip the top of my ear. Screaming again, not because of the pain, but because of something worse, I ripped his shirt open and thrust my hand onto his warm skin. His heart strained against the thin membrane and thudded against my palm.

I felt it thump, thump.

Seize.

"We need backup!" Another yelled, but I couldn't see who in the squirming pile of flesh. "God, we need backup! Nothing's working!"

Over the radio left to me, a voice crackled back, but it was unintelligible.

"Send someone, anything!"

I stood, striding over the bodies the same way I'd walked in, crushing the still static radio beneath my heel. There were only minutes left before another stampede of overzealous guards trampled in to find the carnage.

I didn't plan to be here when they arrived.

The Command door was going to be the only unmarked door on the floor. I had read that, back with Eli.

I stumbled, bracing myself on the wall. Eli.

That's right.

My throat scratched and burned as I remembered. Eli. I was here with Eli.

We are in this together. I pulled myself forward, fighting to keep my head upwards. *Remember that.*

Blood poured from my wounds, leaving a sticky red river that flowed like freedom down the hallway. One of the guards- one I must've missed- fired a shot that whizzed past my ear and hit a table on the left side.

Come on, Valencia. I fought the groggy haze that threatened to consume me. *You're almost there.*

With shaking hands, I felt for the edges of the drive in my breast pocket. Still there, I comforted myself. Still going. I choked back a sob. I was still going.

I wasn't running away.

It would be nice to say that I found the Control room door on purpose. That I had drummed up enough energy to raise my head and squint through the ever-flowing waterfall of blood to make out small numbers on the doors, but when I shoved on that door with the crooked lining, I wasn't thinking of anything.

There was nothing.

"Who the hell-." The watchman started, but he cut himself off as I wriggled and dragged my limp body across the floor. "Goddamn it," he said, as I reached my hand out. He lifted his foot to avoid my grip, but I was still fast, even in the state I was in. My hand connected with the bone of his other ankle, forming a loose fist around the protrusion.

"What-." He never finished his thought, but I was sure it wasn't anything I hadn't heard before. He dropped next to me, his doughy face landing in folds that might've been almost comical.

We laid there together for God knows how long- me, staring at the way the drool dripped from his slack mouth and onto the floor, mixing with the ooze that had dribbled from his eyes.

I was tired. No, too tame a word. My eyes feathered shut. There were no words for this feeling. No words for any of it.

Keep going, Cia. Caleb's voice was warm and light, just like the memory as it flowed freely into me. *Keep going, Cia,* dream Caleb echoed.

I howled out as I pulled myself to a sitting position, feeling the pain nowhere but everywhere in the most foreign distribution of it. How could something feel like nothing but everything, all at once?

Breathing heavily, I used my feet to cycle-kick the watchman's body to the door. It wouldn't hold it for long, but it might buy me some time.

Keep going.

I flopped my arms into the holes of the chair, hooking them around the back to hoist myself upwards. It was like a dream- a horrible, messed up, backward dream. I'd been in it before, I was sure of it. How could I have been here before? I stared at the hundreds of screens in front of me, unable to identify any of the rooms or people I saw.

How did they know when they saw something worth anything?

Fuck, the drive. Fuck. I wiggled it from my tight pocket and fumbled to hold it in my bloody hands. I didn't know anything about computers. How was I supposed to know where to plug it in? I didn't know anything. As quickly as the panic had vanished, it began to rise again, kicking and screaming as it quivered up to fruition.

Keep going.

I rose onto quaking legs, inspecting the grooves of the machine. There were no lights in the watch room, only two large, diamond-clear windows that let in the natural light. It was barely enough to find the slots on the devices, but I landed on one that seemed to fit the drive. For a moment, everything stayed the same. The drive, unlit. The screens, on.

Then they began to click off.

It started with the ones at the top of the display, then it dropped down like an outdated game, knocking the screens into darkness. Five, six, seven eight.

They dropped like flies, somehow dropping off into the small drive with a blinking red light until all but one remained. One room. One screen.

One camera.

I leaned closer, squinting at the small picture. It looked like someone was moving in there, like the shadows were shifting to accommodate for it, and one small bright light. Why was that the only one left?

Unable to free myself from the strains of my curiosity, I pulled myself closer- so close that my nose brushed the glass of the display- and it was unmistakable, but I wouldn't believe it. A bobbing head of dark black curls.

The air whooshed from my lungs and left me feeling hollow, the deep breeze of dread blowing through me.

Eli.

"No, no, no," I breathed out, the words coming out so fast they left windburn on my cheeks. Frantically, I began to slam at the keyboard. Why wouldn't it go away? Why was it-

Light exploded across the tiny screen, wiping out the notable shape of Eli's head and his computer. More figures stormed in, decked in black with shapes strapped to their sides.

The last screen went dark.

The device- blipped green.

"What-" I said aloud, covering my mouth with my hand as the tears started. Hot and angry, they poured down my face and into the slope of my throat, mixing a milky blend of tears and blood that stained the front of my shirt. "Eli," my voice cracked out, thin with shock.

"In here!" Was the last thing I heard before the door was being shoved open, acting as a battering ram against the limp body that laid as a doorstopper.

Using my last ounces of energy, I ripped the drive from its slot and tossed it into my mouth, pressing it in place between my teeth and cheek.

Nowhere to go. The group of guards flooded in as one solid mass, moving like a sickness invading the body.

"Stop where you are!"

The room suddenly felt impossibly small, the walls closing in with pressure like the waves of the Spillout. Feelings I thought could never happen again- would never, happen again- engulfed me- the feeling of my entire life and death happening all at once.

It was over.

It was over.

There was nothing else.

I dropped my hands in front of me, clasping them together, and closed my eyes once more- always closing my eyes, always hiding behind something even when there was nothing left to hide behind.

"Grab her!" The guard in the back yelled. "We've got to do this together!"

Together. I peeled my eyes open, trying desperately to remember what Eli had said to me earlier.

We'll both be exactly where we are meant to be.

My second wind rushed through me, invigorating me with a current of strength that didn't entirely feel like it belonged to me. I thrust myself forward, rushing at the masked guards. When they fired, and I knew they would, the shots riddled my body like earth tremors, leaving craters in my skin. *Come on, assholes*. I gritted my teeth.

Miss.

The shatter of glass was louder than the shots, tinkling like an engine wind-chime and exploded into debris.

Yes, I thought maniacally, stumbling back towards the open window. It was a simple equation.

Begin with a fall.

End with a fall.

A guard lurched forward, his fingers brushing my arm.

I was halfway over the edge then, my heels hanging among the last shards of standing glass and the wind tossing my hair like an old rag in the dust when our eyes met.

Eyes like a warming chestnut fire. Eyes that twinkled when they laughed, eyes that shone with mischief and promise. Eyes over an old table, behind a barrel, darkened by the shadows of a tunnel. *Caleb? Why was Caleb here?*

"Cia?" he questioned in a voice so soft I barely heard, but I was falling, the air wrapping around me like a funnel, sucking me down. The humming sound started again, just like the first day I fell. I knew what was coming. I knew it was here.

The light. I smiled as it wrapped around me once more, filling my limbs with joy and dusting away the poison. It would end again, that much I knew- but I could celebrate this moment, before the impact, before the running, before the terror began again.

Our truths, once ours, no longer belonged to us. Our truths faded away, like a scrape on our knee or a message once written, flitting away into the churning stomach of something so much bigger than us. Ever filling us with lies and deceit and failure- chewing at us until it's gnawed away what's left of our goodness and leave us wondering when we became so empty. An evil so sinister we must scrape at the edges and clamber for scraps, begging for things we don't even believe in. We became our fear, and our fears became us- until our spirit was all any of us had- stripped of everything and abandoned, this was all we had left.

Our hope- such stubborn, beautiful hope- was all that we had.

It was all that we were.

EPILOGUE

The Follower, and The End

For a place to rest, the Verity Courtyard garden was as good as a place as any. I hit the ground with enough force that every bone I'd ever cracked, bent, or dislocated snapped like it had just been waiting for a fall like this one. Really, the blinding pain was a bit like coming home. A message to my body of, *'oh, there you are'* and *'I see you.'* If I didn't know that the guards would be coming after me, I would've just stayed in the turf, crumpled in a heap. The sky was clear, the breeze was light, and the turf was the softest I'd ever felt the fake grass to be. It wasn't so bad, even with the splitting pain in the back of my skull and the way my eyes couldn't see to focus anymore.

It wasn't until I heard the sound of commotion just behind the Centre's doors that I managed to bring my feeble arms beneath me, pulling my weight with everything I had left. There, in the flower bed, disguised by the heads of flowers too bright, too cheerful, too false for this city, and everything that was in it, I held my breath as I listened to the stampede of guards enter the Courtyard. It sounded like many, but I knew it was only a few when they began to talk. When they came across the smashed turf and the bloody ring in the dirt like a wet glass on a countertop, they started to laugh, and I had to close my eyes against the fresh wave of hatred that came over me.

"She couldn't have gone far," one muttered, and I heard the easily distinguishable sound of boot into ground.

"It doesn't matter if she did. She'll be dead in a minute just like every other dirtbag down here once the stuff kicks in." Some rustling, then, "Don't think the Senator will mind if we bring back a dead body instead, will he?"

Then they laughed again, and my entire body tensed. My bones were knitting themselves back together, my skin rippling and moving around my wounds like a hungry, pulsating sinkhole, and I was too tired to think of anything but the sun in my eyes and the plush warmth of the soil beneath me. Real soil-fake flowers? I was so tired my eyelids were drooping.

There was someone else coming into the Courtyard, someone who was calmer than the other men. He stepped purposefully, calmly, and spoke with muted, unhurried tones. The guards seemed to disagree at first, but soon the Courtyard was as quiet as it had ever been, nothing but the sound of my deep breathing through punctured lungs and the stiff creaking of the calm man's boots.

"I know you are here," he said, and it was low but unthreatened. "And I know you are hurt."

I didn't even have enough to whimper in protest. I didn't have enough to do anything but lay here, hoping that the flowers covered me enough.

"I am not going to look for you," he continued, and I shifted in surprise.

"But understand this:

Today, I am not looking. But this is in no way clemency."

There was a long pause, a shifting one, something that felt like it weighed a hundred pounds. "You *belong* to me." A pause, a half-second too long that it became obvious it was a threat. "I will find you."

I was going into shock, my vision blackening and my body trembling uncontrollably. I was quickly falling into dreamless sleep, fighting to stay alert and aware when I knew he was still out there, but I was quickly losing the battle. I was seconds away from death when I heard it.

"I will *always* find you, Valencia."

-

ACKNOWLEDGMENTS

The largest and most poignant of thank-you's goes to you, the reader, for being willing and open to support this debut novel. As I've mentioned before, there is no story without active participants like you, and I'd be eternally grateful to you if you were willing to leave a review encouraging others to do the same. Please feel free to join my community on any of my social media, I am most active on Instagram @tjswackhammer, or through my website tjswackhammer.com.

Next, I must extend the most heartfelt of thank-you's to my family: my mother, who tirelessly supported my dream and believed unerringly that it was within reach. My sister, whose sharp eyes and vast intelligence helped me build this world from the ground up and make sense of the all these tumbling worlds. And of course, my beautiful and gifted fiancé, who sat with me as we did countless concept designs and polished all my rough ideas into diamonds.

And thank you to my other friends and family for their pride, excitement, and joy leading up to this release. It was, and remains to be, the breeze that keeps this kite flying high.

T.J. SWACKHAMMER

Is a passionate creative hailing from Ontario, Canada, where she resides with her equally bizarre family, a trio of half-feral cats and one spoiled dog.

She has been writing works of fiction since childhood and has long since decided that these 'imaginary' worlds are where she wants to be.

City of Immortal Shadows is her debut novel and introduces the first of many worlds to discover.

She is of endless gratitude for the people who will bear witness.

Manufactured by Amazon.ca
Bolton, ON

15095686R00296